Hiking Trails of Ottawa,
the National Capital Region, and Beyond

Also by Michael Haynes

Hiking Trails of Nova Scotia
Trails of Halifax Regional Municipality
Hiking Trails of Cape Breton

MICHAEL HAYNES

Hiking Trails of OTTAWA
the National Capital Region
and Beyond

Edited by Charles Stuart.
Cover and interior photographs by Michael Haynes,
unless otherwise stated.
Maps prepared by Heather Newson and Digital
Projections.
Cover and page design by Julie Scriver.
Printed in Canada on recycled paper.
10 9 8 7 6 5 4 3 2 1

Library and Archives Canada Cataloguing in Publication

Haynes, Michael, 1955-
  Hiking trails of Ottawa, the National Capital Region and beyond /
Michael Haynes.

Includes index.
ISBN 978-0-86492-484-1

1. Trails — Ottawa River Valley (Québec and Ont.) — Guidebooks.
2. Trails — National Capital Region (Ont. and Québec) —
   Guidebooks.
3. Hiking — Ottawa River Valley (Québec and Ont.) — Guidebooks.
4. Hiking — National Capital Region (Ont. and Québec) —
   Guidebooks.
5. Ottawa River Valley (Québec and Ont.) — Guidebooks.
6. National Capital Region (Ont. and Québec) — Guidebooks.
I. Title.

GV199.44.C22O88 2010   796.5109713'8
C2009-907518-0

Goose Lane Editions acknowledges the financial support of the
Canada Council for the Arts, the Government of Canada through
the Book Publishing Industry Development Program (BPIDP), and
the New Brunswick Department of Wellness, Culture, and Sport for
its publishing activities.

Goose Lane Editions
Suite 330, 500 Beaverbrook Court
Fredericton, New Brunswick
CANADA E3B 5X4
www.gooselane.com

Contents

7   Preface

9   Introduction

17   Note for New Canadians

18   Overview Map

19   Trails at a Glance

23   Ottawa – City and Greenbelt

77   Western Québec – Gatineau Park

127   Western Québec – Beyond Gatineau Park

179   Eastern Ontario – Beyond Greenbelt

237   Eastern Ontario – Frontenac Arch

279   Acknowledgements

281   Web Pages

285   Index

Preface

More than anything else, Ottawa is an outdoor city. This might surprise those who think of it only as the political centre of Canada, or others who know it principally for its dynamic artistic and cultural community. Yet spend only a short time here and you will soon realize how much the region is dominated by its natural environment and how its population actively interacts with it.

Foremost in people's affections are the Gatineau Hills, particularly with Gatineau Park, with its magnificent networks of summer and winter trails. Its high escarpment dominating Ottawa's northwestern skyline, Gatineau Park's 361 km^2 (140 mi^2) natural space, extending into the urban core, is the forest playground of choice for tens of thousands. And, with its rugged hills, lakes, and winding river valleys, many other options for outdoor activity are available throughout this section of Western Québec.

Perhaps even more central to the region's identity are its rivers. The Ottawa, Rideau, and Gatineau were once major routes for industry and trade, and now their banks are home to numerous parks and conservation areas, and many of its most popular trails. Smaller tributaries such as the Mississippi, Petite Nation, Madawaska, Lièvre, and South Nation rivers helped define the pattern of settlement and are themselves major recreational corridors for canoeists and kayakers.

Ringing Ottawa to the west, the Opeongo Hills and the Frontenac Arch are extreme southern extensions of the Canadian Shield. Once as high as the Himalayas, the eroded remains of the Shield are made up of some of the most ancient rock on earth, nearly four billion years old. The granitic and gneiss-type rocks of this area produce thin, acidic soil, which has prevented much agriculture or dense settlement. However, its hills and lakes have attracted hikers and other recreationists for decades.

In sharp contrast to much of the region, the sedimentary lowlands extending south and east of Ottawa make up some of the smoothest land in Ontario. Largely the result of glacial deposition when the entire area was submerged during the last Ice Age, this prairie-flat area supports extensive agricultural activity and its trails present a distinctly pastoral aspect found nowhere else in the region.

In short, Ottawa offers an almost limitless variety of outdoor experiences, and its residents respond by hiking, biking, canoeing, cross-country skiing, and participating in every form of outdoor recreation available. The city is home to one of the largest hiking clubs in Canada, the Rideau Trail Association. Nakkertok Nordic Cross Country Ski Club may be the largest skiing club in the country, with more than 1,000 members. Similar claims can be argued for many of Ottawa's other recreational associations, and many of the region's smaller communities themselves have a local walking or ski club.

Yet, despite all this organized outdoors activity, and the brochures published by parks, tourist associations, and the National Capital Commission, newcomers still often find it difficult to know how and where to start to enjoy the outdoors. The purpose of this book is to make that easier, both by providing detailed examples of a number of the hiking paths that may be found throughout the Ottawa area and by supplying links to many of the clubs and outdoor groups that enjoy the region's natural landscape.

I hope that you find *Hiking Trails of Ottawa* to be helpful in your personal discovery of the outdoors, both within the National Capital Region, and beyond.

Introduction

SELECTION OF TRAILS

Eastern Ontario and western Québec are blessed with thousands of kilometres of managed trail. *Hiking Trails of Ottawa, the National Capital Region, and Beyond* does not attempt to list them all. Instead, it provides a detailed profile of fifty representative routes, distributed throughout a circle radiating approximately 100 km (60 mi) from downtown Ottawa. I have divided this circle into five districts — Ottawa within the Greenbelt, Gatineau Park, Québec outside of Gatineau Park, Ontario beyond Ottawa's Greenbelt, and the Frontenac Arch — and provided options in each, ensuring that in every area there is a variety of challenges available.

I chose to balance the number of selections in each of the five districts, and to ensure that each region contained variety, by selecting ten hiking trails: a few easy, some moderately challenging, and at least one or two more demanding. This occasionally meant that I left out very good trails — in Gatineau Park, for example — but was able to profile a wider geographic area than I might if I had attempted to mention every trail found inside the National Capital Region.

The selection of the routes in *Hiking Trails of Ottawa, the National Capital Region, and Beyond* was mine alone. If I left out your favourite trail, please let me know.

HOW TO USE THIS BOOK

You should begin with the **Trails at a Glance** table (pp 19-21). This lists all the trails found in the book, showing their length and degree of difficulty, indicating the uses permitted, and whether you must pay to use it. It also provides an estimated time required to complete the walk profiled.

The **Trails at a Glance** uses a number of abbreviations and notations of which you should be aware:

Permitted Uses
No-snow Season:
W = walking/hiking
B = bicycling, either touring or mountain biking
A = ATV and other off-highway vehicles
H = horseback riding

I = in-line skating and (usually) skate
        boarding
Snow Season:
S = snowshoeing (and walking)
X = cross-country/Nordic skiing
Sm = Snowmobiles and other motor-
        ized winter vehicles

Any use marked with an asterisk (*)
means that it is permitted, and might
be encountered, along some sections of the profiled route but is not
permitted throughout the entire
distance.

Dogs: Dogs enjoy the outdoors as
much as, or more than, any human,
and their owners are always looking
for dog-friendly routes. Many of the
trails profiled have strict regulations
about dog use, particularly those on
National Capital Commission properties. Please observe rigorously
— and always "poop & scoop" no
matter where you take your canine
companion.

N = no dogs permitted
L = dogs permitted on leash
0 = dogs permitted off-leash

When marked with an asterisk (*),
this means access permitted April
15 to November 30, but no dogs al-
lowed December 1 to April 14.

Fees:
N = no fees
Y = there is a fee to use this trail, usual
        in provincial parks and conservation
        areas.
Y* = there is a fee to park at the
        trailhead specified — usually only
        during the summer.

Once you have selected the trail you
wish to hike, turn to the trail; there
you will find access information and
details of the route being profiled.
Every trail description follows the
same basic format. At the start of
each profile is a capsule description
of the walk:

Name of Trail: official name if it is a
maintained pathway or start/finish
for portions of longer trails.

Length: gives return-trip distance in
kilometres and miles, rounded up
to the nearest half kilometre (and
quarter mile).

Hiking Time: based on an average
walker's rate of 4 km (2.5 mi) per
hour. This may not accurately re-
flect the time that you will require
to complete any particular hike.
Each person sets his or her own
pace, which will vary according to
weather conditions, length of the
trail, and fitness level.

Type of Trail: indicating the footing that will be encountered.

Uses: mentions possible types of recreational use, including hiking, biking, cross-country skiing, in-line skating, horseback riding, snowshoeing, snowmobiling, and ATVing.

Facilities: services such as washrooms or water that will be found along the trail, or at the trailhead.

Gov't Topo Map: the National Topographic System 1:50 000-scale map showing the terrain covered by the trail.

Rating: a designation from 1 to 5. 1 indicates suitability for all fitness and experience levels; 5 is recommended only for experienced and very fit outdoor people. These ratings are based on length, elevation change, condition of treadway, and signage. Novices should choose level 1 and 2 hikes initially, and work up with experience. Level 4 and 5 hikes include an indication of what qualifies them for a higher rating.

Trailhead GPS: the latitude and longitude of the start/finish of the hike. This data was collected using a GARMIN GPS 12XL Receiver. It is accurate to within 25-30 m/yd.

The detailed trail outline is divided into the following sections:

Access Information: how to drive to the trail's starting point from a convenient landmark:

For trails in Gatineau Park and Western Québec, directions will begin from the mid-point of the Macdonald-Cartier Bridge.

Directions for trails west of Ottawa will begin at the junction, known locally as the "split," of Highway 416 and Highway 417.

Directions for trails east of Ottawa will begin at the split of Highway 174 and Highway 417.

Directions for trails within or close to the city of Ottawa begin at the closest exit of Highway 417.

Introduction: background about the trail, possibly including historical, natural, or geographical information, as well as my personal observations or recommendations.

Route Description: a walk-through of the hike, relating what I found when I last travelled this path. In every case, I describe junctions and landmarks from the perspective of someone following the trail in the direction I have indicated. If travelling in the opposite direction, remember to reverse my bearings.

Cautionary Notes: hunting season, cliffs, high winds, road crossings, or anything I believe you should be especially cautious about on this route will be mentioned here. All wildlife hazards, such as bears, coyotes, and/or wolves, are represented by the word "animals."

Cellphone Coverage: how well a cellular phone will work on this trail, including locations of dead spots.

Further Information: Websites are available for many trails, particularly those in parks, and I mention if brochures are printed.

SIDEBAR NOTES

Scattered throughout the book are brief capsule descriptions of some of the plants, animals, geological features, and human institutions that you might encounter on the various trails. These are intended to be brief samples to whet your curiosity about the world through which you are hiking and to encourage you to learn more.

QUICK TIPS

Unless you are an experienced hiker, you might not know how much water to carry on your hike or why wearing blue jeans is not the best idea. An assortment of helpful hints is sprinkled among the trail descriptions.

GETTING STARTED

New walkers should begin by selecting routes with a difficulty rating of "1" or "2." These are likely to be completed within one or two hours by people of almost any fitness level. With experience, trails with a higher difficulty level can be attempted.

Clothing and footwear are extremely important. For shorter walks in comfortable weather, there is little need for specialized gear. However, as distance and time walked increase, comfort and safety will be substantially improved by wearing hiking shoes and outfits specially designed for outdoor activity. There is a bewildering array of products available, more than enough for a book of its own, and choosing the right gear is also dependent upon individual preferences. I, for example, like to hike in sandals, while friends often wear heavy boots. Once you have decided that hiking is a regular part of your lifestyle, you can visit the outdoor stores and find what works for you.

However, there are a few items that should always be carried, even if only going for a short hike. Doing so may help make every hiking experience an enjoyable and safe one.

Water: Nothing is more important than water. You can survive up to two weeks without food; you may die in as few as three days without water. I carry one litre per person on a hike up to 10 km (6.25 mi), more if the distance is greater, if the day is particularly hot or humid, or if I am taking children with me. Dehydration occurs rapidly while hiking, and the accompanying headache or dizziness diminishes the pleasure of the experience. Drink small sips of water often, and do not wait until you are thirsty to do so. Portable water filtration systems are available in any outdoor store and are worth carrying, especially on hot summer treks.

Map: I consider a map crucial. With a map, I have a context of the terrain through which I will be hiking. Is it swampy? Are there hills? If I get confused, what direction do I follow to find people? In parks, a special map of the trail is often available. Otherwise, I carry the National Topographic System of Canada 1:50,000-scale map of the area.

Food: Though not essential on a day hike, I always carry something to snack on while I walk, and who does not enjoy a picnic? Apples, trail mix, bagels: anything like this is good. Chocolate bars, chips, and other junk food are not the best choice and should be avoided.

Whistle: If you are lost and want to attract attention, a whistle will be heard far better than your voice and is less likely to wear out from continuous use. Test it out. Take one outside the house and give a couple of blasts. See how much attention you attract. (Feel free to blame me for the commotion it causes!)

First Aid Kit: When in the woods, even little problems can become very serious. A small first aid kit with bandages, gauze, tape, moleskin, etc. permits you to deal with blisters and bruises that require attention.

Garbage Bag: You should always carry your trash out: food wrappers, juice bottles, and even apple cores should go into the bag. If you are hiking on a well-used trail, you will probably find litter left behind by others. Take a moment to put as much as you can into your own garbage bag.

Warm Sweater and/or Rain Jacket: Weather is highly changeable, especially in spring and fall. Cold rains and high winds can create uncomfortable, possibly life-threatening conditions. No matter how good the weather seems to be, always carry some protective clothing.

Backpack: You need something to carry everything, so I recommend that you invest in a quality day pack. It should have adjustable shoulder straps, a waist strap, a large inner pouch, and roomy outer pockets. The equipment listed earlier will fit easily inside a good pack and will sit comfortably on your back. After one or two trips, wearing it will become just another part of your walking routine. I never hike without my pack.

Optional (but Recommended) Equipment: sunscreen, hat, bug repellent, camera, binoculars, field guides, extra socks, and toilet paper.

Really Optional Equipment: tarp, rope, eating utensils, flashlight, towel, bathing suit, small stove, fuel, toothbrush, toothpaste, soap, writing paper and pen, and sleeping bag.

HAZARDS

The Ottawa area is home to a number of potential harmful plants and animals. Encounters with large mammals, such as bears, cause more apprehension than necessary. On the well-used trails found in this region, it is even less likely. However, you should be aware of what might share the forest with you.

Bears: Black bears are fairly common in the region. Gatineau Park prints an excellent brochure: www.canadascapital.gc.ca/data/2/rec_docs/231_blackbear_e.pdf. Take time to read it before you hike.

Cougars: In July 2007, a cougar was sighted in Gatineau Park. While extremely rare — only eight are known in Québec — sighting one is not impossible.

Wolf: A wolf looks somewhat like a German shepherd dog but heavier; a large wolf weighs 45 kg (100 lb). They are found in the Ottawa region, but there have been virtually no recorded instances of attacks on humans in North America, although there are numerous reports of attacks on pet dogs on trails.

Bobcat/Lynx: Present, but so wary of humans that few have ever seen one. Consider yourself lucky if you catch a quick glimpse.

Moose: Uncommon in the region, moose can be found in deciduous forests, scrub lands, and swamps. Dawn and dusk are the times they are most likely to be sighted. Bulls weigh up to 550 kg (1,200 lbs) and can be unpredictable, especially during the fall rutting season. Moose are not simply larger deer; treat them with as much respect and caution as you would bears.

Poison Ivy: Extremely common, it is often found along the edges of many trails and fields. Managed trails will usually post warning signs, but as the plant is spreading due to climate change; it could be almost anywhere. Best way to avoid: stay on the path.

Ticks: Also spreading throughout the region, these small brown spider-like creatures live to suck your blood! They do so by burrowing beneath the skin and hanging on until they are engorged (as gross as it sounds). As some ticks can carry diseases dangerous to humans, you should notify your doctor if you find one that has fastened itself on to you.

Hunting Season: Hunting is permitted in many of the areas covered in this book. Usually starting in early October, hunting season varies from year to year for different types of game and in different areas within the region. Contact the Ministry of Natural Resources (Ontario), and Ressources naturelles et Faune (Québec) for detailed information before going into the woods in the fall.

Weather: Ottawa experiences high heat and humidity during the summer and arctic-like cold in the winter. It is essential that you understand the conditions you will encounter, and prepare for them appropriately. Always check the weather forecast: www.theweathernetwork.com/weather/caon0512.

Note for New Canadians

According to the latest census, nearly 4% of the population of the city of Ottawa, or 29,650 people, arrived in Canada between 2001 and 2006. More than 22% of the city's residents, or 178,540 people, were immigrants originally.

For most of these new Canadians, their familiarity with the county's forests and wilderness areas is limited. Indeed, to many, our natural spaces may seem strange and dangerous, the reported haunt of bears and bobcats, coyotes and cougars. If they lived in an urban environment previously, our trails and parks can seem like especially forbidding, dangerous places.

Yet there is little to fear. Bears do live in the nearby forests, but you can hike for many years without being lucky enough to see one. I average more than 1,500 km (932 mi) of walking annually, but have only seen a bear on half a dozen occasions. And the encounters have nearly always been the same: I shriek (or whimper), the bear snorts in surprise, and we both run off in opposite directions. I might as well have run into some nervous person wearing a fur coat.

If you are careful to hike on managed trails in our nearby parks, the most deadly encounter you are likely to have is with mosquitoes. (Don't laugh until you have been bitten a dozen times while on a walk.) And although the weather can be unpredictable occasionally so you might be caught in the rain, the other common challenge is insufficient drinking water leading to mild dehydration. Predatory animals, such as wolf, bobcat, and lynx, have come to equate humans with danger, and stay far away from us. In thirty years of hiking, I have seen a wolf once, a bobcat twice (once from the car), and a lynx never.

Canada's natural spaces substantially define us as a nation. The opportunity to enjoy these areas, whether through hiking, biking, canoeing, or other means, constitutes one of the great benefits of living in this country. So I urge you to take advantage of the opportunities. To get started, join a walking club for one of their organized hikes, and you will soon discover the incredible delights of trekking through the wilderness.

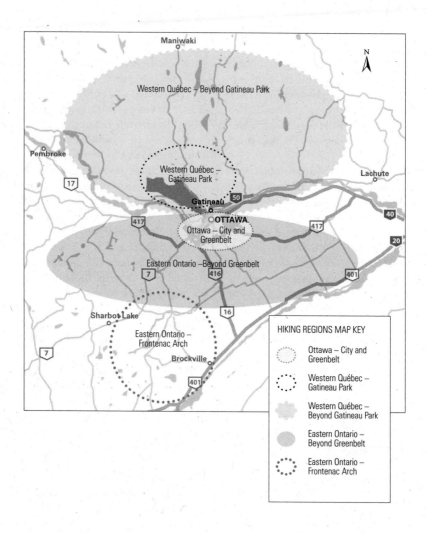

Hiking Trails of Ottawa, the National Capital Region, and Beyond

TRAILS AT A GLANCE

HIKING TRAILS OF OTTAWA, THE NATIONAL CAPITAL REGION, AND BEYOND							
				Features			
Trail Name	Difficulty level 1-5	Length km (mi)	Time to complete (hours)	Permitted Uses (no snow)	Permitted Uses (snow)	Dog Use	Fees

Uses (no snow): W = Walk, B = Bike, A = ATV, H = Horseback Riding, I = In-line Skating
Uses (snow): S = Snowshoe/Walk, X = Cross-Country Ski, Sm = Snowmobile
* = Permitted on some sections of the route, but not all

OTTAWA – CITY AND GREENBELT							
Mer Bleue	2	10 (6.25)	3	W	S, X	L*	N
Old Quarry Trail	2	10 (6.25)	3	W, B*	S, X	N	N
Ottawa River – Aviation Museum	2	8 (5)	2	W, B, I*	S, X	L	N
Ottawa River – Britannia Park	3	11 (6.9)	3	W, B*, I*	S, X*	L	N
Ottawa River – Green Creek	2	7.5 (4.7)	2	W, B, I*	S, X	L	N
Pine Grove Forestry Trail	1	6 (3.75)	2	W	S, X	L*	N
Rideau Canal	2	8 (5)	2	W, B, I	S, X	L	N
Rideau River	3	15 (9.4)	4	W, B, I	S, X	L	N
Rideau Trail – Lime Kiln Loop	3	9.5 (6)	3	W	S	N	N
Shirleys Bay – Trail 10	1	4 (2.5)	1	W	S, X	L*	N
WESTERN QUÉBEC – GATINEAU PARK							
Herridge Shelter	3	10 (6.25)	3-4	W, B	X	L*	N
King Mountain	3	6.5 (4)	2-3	W, B*	—	N	N
Lauriault Trail	1	4.5 (2.8)	1-2	W	S	L*	N

Trail Name	Difficulty level 1-5	Length km (mi)	Time to complete (hours)	Features		Dog Use	Fees
				Permitted Uses (no snow)	Permitted Uses (winter)		
Lusk Cave	5	13.5 (8.4)	4-6	W, B*	S*, X*	L*	Y*
Luskville Falls	4	5 (3.1)	2-4	W	---	N	N
Pink Lake	1	2.5 (1.6)	1	W	---	N	N
Skyline	3	9 (5.6)	2-4	W, B*	X	L*	N
Trail 56	4	12 (7.5)	4	W, B	X	L*	N
Trail 62 (Wolf Trail/Sentier des Loups)	4	9 (5.6)	3-5	W	S	L*	Y*
Western Shelter	5	10.5 (6.6)	4-5	W, B*	X	L*	Y*
WESTERN QUÉBEC – BEYOND GATINEAU PARK							
Cycloparc PPJ	5	26 (16.25)	6-8	W, B	Sm	O	N
Forêt-la-Blanche	2	3 (1.9)	1	W	S, X	N	Y
Lac Leamy to Museum of Civilization	3	13 (8.2)	4	W, B, I	S, X	L*	Y*
Parc du Lac Beauchamp	1	4.5 (2.8)	1	W	S, X	L*	N
Parc linéaire de la Vallée-de-la-Gatineau	4	19.5 (12.2)	5-6	W, B	Sm	O	N
Parc national de Plaisance – Sentier des Outaouais	4	21 (13)	5-6	W, B	S, X	N	Y
Parcours Louis-Joseph-Papineau	5	20.5 (12.8)	5-7	W, B	S, X	O	N
Sentier des Montagnes Noires	3	9.5 (6)	3-4	W, B*	S, X	O	N
Sentiers L'Escapade	5	20 (12.5)	5-8	W, H	X	L*	N
Wakefield to Lac Brown	3	9.5 (6)	3-4	W, B*	S*, X*	L	N
EASTERN ONTARIO – BEYOND GREENBELT							
Glengarry Trails – Alexandria	3	15 (9.4)	4	W, B	S, X, Sm*	L	N
K&P Trail – Calabogie	3	13 (8.2)	4	W, B, H, A	S, X, Sm	O	N
Macnamara Nature Trail	1	4.5 (2.8)	1	W	S, X	L	N

Trail Name	Difficulty level 1-5	Length km (mi)	Time to complete (hours)	Permitted Uses (no snow)	Permitted Uses (winter)	Dog Use	Fees
				Features			
Manitou Mountain	5	11.5 (7.2)	4-5	W	S	O	N
Marlborough Forest	5	14 (8.75)	4	W, B*, H*, A*	S, X, Sm*	O	N
New York Central Fitness Trail	2	12 (7.5)	3	W, B, I	S, X	L	N
Ottawa-Carleton Trailway	5	42 (26.25)	10-14	W, B, H	S, X, Sm	L	N
Prescott-Russell Recreational Trail: Hammond to Bourget	2	12 (7.5)	3	W, B	X, Sm	O	N
St. Lawrence Recreational Path	4	18.5 (11.5)	4-6	W, B	S, X		N
Stonebridge Trail	2	8 (5)	2	W, B	S	O	N
EASTERN ONTARIO – FRONTENAC ARCH							
Cataraqui Trail – Chaffeys Locks	5	19 (11.9)	5-7	W, B, H	S, X, Sm	O	N
Charleston Lake Provincial Park – Tallow Rock Bay Trail	3	10 (6.25)	4	W	S	L	Y
Frontenac Provincial Park – Doe Lake and Arab Gorge	1	4.5 (2.7)	2	W	S, X	L	Y
Frontenac Provincial Park – Slide Lake Loop	5	28 (17.5)	7+	W	S	L	Y
Mac Johnson Wildlife Area – Brockville	1	8.5 (5.25)	2	W	S, X	L	N
Marble Rock	4	11 (7)	3-4	W	S	O	N
Murphys Point Provincial Park	2	7.5 (4.7)	2	W	S, X	L	Y
Rideau Trail – Tay Towpath	2	8 (5)	2	W, B*	S, X	L	Y*
Rideau Trail – Westport	3	9 (5.6)	3-4	W	S, X*	L	N
Rock Dunder	3	6 (3.75)	2	W	S	O	N

OTTAWA — CITY AND GREENBELT

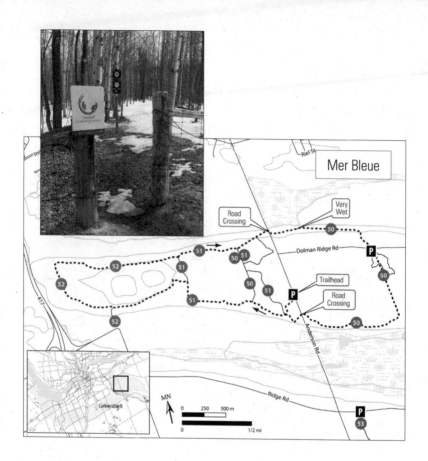

Mer Bleue

Riel St

Road Crossing

Very Wet

50

Dolman Ridge Rd

P

52

51

50 51

50

51

52

50

51

Trailhead

Road Crossing

P

52

51

P

50

Anderson Rd

Greenbelt

Ridge Rd

P

53

MN

0   250   500 m

0   1/2 mi

Mer Bleue

Length: 10 km (6.25 mi) return
Hiking Time: 3 hrs
Type of Trail: natural surface
Uses: walking, snowshoeing, cross-country skiing
Facilities: outhouses, picnic tables
Gov't Topo Map: 031G05
Rating (1-5): 2
Trailhead GPS: N 45° 24' 15.5"
    W 75° 33' 31.4"

Access Information: From the Highway 174/417 split, head east on Highway 417 for 2 km (1.25 mi) to Exit 112/Innes Road. Turn left onto Innes Road and follow for 2.2 km (1.4 mi) to Anderson Road. Turn right and follow for 1.6 km (1 mi) to an intersection, keeping right on Anderson Road for an additional 1.8 km (1.1 mi) to parking area P20.

Introduction: The trails at Mer Bleue are situated on parallel ridges separated by extensive wetlands and make up two stand-alone networks. The ones profiled here — trails 50, 51, and 52, — are organized into three connected, or "stacked," loops that permit users to select the distance

Mer Bleue Bog

One of the largest bogs in southern Ontario, Mer Bleue is a provincial conservation area and an internationally significant wetland protected under the United Nations' Ramsar Convention. This 33.43 km² (12.9 mi²) area is home to a variety of rare creatures, including the spotted turtle and Fletcher's dragonfly, an insect known only in a handful of sites worldwide.

Situated in an ancient channel of the Ottawa River, more than half of the bog is a raised boreal peat dome sphagnum bog, an ecological community usually found much further north in Canada.

appropriate for them. I have elected to describe the outer perimeter, providing the longest hike possible without repeating any section.

One of the highlights of this trail is its many bird feeders. Scattered throughout the route, these attract dozens of chickadees, nuthatches, and other species, especially in the winter. Spread a few sunflower seeds in your palm, hold very still, and within a minute, you will have a procession of these feather-light diners perching tamely on your fingertips.

Route Description: At the trailhead, a wood-rail fence separates the path from the parking lot. Through the opening, you pass a daunting array of regulatory signs to reach a pavilion where a system map is posted. You begin from here, walking past a bear-proof garbage can and outhouse. Underneath some pines on your right, you also will see several picnic tables positioned near bird feeders.

The wide path wends through the hardwoods for 200 m/yd before you reach the first intersection. To your right is Trail 51; you continue straight, which a small blue marker tells you is Trail 50. This easy path stays near the crest of the ridge, with the wetlands of Mer Bleue to your left and below. Bird feeders are frequent and are usually well populated.

At 600 m/yd, in a small clearing fringed by birch, you reach the next junction. Signage is difficult to find, but you continue straight, now on Trail 51. Through this next section you pass several stands of red pine, their ordered ranks filing off to your right. Occasional yellow circles

affixed to trees sign a cross-country ski route. After another 600 m/yd, your path curves right and passes through the open area beneath two high electrical towers. After crossing a small brook 250 m/yd further, you turn left onto Trail 52.

This next 200 m/yd, adjacent to a swampy area, is usually wet. Then you climb onto the slope of a low, gentle hill, reaching another T-junction, where you turn left again. Trail 52 now works around the south side of this hill — forest to the left and semi-open slope to your right — until you reach another junction, at 2.5 km (1.6 mi).

Because of recent work on the power lines, in 2009 the crossing looked like a road used by machinery. To your left, it is a short drop to an informal access point on Walkley Road. Your route is to the right, perhaps 10 paces, then left into an opening in the forest, which is the continuation of Trail 52. This is much more pleasant, shaded by hardwoods, and while still wide enough for two, somehow feels more snug.

This path continues more or less in a straight line, though curving gradually right, for 500 m/yd, with the traffic noise of nearby Highway 417 growing steadily louder. It then turns distinctly right, continuing for 400 m/yd, then sharply right again.

Chickadee

Tiny, energetic birds flitting among the pines and hardwoods, emitting their easily recognizable call of *chik-a-dee-dee*, are common hiking companions. Black-capped chickadees are quite curious and very comfortable around people. Stand motionless and make a low, steady *pish-pish-pish* sound; this should soon result in several of the little birds lighting in nearby trees to get a closer look. Place sunflower seeds in your palm and remain motionless, and they may land momentarily to feed.

A related species, the boreal chickadee, can be distinguished by its brownish-grey head and is normally found only in softwood areas. Both species of chickadee remain throughout the year and in winter can often be seen in company with golden-crowned kinglets and red-breasted nuthatches.

You should notice that the route has returned to the crest of the ridge and cultivated fields are visible left and below. I particularly enjoy the next 500 m/yd, with the path making small turns and passing over low undulating, tiny mounds that have not been levelled. Unfortunately, just before reaching the open land again at 4 km (2.5 mi), you pass through an area that is poorly drained. Expect wet feet.

Continue straight, keeping to the left of a deep drainage ditch, with the open hillside on your right. The nearby apartment towers of Blackburn Hamlet look incongruous sprouting above the distant trees. After 800 m/yd of field, you attain the forest again, keeping straight on Trail 52. About 100 m/yd later, you reach another major junction, where you keep straight/left. You have moved back onto Trail 51.

This section follows the ridge line as before, with the trees on the northern slope changing to include more cedar and some stands of hemlock. After passing a side trail that descends into the wetlands and a junction to the right at 600 m/yd, with a connector trail that will return you to P20, your route becomes Trail 50 and descends the slope to reach Anderson Road at 6 km (3.75 mi). On the descent, you might notice a sign for the Nut Tree Trail to your right; this unnumbered interpretive trail will also return you to P20.

At Anderson Road, you need to carefully cross this busy highway, resuming your hike in very different terrain. The path is now at wetlands level in the open on a soggy meadow, with the ridge rising on your right, and it parallels a fence for the next 1 km (0.6 mi). It then takes a little curve to the left, swings sharply right, and heads directly up the ridge. At the top, it crosses a field diagonally, right to left, and reaches P23, trailhead of the Dewberry Trail, on the opposite side of the Dolman Ridge Road at 7.3 km (4.6 mi).

Turn left on the road for 50 m/yd, avoiding P23, unless you want to walk the Dewberry Trail. Trail 50 recommences on the other side of a wooden fence and stretches straight ahead for the next 800 m/yd, varying only when it bridges an appealing wet area. It makes another sharp right-hand turn and soon reunites with the ridge line. This area is probably my favourite. Little ravines slope off to the left; the trail narrows somewhat, bending more and featuring more undulations; and the afternoon sun filters attractively through the surrounding hardwoods.

After another 500 m/yd, you encounter your first real bridge, sturdy planking and solid railings crossing a narrow but deep gully. From here, it is only another 600 m/yd to Anderson Road.

You have almost finished. Cross the highway and round the fence; the trail drops down the ridge again, bridging a small stream, then turns right to climb back up the hill. About 200 m/yd past this bridge, you complete your loop, connecting at the first junction you encountered. Turn right and retrace you initial 200 m/yd to return to P20.

Cautionary Notes: Poison ivy, road crossings.

Cellphone Reception: Excellent.

Further Information: www.canadas capital.gc.ca/bins/ncc_web_content_ page.asp?cid=16297-16299-9735& lang=1; paper trail map available for purchase.

Old Quarry Trail

Length: 10 km (6.25 mi) return
Hiking Time: 3 hrs
Type of Trail: compacted earth, crushed stone, natural surface
Uses: walking, biking*, snow-shoeing, cross-country skiing
Facilities: benches, garbage cans, interpretive panels, outhouses
Gov't Topo Map: 031G05
Rating (1-5): 2
Trailhead GPS: N 45° 18' 06.3" W 75° 52' 27.5"

Access Information: From the Highway 416/417 split, follow Highway 417 west for 6.5 km (4.1 mi) to Exit 138. Turn left onto Eagleson Road and follow for 2.5 km (1.5 mi). Turn left at the light into P5.

OC Transpo Route 61 stops at Hazeldean Mall, across the road from P5. Multiple routes stop at Eagleson and Hazeldean, 250 m/yd from P5.

Introduction: The Old Quarry Trail is located in the Stony Swamp area of the Greenbelt, which includes its most extensive network of walking trails. Although I have labelled this walk the Old Quarry Trail, it includes that trail plus extensive portions of trails 23, 24, and 25, as well as segments of the Rideau Trail and the Ottawa-Carleton Trailway. You will get lots of variety!

This walk can be undertaken in three loops of varying length. The Old Quarry Trail on its own is a pleasant family walk of less than 3 km (1.9 mi). Hiking as far as the Ottawa-Carleton Trailway and returning on trails 24 and 23 makes a hike of 5.5 km (3.4 mi). Undertaking the route described is 10 km (6.25 mi).

Route Description: The start of the Old Quarry Trail presents you with a bit of a challenge. If you are lucky enough to have a map, this shows two routes from P5. However, even the most casual glance from the fence at the trail map will pick out four distinct trails and little in the way of signage. Fortunately, the third trail from the left features an interpretive panel; start here.

There are two interpretive programs on Old Quarry. One, indicated

The Old Quarry Trail contains several interpretive stations.

by numbered posts, works with an illustrated trail brochure, theoretically available at the trailhead. Unfortunately, there have never been any available the three times I visited P5. The other is a series of plaques mounted on massive concrete panels explaining the fascinating — and not just to us rock nerds — geological foundation of the area. The first plaque, "A," is in sight of P5, then, just over the lip of the first hill, this path connects with one of the others leading from P5; turn right and the panel "B" is 5 m/yd to the left on a side trail. Continue across the open top of the hill, bordered by sumac and pine, on the crushed-stone path until, at 250 m/yd, you turn left to reach "C," "Widening Joints." (I hope you are reading them all carefully.)

Immediately afterwards, the trail turns left 180° and passes slightly beneath "C," quickly heading into an area first of pine and spruce, then

of dense cedar. A very large swamp is visible to your left, and the path traces its perimeter. At 600 m/yd, the path turns left. Watch for post #6; about 100 m/yd later you will cross a long boardwalk over the swamp. Barely 100 m/yd beyond the long boardwalk is panel "D," then another lengthy boardwalk, after which the trail curves left, keeping close to the swamp.

You might occasionally notice the Old Quarry Trail marker, a white-and-blue rectangle sporting a pick and shovel. Back on crushed stone, the trail works around the swamp, and you should keep left at any informal junctions. "E," the final interpretive panel, is reached at 1.4 km (0.9 mi), and 100 m/yd later, the Old Quarry Trail branches left, crossing another long boardwalk over the swamp. Take this to return to P5, for a total walk of less than 3 km (1.9 mi) in length.

However, for a longer hike, turn right. This path takes you 200 m/yd to the junction with Trail 23, where you turn right then right again at another junction 100 m/yd further. You now pass through a tremendously attractive plantation of pine towering high overhead, with very little understorey. After 500 m/yd of nearly straight route, Trail 23 turns almost in a figure "S" to reach within a few metres of the Ottawa-Carleton

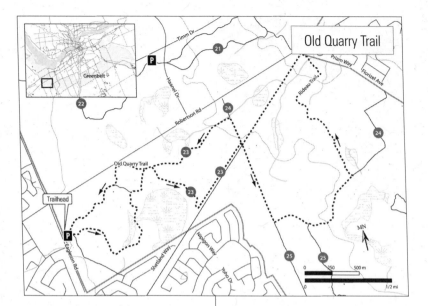

Trailway. There is an informal connector, and you can see a Trans Canada Trail interpretive panel on the Trailway.

You can walk on either trail because they parallel each other for the next 700 m/yd. However, Trail 23 remains more in the forest, providing some shade, and its grass surface makes for pleasant walking. At 3 km (1.9 mi), you reach a major intersection where trails 23 and 24 and the Ottawa-Carleton Trailway all meet. If you turn left, you will return to P5, about a 5.5 km (3.4 mi) total walk. If you still want more, turn right and follow Trail 24 across the Trailway.

The next 800 m/yd are straight and wide, like a forest access road through the younger trees. There is little notable to describe, although the hardwoods on the left grow increasingly impressive during the final 400 m/yd. At the next intersection, turn left onto combined Trail 24/25, which describes a long continuous curve to the right for 400 m/yd, skirting another pine plantation, until it reaches a signed junction where Trail 25 branches right. Keep straight on Trail 24, which is now also signed with the orange triangles of the Rideau Trail. In fact, you will see some trees affixed with the orange triangle, the trail number,

Several trails share the same route: Greenbelt Trail 24, the Rideau Trail, and a cross-country ski path.

and the yellow circle indicating a cross-country ski route.

Trail 24 is easy trekking, wide and grass covered, often overlain with a carpet of pine needles. It curves left initially, reaching a tremendous plantation of red pine, where a Rideau Trail interpretive panel may be found 400 m/yd from the last junction. After only another 300 m/yd the Rideau Trail separates from Trail 24; turn left and follow it onto the first real footpath of the hike, barely distinguishable from the forest floor. I like this section very much, as the narrow track meanders first through the hardwoods on a slope, then downhill through cedar thickets on the shore of a small pond and swamp. You will need to watch carefully for the trail markers

until you emerge, rather abruptly, onto the Ottawa-Carleton Trailway at Robertson Road, practically in the backyard of an adjacent apartment building, after an enjoyable 1.5 km (0.9 mi) ramble.

You are returning to P5 now, turning left onto the Trailway for 1 km (0.6 mi) to the junction with trails 23 and 24 and completing a loop. From here, turn right onto Trail 24 toward Robertson Road, turning left onto Trail 23 over a little bridge 250 m/yd later. This zigzags uneventfully through the forest, the noise of nearby Robertson Road your constant companion. Keep straight at the first junction, 900 m/yd later, and the next 100 m/yd further, following the signs toward P5.

Trail 23 almost touches Robertson Road, coming no more than 10 m/yd away, but it turns back to intersect the Old Quarry Trail 1.4 km (0.9 mi) after leaving Trail 24. Only 700 m/yd of gently walking on a crushed-stone path remains to P5 and the finish.

Cautionary Notes: Animals.

Cellphone Reception: Excellent.

Further Information: www.canadas capital.gc.ca/bins/ncc_web_content_ page.asp?cid=16297-16299-9735& lang=1; paper trail map available for purchase.

Ottawa River – Aviation Museum

Length: 8 km (5 mi) return
Hiking Time: 2 hrs
Type of Trail: crushed stone, asphalt
Uses: walking, biking, in-line skating*, snowshoeing, cross-country skiing
Facilities: benches, garbage cans, trail maps
Gov't Topo Map: 031G05
Rating (1-5): 2
Trailhead GPS: N 45° 27' 23.7" W 75° 38' 42.3"

Access Information: The Aviation Museum is at the north end of the Aviation Parkway, 4.2 km (2.6 mi) from the Highway 174/417 split. However, the only direction from which the Aviation Parkway can be accessed is from Exit 112/Innes Road on Highway 417. There is no access from Highway 417 from the west or from Highway 174 to the east. Park in the south end of the parking lot; the trail starts in the southwest corner.

OC Transpo Route 129 stops at the Aviation Museum, 100 m/yd from the trailhead.

Introduction: Few trails offer the possibility of combining a hike with a visit to a nationally famous museum. By itself the loop includes 3.5 km (2.2 mi) of the most exquisite scenery along the banks of the Ottawa River, making it one of the better walks available within the Greenbelt. Add to that the possibility of spending a few additional hours exploring the Aviation Museum, and I think you have a most enjoyable way to spend a day.

I am particularly pleased that those who don't own cars, or those who wish to reduce their car use, can take the bus to within 10 m/yd of this route.

Route Description: Next to the Aviation Museum parking lot is a map pavilion, which often contains free brochures outlining the National Capital Region's bike paths, and a few other regulatory and informational signs. Turn left and follow the paved trail — keeping to the right of the yellow centre line, of course — as it crosses Aviation Parkway and heads through a very large grassy field. To your right is the Rockcliffe Parkway, which your route will parallel; to your left are the huge hangers of the Aviation Museum and, behind that, Rockcliffe Airport. This entire area was home to the former Rockcliffe Airbase.

For the next 800 m/yd you march across the wide open grassland. A few ornamental trees have been planted, and two benches at 500 m/yd permit you to watch the continual procession of small aircraft taking off and landing. At the far end of the open ground, you cross Polaris Avenue, finally obtaining a little forest cover, although mostly young trees. The paved pathway also begins to curve somewhat, but it continues to follow alongside Rockcliffe Parkway for another 300 m/yd before turning sharply left, away from the road and toward the Ottawa River.

The trail coils pleasantly through the young hardwoods, crossing a small railed bridge at 1.5 km (0.9 mi). Immediately afterwards, it curves right and then descends a slope to connect with the Ottawa River Pathway at 1.7 km (1.1 mi).

The view from here is very attractive. Directly across the broad river is the province of Québec; to your right are the Duck Islands and the Ottawa River stretching toward Montréal. A directional sign states that Parliament is 9 km (5.6 mi) to your left. You will not be going that far, but that is the direction of your hike.

You may shut off your conscious mind for the next little while. The crushed-stone Ottawa River Pathway traces the banks of the river closely, tree-covered hillside on your left and water less than 5 m/yd to your right. The broad, smooth pathway is level and without tree roots or rocks to trip you, so you have little to divert your attention from the lovely view. One of the most striking characteristics of this trail is how little evidence there is of human habitation. You are in the middle of the fifth-largest metropolitan region in Canada, yet you can probably see only a few houses at river level on the Québec side, possibly one or two office towers far distant, and the steam from the pulp and paper mills rising above the trees of Kettle Island.

After 800 m/yd along the pathway, the trail passes through the Rockcliffe Yacht Club, crossing its launch ramp. Those wishing a shorter walk can turn left here and walk along Polaris Avenue back to the Aviation Pathway. But I recommend you continue. On the far side of the RYC is the first of many benches, so you may enjoy the sight of sailboats plying the river. There is also a sign thoughtfully warning of the presence of poison ivy.

For the next 3.5 km (2.2 mi), there is little to describe. Numerous benches on your left face the water, providing opportunities to relax and contemplate the scenery. There are several possible exits, well signed and announcing the steadily decreasing distance to Parliament. Take any of these up the hillside to shorten your trip. But I consider the river view so pleasing that I recommend that you continue until you are almost within hailing distance of a large white building, the historic Ottawa New Edinburgh Club. Just 200 m/yd beyond the Hillside

Road exit, where you are told that Parliament is only 5.7 km (3.6 mi) distant, an unmarked, but paved, route heads left up the slope. Take it. At this point you have walked 5.2 km (3.25 mi).

At the top of the hill, you rejoin the paved Aviation Pathway. Turn left and follow this as it parallels

Ottawa River – Aviation Museum

Rockcliffe Parkway back to the Aviation Museum. Your route now remains on the embankment above the river and mostly on open ground. Occasional benches look toward the water whenever any view presents itself, and you will cross the entranceways to P4 and P5, which are often very busy. The only services at each are garbage cans and trail maps.

You will also pass the other routes connecting to the Ottawa River Pathway, permitting you to return to the river should you wish. At 6.4 km (4 mi), you pass the last connecting path. On your right, across Rockcliffe Parkway, you can see the fields and structures where the horses for the RCMP's Musical Ride are stabled. Directly ahead, the massive buildings of the Aviation Museum dominate.

In the last 600 m/yd, the trail curves away from the river, working around the end of Rockcliffe Airport's runway. On weekends, planes fly directly overhead, and a few last benches provide ideal viewing. The path continues around the museum, reaching the museum's parking lot at the Capital Pathways pavilion at 7.8 km (4.9 mi).

Cautionary Notes: Poison ivy.

Cellphone Reception: Excellent.

Further Information: www.canadas capital.gc.ca/bins/ncc_web_content_page.asp?cid=16297-16299-9735&lang=1; paper trail map available for purchase.

National Capital Commission

Created in 1959 to "create pride and unity through Canada's Capital Region," the National Capital Commission, a Crown corporation of the Government of Canada, in addition to its management of the Houses of Parliament and all other federal public structures in the Region, administers the Greenbelt, the Capital Pathway, and Gatineau Park. These three areas combined contain more than 450 km (280 mi) of managed trails available for public use, one of the largest recreational trail networks of any city in North America.

Ottawa River – Britannia Park

Length: 11 km (6.9 mi) return
Hiking Time: 3 hrs
Type of Trail: crushed stone, natural surface, asphalt
Uses: walking, biking*, in-line skating*, snowshoeing, cross-country skiing*
Facilities: barbeque pits, beaches, benches, covered tables, garbage cans, interpretive panels, outhouses, picnic tables, playgrounds, restaurant, water

Gov't Topo Map: 031G05
Rating (1-5): 3
Trailhead GPS: N 45° 21' 48.2"
W 75° 48' 04.0"

Access Information: From Highway 417, take Exit 129, following Pinecrest Road north for 1.2 km (0.75 mi) to the intersection with Carling Avenue. Continue straight on Greenview Avenue for 800 m/yd, parking in the lot opposite Ron Kolbus

Lakeside Centre. Start the trail from where it crosses Greenview Avenue.

OC Transpo Route 18 stops at Ron Kolbus Lakeside Centre.

Introduction: The Ottawa River Pathway West is far less isolated than its eastern relation. The houses of the city extend almost to the water, cramming the National Capital Commission's parkway and trail into a narrow coastal strip. Even so, it is a popular trail, all the way from the downtown to its end at Andrew Haydon Park. Any part of it is worthwhile, but the section between Britannia Beach and Westboro Beach offers one of the few chances you will have to hike between two supervised swimming locations and explore an adjoining conservation area.

The portion of the route profiled in the Mud Lake Conservation Area regularly floods in the spring. It is also the only part of this route not suitable for biking, in-line skating, and cross-country skiing. You may avoid this section, should you choose, simply by remaining on the Ottawa River Pathway.

Route Description: The paved Ottawa River Pathway crosses Greenview Avenue near the lakeside centre, and heads both west and east. Follow it east, past the Trolley Station and its sheltered picnic tables and past the

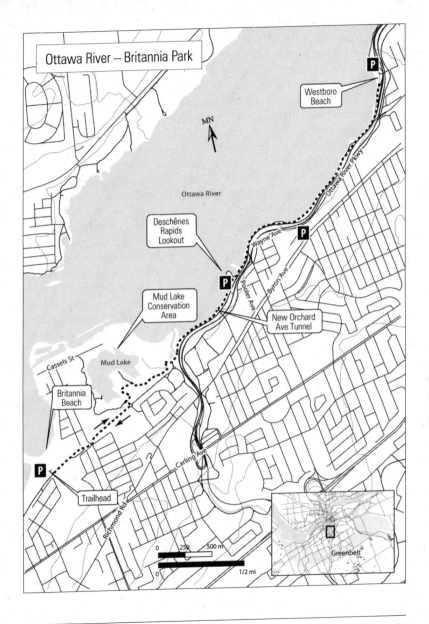

Ottawa River – Britannia Park

MN

Ottawa River

Westboro Beach

Ottawa River Pkwy

Deschênes Rapids Lookout

Wayne Ave

Byron Ave

Pooler Ave

New Orchard Ave Tunnel

Mud Lake Conservation Area

Cassels St

Mud Lake

Britannia Beach

Carling Ave

Trailhead

Richmond Rd

0   250   500 m

0   1/2 mi

Greenbelt

map sign and directional marker indicating that Parliament is 12.1 km (7.6 mi) away. On your right is a large parking lot and, beyond that, some of Britannia Park; to the left are the beach, picnic tables, benches, and a playground. Early on, you might notice markers for both the Trans Canada Trail and the orange triangles of the Rideau Trail.

You leave Britannia Park after 300 m/yd, almost touching the houses of Britannia Village on your left. The path makes a gentle curve right, to reach the intersection of Britannia Road and Howe Street, which it crosses. It then curves left, and after 500 m/yd, you reach the entrance to the Mud Lake Conservation Area, where there is a bike rack, a garbage can, and various regulatory signs. Turn left off the Ottawa River Pathway; follow the narrow natural-surfaced footpath into Mud Lake's enticingly thick tangle of vegetation.

This path initially runs parallel to the backyards of the nearby houses; turn right at the first junction at 200 m/yd. The trees here are mostly young and low, although many old pines tower high above. After 100 m/yd, keep right at the next junction, and you soon reach the south edge of Mud Lake. This is a bird-watcher's paradise, home to more than 200 species and many friendly chickadees.

At 1 km (0.6 mi), you cross a little boardwalk/bridge, and you keep left at the next junction 100 m/yd later. Within 100 m/yd, you reach a long railed bridge that crosses an arm of the lake, an excellent area from which to view wildlife with a good view of a beaver lodge. Once across, climb three stairs to the top of a low ridge; turn left and follow the path alongside the lake for another 100 m/yd, where you will need to turn right and follow a narrow gravelled track. Turning right again 100 m/yd later, this twisty route passes through a semi-open area growing back into woodland before heading beneath a forest canopy and alongside a wet area. At 1.7 km (1.1 mi), the trail crosses a tiny footbridge then turns left to end in front of another conservation area gate. Turn right, and follow the crushed-stone path to return to the Ottawa River Pathway.

At the pathway, turn left and follow it through the narrow space between the Ottawa River Parkway on the right and the river on the left. After 200 m/yd, you will pass the first of many benches facing the water, and 500 m/yd further, you pass a turn off to New Orchard Avenue through a tunnel beneath the parkway. Only 250 m/yd further,

2.8 km (1.75 mi) from Britannia Beach, you reach the Deschênes Rapids lookout, a lovely area with benches facing the rapids upstream and interpretive panels profiling the abundant birdlife and river history. Follow the pathway left around the outside of the parking area and you will not need to cross the road.

For the rest of the walk, your route parallels the river on the paved Ottawa River Parkway, wedged in the relatively small space between the busy road and the broad river. This is almost always a very busy trail and one popular with cyclists, so be sure to keep to the right of the median line. You might notice a well-worn track in the grass next to the pavement, where walkers often retreat.

At 500 m/yd from the Deschênes Rapids lookout, you will find a Trans Canada Trail discovery panel about white elm near one of those now-rare trees. There are also occasional sidings — walker-only sections briefly separating from the main path that veer closer to the water and where clusters of fences face toward the river. There is one at 3.5 km (2.2 mi), another at 4.5 km (2.8 mi), and a third, and final, at 5.1 km (3.2 mi). You will appreciate these because they are the only times you are away from the roadside and almost the only time you are even slightly shaded by trees. At the end of the third siding, the path splits, with the left fork descending to your destination: Westboro Beach. You reach it 5.4 km (3.4 mi) from Britannia Beach. Here you will find tables, a restaurant open during the summer, and a popular swimming area.

To return, either retrace your approach route, or take the tunnel underneath the parkway and turn right at the trail junction on the other side. An older, less heavily used paved trail parallels the road on the city side. You can follow this almost 3 km (2 mi) to the New Orchard Avenue tunnel, where you need to cross back onto the river side. In many ways this is a more relaxing walk, with almost no cyclists but farther from the river.

Cautionary Notes: Poison ivy.

Cellphone Reception: Excellent.

Further Information: www.canadas capital.gc.ca/bins/ncc_web_content_ page.asp?cid=16297-16299-9735& lang=1; paper trail map available for purchase.

Ottawa River – Green Creek

Length: 7.5 km (4.7 mi) return
Hiking Time: 2 hrs
Type of Trail: crushed stone, asphalt
Uses: walking, biking, in-line skating*, snowshoeing, cross-country skiing
Facilities: benches, interpretive panels, outhouses
Gov't Topo Map: 031G05
Rating (1-5): 2
Trailhead GPS: N 45° 28' 00.8" W 75° 34' 53.8"

Access Information: From the Highway 174/417 split, follow Highway 174 for 4.5 km (2.8 mi) to the Montreal Road exit. Turn right onto Montreal Road, and in 1 km (0.6 mi), turn left onto Rockcliffe Parkway. Follow Rockcliffe Parkway for 3.2 km (2 mi); turn left into parking area P8. The trail starts on the east side of the lot.

Introduction: One of the most striking characteristics of the city of Ottawa is how much of its shoreline along the Ottawa River is preserved as public space. In the east, from Rockcliffe Park to Petrie Island, a distance of nearly 18 km (11.2 mi), the shoreline is public land, and trails run almost the entire distance.

In my opinion, these are among the most scenic paths in the city, and all are worth walking any time of the year. I have profiled a section that leads from the parking lot at Green Creek toward Orléans and includes the best view on the river. Moreover, this is best hiked late in the day, when the sun is setting behind the Gatineau Hills and the river is a ribbon of gold stretching from your feet toward the horizon.

Route Description: From the parking lot, cross Rockcliffe Parkway and, on the paved pathway, head in the direction of the river. At 150 m/yd you reach a junction, where there is an outhouse and a trail map. Turn right and head into the forest in the direction indicated by the sign saying Orléans is 3 km (1.9 mi). Do not worry! You will see the river on the return walk.

These woods are very attractive, especially in the late afternoon,

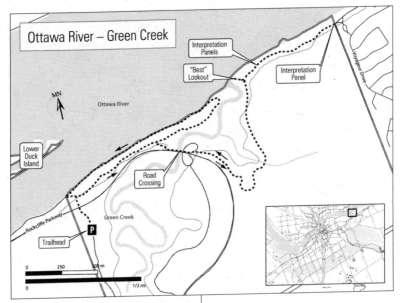

even though they do thin out within 150 m/yd. The paved trail meanders nicely, never settling into an extended straightaway for long. This is an attractive path, with lush vegetation growing to the edge of the asphalt. By the way, pay attention to the yellow line in the middle and stay to the right. This is a busy bicycle route, and sharing the trail means staying in the proper lane. Bikes are required by law to have bells, so if you suddenly hear jingling just continue in a straight line and let the bikes pass safely.

Regrettably, the path comes within 20 m/yd of Rockcliffe Parkway, traffic on which can sometimes be busy, but when there are leaves on the hardwoods, it is usually well buffered. After 800 m/yd, you reach a junction with a crushed-stone path. Keep right, and follow the trail as it emerges from the forest and crosses Green Creek on the sidewalk of the road bridge.

On the opposite side, you will see a gravel path make a wide sweep to the left, and you might notice another trail on the far side of the road, but there is another map here if you are unsure of your route. There is also a sign warning about poison ivy; please take it seriously (personal experience).

Continue straight on the paved

Water

Summers in Ottawa are roasting and dehydration can occur in less than an hour. Nothing is more important than having enough drinking water, and safe sources are rarely available. I like to carry one litre per person for each hour.

pathway, which crosses a field while moving slightly further from the road. It enters my favourite part of this walk, an area beneath towering hemlock and other softwoods. On summer days, it is always much cooler under their shade. The trail skirts around the tops of several ravines while curving wildly around several large trees.

Though pretty, it is an all-too-brief 250 m/yd before you emerge from the forest into a long sweeping curve that arcs through 180° while crossing a little brook. Cultivated fields stretch from the far-off Highway 174 almost onto the path, and the trail describes two more curves, and crosses another tiny brook, before settling into a long straightaway 2 km (1.25 mi) from P8. For the next 500 m/yd, you follow the wide-open paved path through the field, with farmland to your right and trees left.

At 2.5 km (1.6 mi), you reach a junction. On your left is a short 80 m/yd side trail to a bench located on a hill above Green Creek where it enters the Ottawa River. The view from this knoll, facing toward the Gatineau Hills but with sightlines north and east as well, is grand. Quite possibly this is the finest view along the entire river, particularly at sunset. The bench is almost always occupied by someone enjoying the scenic vista. Unofficial footpaths permit you to drop down to water level.

From this location, continue on the main trail a little further. After about 100 m/yd, you will find two interpretive panels that provide an excellent overview about the farming operations carried out in Ottawa's Greenbelt, and 600 m/yd beyond that you reach the community of Orléans. There is a bench here, an imposing array of directional and regulatory signage, and another interpretive panel, this one explaining the Greenbelt concept.

You have now walked 3.2 km (2 mi), and it is time to turn around, although the path ahead continues all the way to Petrie Island, more than 6 km (3.8 mi). Retrace your route back across Green Creek until you come to the intersection with the crushed-stone path, about 2.4 km (1.5 mi). A directional sign, next to a garbage can, says that this is an alternate route to Parliament, 14.7 km (9.2 mi) away. Turn right; you will be walking only 2 km (1.25 mi).

This track is marginally narrower than the main route, with vegetation closer to its edge. It starts on a small ridge above Green Creek, which you will soon see on your right, but within 500 m/yd, it drops down to pass next to the narrow, slow-moving stream. Within another 100 m/yd, the trail swings 180° in a tight circle, and you find yourself on the bank of the broad Ottawa River, at this point more than 1 km (0.6 mi) wide. You can see the houses of Gatineau on the far bank, and there are almost always many recreational boaters in the river. Visible directly ahead are the low bulks of the Duck Islands.

This is the view you will enjoy for the next 1.1 km (0.7 mi), as the wide trail traces the bank of the river. There are even several benches along the way, tempting you to sit and absorb a few tranquil moments. At 7.4 km (4.6 mi), you encounter an intersection with a paved trail descending the hill on your left. That is your return route; turn left, it is less than 200 m/yd back to P8.

Of course, the Ottawa River Pathway continues ahead, stretching almost all the way to the urban core and running for its entire length along the water. If you are feeling energetic, go for it!

Cautionary Notes: Poison ivy.

Cellphone Reception: Excellent.

Further Information: www.canadas capital.gc.ca/bins/ncc_web_content_ page.asp?cid=16297-16299-9970-9971&lang=1.

Pine Grove Forestry Trail

Length: 6 km (3.75 mi) return
Hiking Time: 2 hrs
Type of Trail: grass, natural surface
Uses: walking, snowshoeing, cross-country skiing
Facilities: garbage cans, interpretive panels, outhouses, picnic tables
Gov't Topo Map: 031G05
Rating (1-5): 1
Trailhead GPS: N 45° 21' 17.7"
W 75° 35' 34.2"

Access Information: From the Highway 174/417 split, follow Highway 417 east for 3.5 km (2.2 mi) to Exit 110/Walkley Road. Turn right onto Walkley Road and continue for 2 km (1.25 mi), turning left onto Russell Road. Russell splits left in 500 m/yd at the first intersection past railway tracks; keep straight on Hawthorne Road. Follow Hawthorne an additional 3.8 km (2.4 mi), turning right onto Davidson Road. P18 is well signed and will appear on the left in 500 m/yd.

Introduction: The majority of Greenbelt trails are found on former forestry or farming roads. Accordingly, they are often wide and level, comfortable for sharing with a companion. And enough time has passed, in most cases, for the vegetation to have grown onto and around them, making them seem less like a corridor for motorized use. The Pine Grove Forestry Trail is ideal for an evening's amble in sylvan surroundings for those who walk more slowly or not so far or for those who simply wish a gentle, relaxing stroll.

Route Description: Start by crossing Davidson Road, entering the forest on Trail 43, which is gated. A large pavilion on your right profiles a history of the region, both its natural and its human past. It also contains a map outlining the tree populations found along the route. Much of the information was provided by the Eastern Ontario Model Forest, which administers the silvicultural maintenance of this property. Text may be found on all sides of the pavilion; do not overlook the part that faces away from the trail.

The first portion of this walk is stunningly attractive, extremely wide,

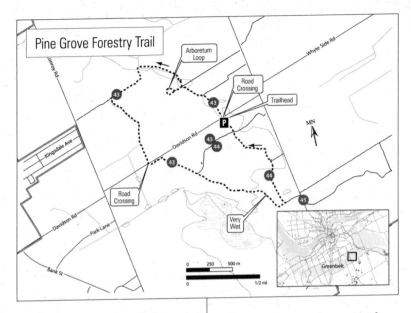

Pine Grove Forestry Trail

and flanked by towering red pines, whose needles help carpet your path. Interpretive panels extend into the distance on the right side of the trail, starting, appropriately, with one about red pine, and followed with others explaining various forest management practices, the effect of the ice storm of 1998, and other natural history topics. At 400 m/yd, you reach a junction with a forest road; keep left, but don't neglect to read all the interpretive panels. (A test will follow!)

At 650 m/yd, you reach a major junction. To your right, the traffic on Hawthorne Road is visible 750 m/yd away down a straight forestry

road. Straight head, more or less, Trail 43 continues, as a posted map indicates. But to your left, a fence funnel invites you to stray from the main trail onto the short Arboretum Loop. No more than 400 m/yd in total, its many interpretive panels are positioned next to the species of tree they describe. This is a worthwhile diversion, particularly if you are interested in trees.

Back on Trail 43, the panels continue relentlessly, but only for an additional 100 m/yd, and you can get down to the business of walking. The trail is at least 5 m/yd wide, grass covered, and sprinkled with pine needles, as it proceeds on a long straight section, flanked first by red pine and maples, then on your left by a wet area. At 1.5 km (0.9 mi), it turns left through 120° to work around the wet area then, within 100 m/yd, cuts sharply right. For the first time you climb, extremely gently, before settling into a long straightaway joined by numerous informal side trails.

At 2 km (1.25 mi), you encounter a junction that is not well signed. Turn left and you will soon notice a trail number. Once past this junction, the path remains a wide, grass-covered track passing through alternating stands of pine and hardwoods, until you emerge onto Davidson Road at 3 km (1.9 mi). You actually need to walk left alongside the road about 150 m/yd until just

before house #3489, then cross the highway and re-enter the forest where you will notice the Trail 43 sign.

This next section is also attractive, with more pines and hardwoods, although you will notice a large swampy area to your left just before you reach the next junction at 3.5 km (2.2 mi). Those who wish may turn left, and Trail 43 will return to P18, 600 m/yd distant. Those wishing to continue, head straight, onto Trail 44.

Trail 44 contains neither interpretive panels nor open views. It remains wrapped in forest, skirting a very large wet area to your left. In the spring, or after a heavy rain, expect substantial portions of Trail 44 to be underwater. From the junction, it continues more or less on a straight path for slightly more than 1 km (0.6 mi) before encountering a wood track, which branches right. Keep left here and, 100 m/yd later, left again at another junction. It is signed, though not well, but if you continue straight you will reach Hawthorne Road in 150 m/yd, where you will spot Trail 45 opposite. A longer walk is possible on it and connecting Trail 46.

However, Trail 44 turns left and on that you should remain. The final 1.5 km (0.9 mi) of your walk returns to P18, passing through more stands

Eastern White Cedar

One of the most valuable trees for wildlife habitat in Ontario, eastern white cedar, sometimes called the "tree of life," grows in abundance in the Ottawa River Valley. With its thick evergreen foliage, white cedar provides shelter and food to deer, small mammals, and many species of birds. It can grow to 15 m/yd high and live up to 400 years in swamps.

White cedar grows best in moist, well-drained soil over limestone bedrock and often develops in pure stands in old fields and pastures. It thrives in areas of thin soil. As a result, much of Ottawa's greenbelt, in particular Stony Swamp, features extensive and dense stands of white cedar.

of pine and crossing numerous wet areas with assistance from board-walks on a wide, easy treadway. When you reach the junction with the connector from Trail 43, less than 200 m/yd remain. One pleasant highlight is found here: a number of feeders have been set in surrounding trees, and these attract large numbers of birds, such as chickadees, particularly in the winter. If you offer them sunflower seeds in your hand, and remain very still, they will probably pluck them skillfully from your palm. Their fluttering wings, cheerful chirp, and delicate touch never fail to delight me.

Cautionary Notes: Road crossings, extremely wet in spring.

Cellphone Reception: Excellent.

Further Information: www.canadas capital.gc.ca/bins/ncc_web_content_page.asp?cid=16297-16299-9735&lang=1; paper trail map available for purchase.

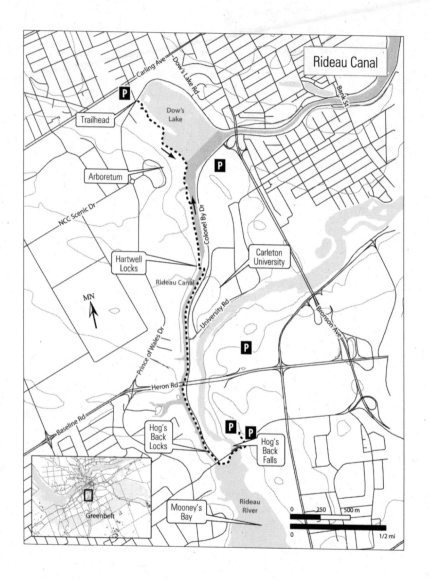

Rideau Canal

Carling Ave
Dow's Lake Rd
Bank St
P
Trailhead
Dow's
Lake
P
Arboretum
NCC Scenic Dr
Colonel By Dr
Hartwell
Locks
Carleton
University
Rideau Canal
University Rd
Bronson Ave
MN
Prince of Wales Dr
P
Heron Rd
Baseline Rd
Hog's
Back
Locks
P P
Hog's
Back
Falls
Greenbelt
Mooney's
Bay
Rideau
River

0   250   500 m

0   1/2 mi

Rideau Canal

Length: 8 km (5 mi) return
Hiking Time: 2 hrs
Type of Trail: crushed stone,
  asphalt
Uses: walking, biking, in-line
  skating, snowshoeing, cross-
  country skiing
Facilities: beaches, benches,
  garbage cans, interpretive
  panels, outhouses, picnic tables,
  viewing platform
Gov't Topo Map: 031G05
Rating (1-5): 2
Trailhead GPS: N 45° 23' 45.6"
  W 75° 42' 24.5"

Access Information: From Highway 417 east, take Exit 121A onto Bronson Avenue. After 500 m/yd, turn right onto Carling Avenue. Follow for 700 m/yd, turning left onto Preston Street. Entrance to a pay parking area is right at the intersection with Prince of Wales Drive. The trail begins on the east side of Prince of Wales Drive beside Dow's Lake.

OC Transpo Route 3 stops on Preston Street 130 m/yd from the trailhead.

Introduction: The Rideau Canal is one of the defining features of the city of Ottawa and was declared a UNESCO world heritage site in 2007. Designed as a secure military supply route, the canal has become one of the Canada's premier recreational facilities, its banks being the most popular destination for the city's walkers, runners, and cyclists.

Anywhere on the canal is a scenic place to hike, but the section between Dow's Lake and Hog's Back Falls is particularly attractive. Dow's Lake — with its pavilion, its facilities for renting canoes and bikes, and restaurants — is a popular site. The Dominion Arboretum and Central Experimental Farm offer any number of enticing side trips. Hog's Back Falls offers one of the most dramatic natural views in the city.

Route Description: Your route, on the Rideau Canal Western Pathway, begins opposite the parking area, across the intersection of Preston Street and Prince of Wales Drive. There is a large signboard with a map located here, and map brochures might also be available. The wide track, bisected by a bright yellow lane line, begins by skirting so close to the main building of HMCS *Carleton*, the home of the Canadian Forces Naval Reserve in Ottawa and slated for demolition in the near future, that it squeezes between its front doors and two commemorative cannon pointing toward Dow's Lake.

At 200 m/yd, you reach the first of many junctions. Keep left, toward the water, and 100 m/yd later, turn left again onto a little gravel path that leads to the tip of a point of land with four benches and the best view of the lake. The path circles back to the paved pathway, connecting in front of a tiny wetland. Turn left again, tracing the shore of the lake, with the beautiful grounds of the Dominion Arboretum to your right.

At the next gravel pathway, turn right, and in 40 m/yd, you will find three interpretive panels that profile the Arboretum, the Central

Experimental Farm, of which it is part, and the history of the Rideau Canal. Return to the water's edge and resume following the paved pathway. This curves gradually to the right, Dow's Lake narrowing into the canal waterway. Another cluster of four benches sits at its mouth, about 1 km (0.6 mi) from the start.

A signed side trail 100 m/yd later points right, into the Arboretum, but you continue straight, toward the museum, which is 1.8 km (1.1 mi) away. A sturdy bridge crosses a small creek 100 m/yd later, and you will probably notice people on the Eastern Pathway across the canal. Your route soon moves parallel to the water: canal on your left and a long line of pine trees, many of them with donation plaques attached, on your right.

The pathway remains straight for the next 400 m/yd, although numerous side trails branch to the right, with the buildings of Carleton University to the left. You reach a major trail junction within sight of a canal lock, and you should follow the left route as it climbs a small hill to the lock station buildings. This, Hartwells Lock, is a delightful spot, with benches, picnic tables, and interpretive panels that further describe the Rideau Canal's history.

It is also here where you must cross the canal, and this is possible

Rideau Canal

The Rideau Canal Waterway, which links the lakes and rivers between Ottawa and Kingston, is the oldest continuously operated canal in North America, extending 202 km (125 mi). The waterway, which is operated by Parks Canada, is a National Historic Site of Canada, a Canadian Heritage River, and a UNESCO World Heritage Site.

Opened in 1832, the canal features 45 locks in 23 lock stations along the main route of the Rideau plus two locks that link the Tay Canal. Most of the locks are still operated by hand, using the same mechanisms that were installed in 1832. The system is immensely popular with recreational boaters, and many parks and conservation areas have been established along its length.

only on the narrow wooden walkway that is found on top of the lock gates, and which is, fortunately, railed. Cyclists must dismount to get across, and the walkway is too narrow for wheelchairs. On the far side, there is another map station, because you are now on the Rideau Canal Eastern Pathway. A distance sign says that Parliament is 6.9 km (4.3 mi) to your left. However, we are going right, to Hog's Back Falls, which is now 1.7 km (1.1 mi) distant.

This next section, so close to Carleton University, can be exuberantly busy during the school year. Hundreds of university students use the trail to commute to the tall apartment buildings rising above the trees in the distance, and so there are benches and lighting. For 1.5 km (0.9 mi), the trail is flush to the stone wall bordering the Rideau Canal, with busy Colonel By Drive only a few metres to the left.

As you round the next curve, you should notice the golden dome of St. John the Baptist Ukrainian Catholic National Shrine. The far bank is thickly wooded, with occasional small streams feeding into the canal. About 600 m/yd from Hartwells, a lighted crosswalk on your left indicates the last opportunity to turn into Carleton University, and 300 m/yd further the pathway passes under-

neath the massive bridges of Heron Road. Stairwells connect to the sidewalks above.

At 3.5 km (2.2 mi) into your walk, you reach the Hog's Back Lock Station. If you cross the lock, there is a small field with picnic tables, garbage cans, and a bench. However, if you continue along the pathway, in 100 m/yd, it passes through a small tunnel and emerges onto Mooneys Bay, an artificial lake created by the dam built here to raise the water level for the canal.

On your right is the Rideau Canoe Club. Ahead and across the lake you can see Mooneys Bay Park and its beach. Turn left as you exit the tunnel. Follow the lakeshore, where there are benches, a viewing platform, and an interpretive panel. Continue left along the pathway, through another tunnel, and you come out at the top of vibrant Hog's Back Falls, your destination. Across a walkway on the top of the dam is a canteen with washrooms (seasonal) and benches, a good place to turn around.

There are walkways on both sides of the falls, providing excellent views of the swirling waters. Several interpretive signs explain both the geology and the construction challenges of damming the Rideau, and there are numerous benches where you may sit and contemplate the power and beauty of the natural world. Enjoy the view, then retrace your route back to Dow's Lake.

Cautionary Notes: Waterfall.

Cellphone Reception: Excellent.

Further Information: www.canadas capital.gc.ca/bins/ncc_web_content_page.asp?cid=16297-16299-9970&lang=1&bhcp=1: paper copies of map also available.

Spare Socks

After walking for a couple hours, changing into a fresh pair of socks is almost as refreshing as soaking your feet in water, and you will find a new spring in your step. I carry two extra pair so I have one to change into at the end of the hike.

Rideau River

Length: 15 km (9.4 mi) return
Hiking Time: 4 hrs
Type of Trail: pavement
Uses: walking, biking, in-line skating, snowshoeing, cross-country skiing
Facilities: benches, garbage cans, interpretive panels, outhouses, picnic tables
Gov't Topo Map: 031G05
Rating (1-5): 3
Trailhead GPS: N 45° 25' 33.4" W 75° 40' 15.6"

Access Information: From Highway 417 east, take Exit 118 onto Lees Avenue. After 400 m/yd, turn right onto Mann Avenue. Follow for 700 m/yd; Mann Avenue turns left and becomes Range Road. At the intersection with Somerset Street East, 400 m/yd further, turn right into the parking area.

From Highway 417 west, take Exit 118, turning left onto Lees Avenue. Follow for 900 m/yd, turning right onto Chapel Crescent. After 300 m/yd, turn right onto Mann Avenue and follow as outlined above.

OC Transpo Route 16 stops on

Somerset Street East 150 m/yd from parking area.

Introduction: The Rideau River cuts through the middle of Ottawa, and for much of its length, it is bordered by a superb pathway system. This route is so attractive that it is among the busiest in the city, particularly on sunny summer evenings and during the morning and evening commute. Walkers need to stay on their side of the path, as cyclists are

frequent and often travelling quite fast.

Hiking anywhere along the river pathways is worthwhile, but I have selected a route beginning from Strathcona Park in the trendy Sandy Hill neighbourhood to Vincent Massey Park opposite Carleton University. Strathcona Park is lined by elegant buildings housing numerous embassies; this area is known as Embassy Row. Vincent Massey Park is more remote, a popular picnic spot featuring wooded areas and large fields. This walk permits a picnic at either end, with several locations in between where extended stops may be made.

Route Description: From the parking area, head directly to the water's edge and turn right onto the paved walkway that parallels the Rideau River. Strathcona Park is filled with benches and picnic tables, with ducks, geese, gulls, squirrels, and people mixing freely among them. The river path is illuminated, and the playing field on the right is frequently used; watch for cricket matches during the summer.

Huge old trees line the wide path, which is situated well above the water, and within 150 m/yd it passes into a wooded area, where a forested hillside on the right insulates you somewhat from the apartment building, and other residences, above. About 250 m/yd later, you emerge next to a parking lot at the end of Range Road. A small field follows, then a wading pool and playground with change rooms, open only in the summer.

Once past this building, a side path joins from the right, and the

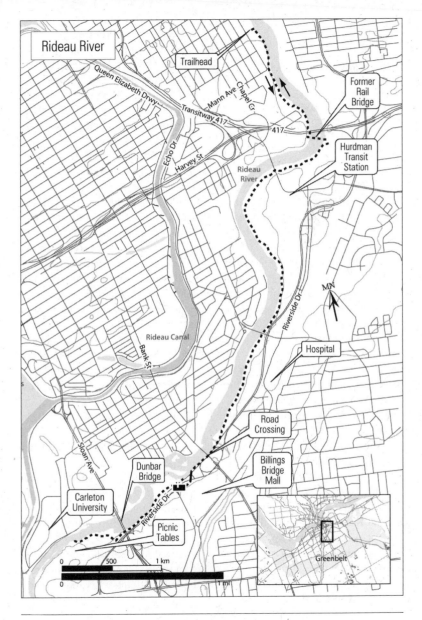

Rideau River

Trailhead

Queen Elizabeth Drwy.

Transitway 417

Mann Ave

Chapel Gr.

Former
Rail
Bridge

Echo Dr.

Harvey St.

417

Rideau
River

Hurdman
Transit
Station

Riverside Dr.

MN

Rideau Canal

Bank St.

Hospital

Road
Crossing

Sloan Ave.

Dunbar
Bridge

Billings
Bridge
Mall

Carleton
University

Riverside Dr.

Picnic
Tables

0   500   1 km

0   1 mi

Greenbelt

trees give way to grassy fields that run right into the river, with more benches to enjoy the view. To the right is the large playing area of Robinson Field. At 900 m/yd, the trail curves left around some new condominiums, pressed into the narrow space remaining between them and the river. After only 100 m/yd, you are past these houses, with the roar of the traffic on Highway 417 dominating. A city works area is on your right for another 100 m/yd, after which you reach the Queensway.

A path to your right leads to a nearby street, but your route is left and through the tunnel-like bridge beneath Highway 417. On the far side you connect to the Rideau River Eastern Pathway, where you cross a former railway bridge over the Rideau River. The views from here are excellent; watch for the city's swans, which like to nest on the tiny island below.

Once across the river you have walked 1.5 km (0.9 mi). Turn right, and follow the path as it curves back almost to the water's edge. A sign indicates that the Via Rail station is to the left, and Hog's Back Park, the direction you are heading, is 7 km (4.4 mi).

You now enter the most interesting section of the walk, as the trail moves into an area of thick vegetation where, with the exception of several high apartment towers to your left and some buildings across the river, almost no houses are visible from the trail. For the next 2 km (1.25 mi), the trail meanders through dense forest, sometimes seeming like a tunnel carved through the thick vegetation. Benches are available every few hundred metres, and there are frequent views of the river, but it is easy to convince yourself that you are in a far more remote location.

There are major junctions at 1.9 km (1.2 mi), to the Hurdman Transit Station, and 300 m/yd later when the trail passes beneath the Transitway Bridge crossing the Rideau. There are also very many informal paths that join the Pathway, crossing the former landfill site converted to parkland.

At 3.8 km (2.4 mi), you emerge from this sylvan refuge to an open field close to busy Riverside Drive

at Smythe Road. Instead of being sheltered, as you were for the past 2 km (1.25 mi), you are now exposed across an open field to the hectic traffic, the tranquil river on your right, until road and path converge at 5.2 km (3.25 mi). The Pathway continues for 500 m/yd across Bank Street to Rideau River Park, opposite Billings Bridge Mall, where you may rest in a lovely area popular for feeding ducks. Interpretive panels discuss the river ecology and the various waterfowl species.

This could be a good spot to turn back, but should you continue, the Rideau River Pathway parallels and remains exposed to Riverside Drive for nearly another 1 km (0.6 mi), crossing beneath the massive Dunbar Bridge at 6.5 km (4.1 mi). But barely 100 m/yd beyond that you return to the forest, the path turning sharply right and descending to the river. Your route meanders through the low ground, with Carleton University visible across the river. About 400 m/yd into the trees, the trail passes beneath a 19th-century rail bridge now used by the O-Train.

Continue a final 400 m/yd to Vincent Massey Park. The trail climbs noticeably for almost the first time and narrows slightly on the wooded slope. With rapids to your right, continue along the pathway until you sight picnic tables to your left. You have arrived. To return, retrace your route.

Cautionary Notes: Road crossing.

Cellphone Reception: Excellent.

Further Information: www.canadas capital.gc.ca/bins/ncc_web_content_ page.asp?cid=16297-16299-9970& lang=1&bhcp=1: paper copies of map also available.

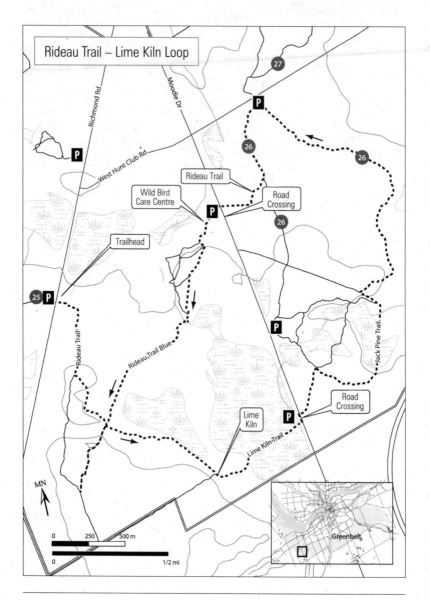

Rideau Trail – Lime Kiln Loop

Richmond Rd

Moodie Dr

West Hunt Club Rd

Rideau Trail

Wild Bird
Care Centre

Road
Crossing

Trailhead

Rideau Trail

Rideau Trail Blue

Jack Pine Trail

Road
Crossing

Lime
Kiln

Lime Kiln Trail

MN

| 0 | 250 | 500 m |

| 0 | | 1/2 mi |

Greenbelt

Rideau Trail – Lime Kiln Loop

Length: 9.5 km (6 mi) return
Hiking Time: 3 hrs
Type of Trail: crushed stone,
    boardwalks, natural surface
Uses: walking, snowshoeing
Facilities: garbage cans,
    interpretive sites, outhouses,
    picnic tables, trailhead maps
Gov't Topo Map: 031G05
Rating (1-5): 3
Trailhead GPS: N 45° 17' 40.2"
    W 75° 50' 04.2"

Access Information: From the Highway 416/417 split, follow Highway 416 for 3 km (2 mi) to Exit 72. Turn right onto West Hunt Club Road and follow 3.3 km (2.1 mi) to Richmond Road. Turn left and drive 700 m/yd to P6, on the right.

OC Transpo Route 66 stops on Richmond Road, opposite.

Introduction: Most serioius hikers know that the Rideau Trail connects the cities of Kingston and Ottawa with a hiking path more than 300 km (188 mi) in length. Less well known, the Rideau Trail system includes a number of side trails, some of them quite extensive. One of these is the Lime Kiln Loop within the National Capital Commission's Greenbelt, excellent for watching nature, especially waterfowl. This loop also passes its namesake Lime Kiln, a historic site featuring several interpretive display panels. The Lime Kiln Loop is a good choice when you wish to hike for several hours but do not wish to drive too far to do so.

Route Description: Start by crossing busy Richmond Road. Then enter the forest on a path marked by the orange triangles of the Rideau Trail. This track is narrow, with a dirt strip in the middle and grass on the edges. It is also unimproved, so it is rocky and rough and quite twisty. Within a few hundred metres/yards, you encounter the remains of an old wood road; turn right onto it. The forest here is mostly young hardwoods, primarily maple.

At 600 m/yd, the footpath separates from the wood road, heading left. Watch for the orange markers. This is much rougher walking, and far more twisty until you reach a bridge crossing a tiny creek, at 1.2 km (0.75 mi). The sign on the far side tells you that you are on the Rideau Trail and that Kingston is 275 km (172 mi) to your right. (If you impulsively decide to trek to Sir John A. Macdonald's city, I hope you at least packed a lunch!) But the sign also indicates that it is 900 m/yd to the Lime Kiln, your first destination.

The route becomes very rocky, with thick stands of cedar predominating. At about 500 m/yd, you sight a large swampy area on your left, and your treadway is almost all massive flat rocks. It is easy to understand

why this area was named "Stony Swamp." Original, no; accurate, yes. You quite suddenly reach a gravelled pathway, the site of the Lime Kiln, where interpretive panels explain the ruins around you.

Follow the most distinct path. You will pass the remains of several buildings, more interpretive panels, and cross a boardwalk bridging a large wet area. Traverse one small ridge, populated by maples, before this section finishes at a spot that is elevated above the large swamps on either side. About 700 m/yd from the ruins, you reach P10 on Moodie Drive. A bear-proof garbage can and another interpretive panel can be found in this small parking lot.

To reconnect with the trail, you must turn left onto Moodie Drive and walk perhaps 200 m/yd. When you see the blue Rideau Trail triangle, cross the road (cautiously!) and re-enter the forest. This is now a conservation area where no dogs are permitted. After following an old wood road for 150 m/yd, you reach a junction, where you turn right. You have joined the NCC's Jack Pine Trail, on Loop C. This is very wide, with a high hardwood canopy on a compacted earth pathway. It emerges into a regenerating field, where you will probably hear nearby Highway 416. Fortunately, the path turns away, gradually curving left; ignore

frequent side paths from your right. It enters a long causeway bisecting an extensive wetland that provides excellent opportunities for viewing waterfowl.

Once across the wetland, you cross several small boardwalks before turning left 90°, after which you reach a junction. Here Jack Pine Trail goes left; continue straight on Trail 26, which is marked by blue Rideau Trail triangles. Almost immediately Trail 26 splits; turn right toward Hunt Club Road. For the next 2 km (1.25 mi), you pass through a fairly featureless section that is home to many jack pines. You will notice a small pond on your right as the woods change to exclusively cedar. About 500 m/yd later, you

briefly emerge from the woods to pass beneath some power lines, and after that, it is only another 500 m/yd until the trail reaches P11 at West Hunt Club. You will find a trail map and garbage cans.

You come out into the parking lot, turn right, and re-enter the forest, still on Trail 26. Many flat rocks line the trail, covered generously with pine needles. You cross beneath the power lines again, and 200 m/yd later, 700 m/yd from P11, at the edge of a lovely field, the Rideau Trail turns right, separating from Trail 26. The narrower footpath passes among beautiful red pine then thick cedar swamp. It can be quite messy in wet weather. You emerge into an open area then soon reach Moodie

Road opposite P8, 400 m/yd from Trail 26. Cross the road.

In P8, in addition to garbage cans and a map, there is also an outhouse. Follow the Beaver Trail, a wide crushed-stone trail surrounded by hardwoods. It passes the Wild Bird Care Centre, a facility dedicated to the rehabilitation and release of injured wild birds. Not surprisingly, there are quite a few bird feeders in the nearby trees. Keep left, as the Beaver and Chipmunk trails separate into a maze of interconnecting paths, until you reach a major boardwalk/bridge structure, 2 km (1.25 mi) from P11. Take this across the major wet area, where there is also an observation deck overlooking a beaver lodge.

On the far side of the boardwalk, you are delivered to a narrow natural-surface footpath with many rocks protruding. It continues for 1 km (0.6 mi), including a climb that, while minor, is still the most significant of the walk. You reach the intersection with the main route of the Rideau Trail at the first bridge. To return to your start, turn right and retrace your first 1.2 km (0.75 mi).

Cautionary Notes: Animals, multiple busy road crossings.

Cellphone Reception: Adequate throughout.

Further Information: www.canadas capital.gc.ca/bins/ncc_web_content_page.asp?cid=16297-16299-9735&lang=1; paper trail map available for purchase.

Common Yellow Warbler

Ottawa River, Ottawa – City and Greenbelt

Pine Grove Forestry Trail, Arboretum Loop,
Ottawa – City and Greenbelt

Rideau River, Ottawa – City and Greenbelt

Hog's Back Falls on the Rideau River, Ottawa – City and Greenbelt

Rideau Trail – Lime Kiln Loop, Ottawa – City and Greenbelt

Snowshoeing, Western Québec – Gatineau Park

Lusk Caves, Western Québec – Gatineau Park

Shirleys Bay – Trail 10

Length: 4 km (2.5 mi) return
Hiking Time: 1 hr
Type of Trail: crushed stone, natural surface
Uses: walking, snowshoeing, cross-country skiing
Facilities: garbage cans
Gov't Topo Map: 031G05
Rating (1-5): 1
Trailhead GPS: N 45° 21' 15.7" W 75° 51' 38.3"

Access Information: From the Highway 416/417 split, follow Highway 417 for 2.5 km (1.6 mi) to Exit 134, turning right onto Moodie Drive. Continue on Moodie for 1.7 km (1.1 mi), turning left onto Carling Avenue. Take Carling for 1.2 km (0.75 mi); P2 is on the right.

There is no nearby bus stop at P2. However, routes 169 and 182 stop at Carling Avenue and Rifle Road. The Greenway Pathway West starts in that intersection's northeast corner and connects to Trail 10 after 700 m/yd.

Introduction: Sometimes you do not have the time to travel to a remote location for a hike, but you really have a yearning to walk away from habitation. Shirleys Bay offers the pleasures of a woodland stroll without the necessity of leaving the city. Trail 10 consists of a short, easily walked loop that includes a brief stretch near the Ottawa River. It is good for families and is quite popular in the winter for cross-country skiing.

The name "Shirleys Bay" sometimes causes confusion among longtime residents. The land around the Ottawa River was originally deeded to Thomas Shirley and became known as "Shirley's Bay." A government research facility on Carling Avenue and the adjacent Connaught Rifle Range became known as "Shirley Bay" during World War II. However, in 1962, the Committee on Geographical Names decided on "Shirleys Bay," keeping with its policy to delete apostrophes or other punctuation in Canadian place names. This is the version used on all official maps and references.

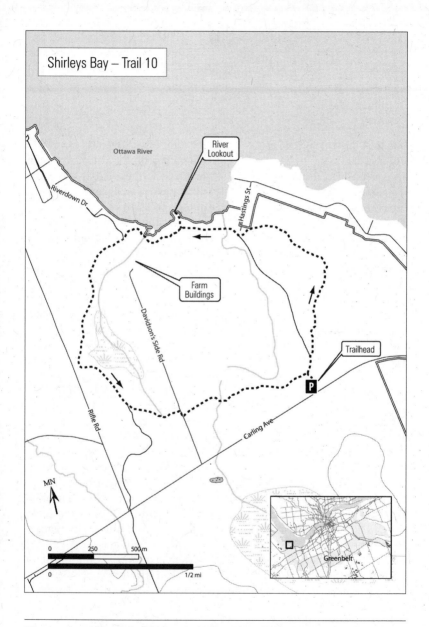

Shirleys Bay – Trail 10

Ottawa River

River Lookout

Riverdown Dr

Hastings St.

Farm Buildings

Davidson's Side Rd

Trailhead

P

Rifle Rd

Carling Ave

MN

0   250   500 m

0   1/2 mi

Greenbelt

Route Description: From the small, fenced-in parking area, which contains only a garbage can and a trailhead pavilion, Trail 10 heads into forested land populated by very young hardwoods. At a first junction, less than 50 m/yd from P2, keep right, and keep right again at 120 m/yd when Trail 10 separates from a wood access road. For the next few hundred metres/yards, the path is bordered by low vegetation, sparsely growing over land being reclaimed from pasture. Only occasional larger trees, or pine, may be sighted.

At 500 m/yd, you reach virtually the only rock to intrude upon your path. It is quite small, and if the trail were not forced to narrow somewhat to pass a large tree, you might not even notice the stone. For the first time, the trees almost close in, and the trail twists and turns a little as it passes through a wet area. At 700 m/yd, you emerge into a clear area, a trail marker in sight affixed to a jack pine. Look to your left, and you should see the remains of an old fireplace. After the field, the trail continues to meander through the brush, with sporadic pine and cedar. To your right, the outlines of houses might be visible through the leaves, and frequent side paths lead off in that direction. At 1 km (0.6 mi), you cross the first unrailed bridge of the walk, and 100 m/yd further, the path comes within a few metres of the end of Hastings Street, where there is another access point.

You reconnect there with the wood access road. Turn right, where you should now be able to see the Ottawa River ahead. The route remains about 25 m/yd from the water's edge, although 100 m/yd from the road, there is a side trail to the river, and 100 m/yd beyond that, a very prominent side trail heads out to the tip of a tiny point, where you will obtain the best view of Shirleys Bay, the Gatineau Hills, and the community of Aylmer on the far side of the very broad river.

Trail 10 stays in the forest, however, threading its way through the wet areas, crossing a creek on a fairly substantial bridge perhaps 200 m/yd later. You might notice farm buildings to your left. Once across, Trail 10 comes its closest to the Ottawa River, then turns away for good, so visit the river now if you want. The trail turns again, to the right, with the straight path continuing toward the farmhouses. Then, at 1.8 km (1.1 mi), Trail 10 links with the wide, crushed-stone Greenbelt Pathway West. You should turn left and follow the trail as it goes gently uphill, away from the river.

For the next 1.1 km (0.7 mi), you follow this easy walking route. It is mostly open, with only small, young

crosses a number of small bridges as it works its way back toward P2. One of these, at about 3.5 km (2.2 mi), is next to some larger trees and a wider creek and might be a pleasant place to stop and dip your feet. Around 700 m/yd after crossing the dirt road, your path intersects the starting trail, completing the loop. To your right, at 50 m/yd, is P2 and the end of your walk.

Cautionary Notes: None.

Cellphone Reception: Excellent.

Further Information: www.canadas capital.gc.ca/bins/ncc_web_content_ page.asp?cid=16297-16299-9735& lang=1; paper trail map available for purchase.

trees bordering it and virtually no shade, except for the occasional pine. It begins passing through a field, with clear views of the farm on your left, and after 700 m/yd, makes a sharp left turn after coming within 40 m/yd of Rifle Road. Up to that point, it has seemed as if a distant communication tower was your objective.

At 2.9 km (1.8 mi), Trail 10 separates to the left from the Pathway, returning to a grass-surfaced, somewhat narrower path. For the next 300 m/yd, you pass underneath the best shade of the walk, a dense stand of cedar. Trail 10 crosses the dirt Davidsons Side Road just in front of the gate to Riverglen Farm. Back among young hardwoods on what looks like an old wood road, Trail 10

GPS/Compass

Nothing has revolutionized wilderness travel recently as much as Global Positioning System satellite navigation. With a GPS unit, you can travel directly to any location for which you have the coordinates. I use one, but also carry a compass as a backup. Its batteries never go dead.

WESTERN QUÉBEC – GATINEAU PARK

Laurentian Highlands

The rugged hills of Gatineau Park look like a different world from the flat lands of the city of Ottawa. They are, in fact, part of the Canadian Shield, a portion of the land mass called the Laurentian Highlands that extends from the Gatineau and Ottawa rivers in the west to beyond the Saguenay River in the east.

Unlike the sedimentary lowlands of eastern Ontario, the Laurentian Highlands are composed of frequent intrusions of tough igneous and metamorphic rocks. Many south-facing escarpments give the area a mountainous appearance, and its rolling terrain is full of lakes surrounded by hills ranging in elevation from 400 to 800 m/yd.

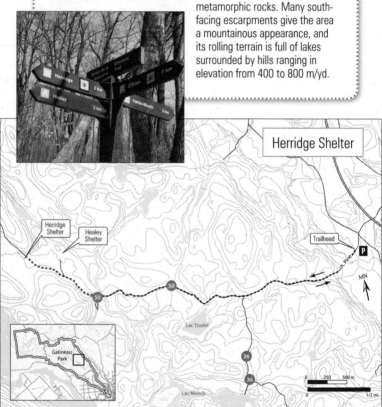

Herridge Shelter

Herridge Shelter

Length: 10 km (6.25 mi) return
Hiking Time: 3-4 hrs
Type of Trail: compacted earth
Uses: walking, biking, cross-country skiing
Facilities: garbage can, interpretive panels, outhouse, shelter, trailhead marker
Gov't Topo Map: 031G12
Rating (1-5): 3
Trailhead GPS: N 45° 34' 20.1" W75° 53' 08.2"

Access Information: From the Macdonald-Cartier Bridge, follow Highway 5 for 21 km (13 mi) to Exit 21. At the stop sign, turn right. At the streetlights at the junction with Highway 105, turn left, drive for 1 km (0.6 mi), turning left again onto Pine Street. The road becomes dirt 400 m/yd later. Keep left at a stop sign at 900 m/yd; the parking area P16 is 200 m/yd further.

Introduction: Originally constructed in 1880 as the home for an Irish immigrant family trying to farm the thin soil of the Gatineau Hills, Herridge Shelter is now a year-

round destination for thousands of outdoor enthusiasts. This would have pleased its namesake, Duncan Herridge, a former Canadian Ambassador to the United States and avid outdoorsman, who, for almost forty years from the early 1920s, used the house as his base to explore the surrounding countryside. The Herridge Shelter is well positioned to be accessed from park trailheads in Wakefield, Lac Philippe, and O'Brien Beach. The trail from less well-known P16 is the shortest and often the least busy.

Because of the many hardwoods, this is an excellent "fall colours" hike. In spring, white trilliums are very common, making this a wonderful

Trillium

The provincial flower of Ontario, the white trillium carpets the hardwood forest floor of Gatineau Park and other parts of the region for a few weeks each year in April and early May. Usually blossoming before leaves have opened on the trees, the distinctive three-leafed trillia glow brightly in the spring sunlight in their clusters of hundreds or thousands. The less common purple trillium, shyly hiding its flower, may also often be found mixed among its more visible relative.

Picking trillia for their flowers can seriously injure or kill the plant. Don't do it.

wildflower walk as well. But beware: the first 2 km (1.25 mi), mostly uphill, make the start somewhat daunting if you have been inactive all winter, so this is not a good hike for novices.

Route Description: Trail 50 is a continuation of a former settler road, so it is wide and almost completely free of potholes and tree roots. Except for a very brief dip at the start, to cross

Meech Creek, the first 1 km (0.6 mi) is uphill, as you cross the fields by the trailhead and enter the forest, which is mixed hardwoods and softwoods. The first level section, at 1 km (0.6 mi), is brief, and the path climbs again, continuing uphill until reaching the junction with Trail 36, at 2 km (1.25 mi).

A sign directs you right, indicating that Herridge Shelter is 3 km (1.9 mi) further. If you head left, expect a long 7 km (4.4 mi) hike in the wrong direction before you reach P11 at O'Brien Beach. Your route, which thankfully finally drops downhill somewhat, is now part of both the Trans Canada Trail and the National Hiking Trail. You should notice the signs for each affixed to some trees.

Small Lake Trudel appears on your left about 500 m/yd further. Beyond that, after a short climb, you should sight a Trans Canada Trail Discovery Panel about the ruffed grouse. The terrain becomes more rolling, with many small hills bordering the path. Continue through the forest for an additional 1 km (0.6 mi), then cross a small creek on an unrailed bridge. Just after crossing, you reach a signed junction that tells you 1 km (.6 mi) remains to Herridge Shelter. Keep right, and climb a little hill to a second junction, where you also stay right. Another Discovery Panel is found here, this describing the pileated woodpecker. Both left-hand paths are closed to the public.

The shelter is easy to find, on the left of the path, about 100 m downhill from another junction, this one

to the prime minister's Mousseau residence. The trail signpost, next to the stone gates in front of the shelter, tells you that it is an additional 10 km (6.25 mi) to P17 at Wakefield and also 10 km (6.25 mi) to P19 at Lac Philippe. The campground there, however, is only an additional 6.5 km (4 mi), should you decide you want to spend an evening inside the park.

Herridge Shelter is excellent. There are benches and picnic tables outside, as well as both "his" and "hers" outhouses. Inside are a woodstove, picnic tables, and an emergency phone. The building contains two levels and features an interpretive panel that provides the history of the house and the property. Firewood, should you need it, may be found out back.

This is a wonderful location for a lunch, and when you are finished, you retrace your route back to P16.

Cautionary Notes: Animals.

Cellphone Reception: Adequate throughout.

Further Information: www.canadas capital.gc.ca/data/2/rec_docs/3414_ SummerTrailMap.pdf; paper copy of map available for purchase.

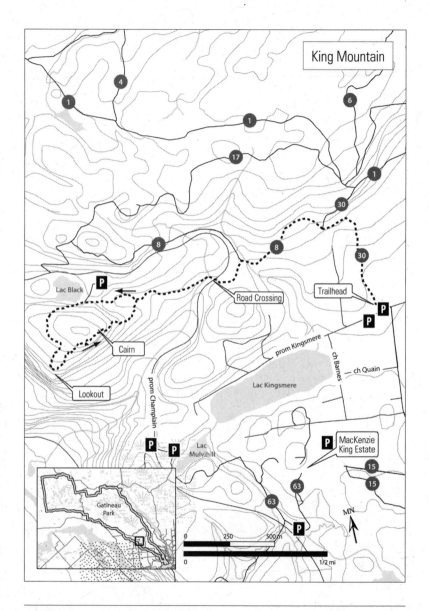

King Mountain

Lac Black

Road Crossing

Trailhead

Cairn

Lookout

prom Kingsmere

ch Barnes

ch Quain

Lac Kingsmere

prom Champlain

Lac Mulvihill

MacKenzie King Estate

Gatineau Park

0   250   500 m

0   1/2 mi

MN

King Mountain

Length: 6.5 km (4 mi) return
Hiking Time: 2-3 hrs
Type of Trail: compacted earth,
  natural surface, rock
Uses: walking, biking* [closed in
  winter]
Facilities: benches, garbage cans,
  interpretive panels, outhouses,
  picnic tables
Gov't Topo Map: 031G12
Rating (1-5): 3
Trailhead GPS: N 45° 29' 27.3"
  W 75° 50' 31.7"

Access Information: From the
Macdonald-Cartier Bridge, follow
Highway 5 for 12 km (7.5 mi) to Exit
12/Chemin Old Chelsea. Turn left
and continue straight through the
community of Old Chelsea, turning
left after 1 km (0.6 mi) onto Chemin
de Kingsmere. Follow for 3 km
(1.9 mi) into Kingsmere; turn right
into P7.

Introduction: The 2.5 km (1.6 mi)
King Mountain Trail loop starting
from Lac Black is one of the most
popular trails in Gatineau Park and
features some of its most highly

structured boardwalks and stair
systems. The King Mountain Trail is
also home to an elaborate system of
interpretive panels. It is constantly
busy, so to provide some relief from
the crowds, I have included a relatively easy 2 km (1.25 mi) approach
walk from P7 on the Kingsmere
Road along quiet Trail 8.

Those wishing dramatic scenery without quite so much walking
should begin from the King Mountain parking area off the Champlain
Parkway.

Route Description: Wide and firm,
Trail 30 climbs almost straight from
P7 before turning sharply to arrive,
at 700 m/yd, at a junction with Trail
8. Trail 30 veers right, but you continue straight on Trail 8. From this
point, bicycles are not permitted.
Occasional glimpses of the homes of
Kingsmere are possible to your left
through the beautiful hardwoods.
Although Trail 8 climbs initially, it
soon drops back down to cross an
unbridged brook, just past a house
that is almost in the path. Once
over the stream, you find a signed

Continue straight/right toward the King Mountain parking lot 500 m/yd away. You climb constantly, but gradually, often assisted by boardwalks in wet areas, passing interpretive panels such as the "Ancient Maples." It mentions that many of these glorious maples are already more than 200 years old and perhaps approaching the end of their lives. The next, challenging, 50 m/yd are up a constricted, rocky defile, enhanced by logs placed to manage drainage and erosion, but at the top, you have only to go 100 m/yd to your right to reach the King Mountain parking area, where there are outhouses and picnic tables overlooking tiny, picturesque Lac Black.

junction, where you turn left onto an unnumbered footpath, at 1.5 km (0.9 mi).

This narrow footpath heads toward Champlain Parkway, which you should be able to see through the trees, and crosses it. (You should be particularly cautious. There are no signs warning motorists of this crossing, and the sightlines are poor). Once across, the path briefly follows another small brook and then works its way along a slope through more hardwoods, climbing gradually until it connects to the King Mountain Trail, 2 km (1.25 mi) from P7.

The main trail continues straight, however, where you face the most daunting section of the walk. As the conveniently placed, (and almost gleeful), interpretive panels explain, you are about to climb to the southern edge of the Canadian Shield, the lip of the Eardley Escarpment, more than 300 m/yd above the floor of the Ottawa River Valley. Fortunately, you only have about 30 m/yd remaining, but it is tough. You are assisted by elaborate stairs, shaded under towering hemlocks, occasionally ornamented by interpretive panels that you can pretend to find absorbing while you catch your breath.

But the effort is worthwhile, for although you must continue a further 500 m/yd beyond the stairs while the trail meanders through groves of red and white oak, after a short descent, you arrive on a bare rock perched on the edge of the mountain with views in almost every direction. Directly beneath sits small Lac Mountains and farmland stretches away like a dappled carpet to the distant blue sliver that is the Ottawa River. There is even a bench.

This view by itself might be worth the climb, but there is more. For the next several hundred metres/yards, the trail scampers over the bare slope of the mountain, climbing constantly while detouring occasionally into forested folds between rocky spurs. The views are magnificent, particularly later in the day when the sun is behind you. Even the towers of Ottawa can be sighted, peeking over the hills to the southeast. Frequent interpretive panels provide context.

The final highlight is a massive stone cairn, fronted with a bronze plaque, marking a National Historic Site: commemorating the first

Eardley Escarpment

The most prominent geographical feature of Gatineau Park, the Eardley Escarpment, towers 300 m/yd above the Ottawa River Valley and stretches like a defensive wall facing the housing developments of the city of Gatineau. This volcanic rock face is a southern extension of the Canadian Shield and during the last ice age, formed the northern boundary of the great Champlain Sea, which covered most of eastern Ontario.

The top of the escarpment affords magnificent views of the Ottawa Valley, and the many trails and lookouts found there are among Gatineau Park's busiest, especially during the fall when the hardwoods that cover its slopes change colour.

the path from Kingsmere. You have completed a challenging 4.5 km (2.8 mi) hike. Turn right and retrace your 2 km (1.25 mi) approach walk to finish.

Cautionary Notes: Animals, cliffs, road crossing, steep climbs.

Cellphone Reception: No signal along Trails 30 and 8 or on the reverse side of King Mountain. Good signal on summit.

Further Information: www.canadas capital.gc.ca/data/2/rec_docs/3414_ SummerTrailMap.pdf. Paper copy available for purchase. Also: www. canadascapital.gc.ca/bins/ncc_ web_content_page.asp?cid=16297-16299-10170-49685-49721-49725& lang=1.

triangulation station of the Geodetic Survey of Canada, erected in July 1905. If that means little to you, you are not alone, but before the advent of satellite navigation, detailed surveys could only be conducted with the assistance of stations where the exact latitude and longitude were precisely calculated. King Mountain's was the first in Canada.

Afterwards the trail moves away from the crest and, after 300 m/yd of matchless views, begins to descend the reverse slope of King Mountain. It is quite steep, but there are stairs. One interpretive panel remains, pointing out, to your undoubted delight, scars on flanking trees made by bear claws. You might be tempted to break into a jog, but 100 m/yd later, you return to the junction with

Map

Hiking without a map is like walking with one eye closed. What is the name of that lake? How high is that hill? How much further to walk? With a map, you have answers to all those questions, an indispensible guide to your surroundings, and an important safety tool.

Lauriault Trail

Length: 4.5 km (2.8 mi) return
Hiking Time: 1-2 hrs
Type of Trail: compacted earth,
    natural surface
Uses: walking, snowshoeing
Facilities: benches, garbage cans,
    interpretive panels, outhouses,
    picnic tables
Gov't Topo Map: 031G05
Rating (1-5): 1
Trailhead GPS: N 45° 29' 02.5"
    W 75° 51' 30.0"

Access Information: From the Macdonald-Cartier Bridge, take Exit 1/ Boulevard Maisonneuve for 1 km (0.6 mi) toward Centre-Ville. Turn right onto Boulevard des Allumettières. Follow des Allumettières for 3 km (1.9 mi), then turn onto the exit ramp for Gatineau Park. After 300 m/yd, turn left onto Promenade de la Gatineau and follow for 11 km (6.9 mi), turning left onto Promenade Champlain. Continue for 1.3 km (0.8 mi), turning left into the parking area.

Introduction: William Lyon Mackenzie King was one of Canada's greatest, and most fascinating, prime ministers. A master politician, and the longest ever to serve as prime minister at nearly 22 years, he was a lifelong bachelor whose diaries reveal a deep interest in the occult.

King also lived a love affair with the hills and forest surrounding Kingsmere Lake, and the trails, gardens, and estate he created in his country home in Kingsmere. The estate's ruins, which are open to the public and can be accessed from the Lauriault Trail, include stones from the original Canadian Parliament Buildings and Westminster Palace in England.

Mackenzie King donated his estate, and the 231 hectares (570 acres) in the area he had acquired, to the Canadian people on his death in 1950. His gift became the core of Gatineau Park, the federal government's great natural green space that extends into the area of the fifth largest urban centre in the country.

Route Description: Due to the popularity of the Lauriault Trail, the parking area is quite large and bordered

by a shaded picnic area with tables and other amenities, including an outhouse. Your route begins in the southeast corner, marked by a map pavilion and trailhead sign, which indicates that the lookout is at 400 m/yd and the waterfall is at 1.5 km (0.9 mi).

The path starts very wide, the ground worn from heavy use. A set of stairs assists you in climbing the first short hill. You will notice rocks peeking through the thin soil and the escarpment sloping away steeply on your right. There are even a few boulders in that first 100 m/yd, balanced on the edge of the slope as if positioned deliberately. (Oh, those tricky glaciers!) In mere minutes, you arrive at a rocky outcropping where a bench faces south; you

have reached the Lauriault Lookout, although the view is not terribly great.

From here the trail changes briefly, narrowing, becoming rocky, and descending through an area of tall, gorgeous maples that form a leafy canopy high overhead. After traversing a rocky outcropping near the lookout, the route returns to being a path wide enough for two. About 300 m/yd beyond the lookout, you cross a tiny creek over an unrailed bridge. You are in the space between two hills here, and the forest is particularly attractive, with high hardwoods whose leaves intercept, but do not block, the sunlight, imparting a yellow-green tinge to everything.

You cross a wide boardwalk 100 m/yd later and climb more stairs on the far side. As you work uphill, the trail becomes gradually rockier, and since you are working around the escarpment side of the hill, you might catch glimpses of the farmland below. There is another small bridge to cross before the trail turns sharply left and heads back downhill. At 1.4 km (0.9 mi), you cross the wide bridge over the creek feeding the waterfall. Turn right, and in 100 m/yd, descending often on stone stairways, you reach the charming viewing area overlooking the modest cascade. A low stone wall lies

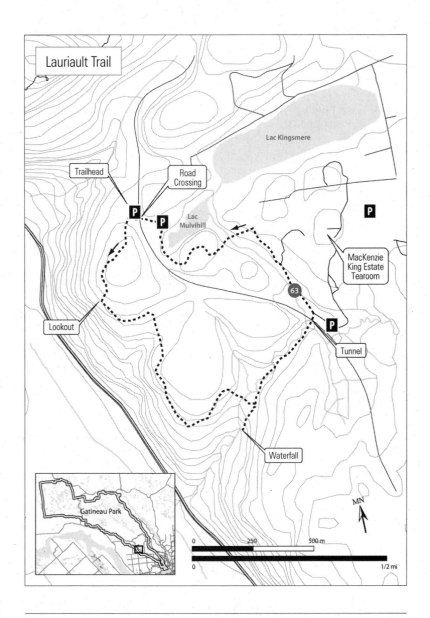

Lauriault Trail

Trailhead

Road Crossing

Lac Kingsmere

Lac Mulvihill

MacKenzie King Estate Tearoom

63

Lookout

Tunnel

Waterfall

Gatineau Park

MN

0   250   500 m

0   1/2 mi

between the path and the creek, a sturdy bench faces the waterfall, and an interpretive panel explains that this was one of Mackenzie King's favourite places.

After a few minutes enjoying this tranquil spot, return to the last junction, but keep straight on the very wide path that parallels the creek up the hill. You soon cross the stream, this time on a bridge with railings, and with the creek on your right, climb the gentle, easy hill along a very pretty route that winds around rocky outcroppings.

Perhaps 600 m/yd after leaving the waterfall, the trail passes underneath the Promenade de la Gatineau through a tunnel. On the far side, there is a junction and an interpretive panel tells you that Moreside Gardens is only 500 m/yd further. This is definitely a side trip worth taking, because you access the Mackenzie King Estate, and during the summer, you can even stop for a snack — pricey but decidedly elegant — at the Mackenzie King Tearoom. The Lauriault Trail turns left and climbs 200 m/yd to another junction, which provides a second opportunity to access the estate. This is also marked by an interpretive panel, which mentions that the trees around you are beech and birch. A sign also tells you that it is

900 m/yd to the Mulvihill parking lot.

You are now passing beneath the first softwoods, still on a wide path. Keep to the left fork at the next junction, and at 300 m/yd, you bridge another small brook. The next 200 m/yd have you climbing up a slope steep enough for another set of stairs. At the top, you should glimpse small Lac Mulvihill to the north. The path drops off this final knoll, skirts the edge of the lake, and reaches the Mulvihill parking lot. To your right, another picnic area may be found beside the water. Cross the road to your left to return to the Lauriault parking lot.

The total distance of the loop, being generous, is 3.5 km (2.2 mi). However, you should definitely take the side trip to the Mackenzie King Estate, which will add no less than 1 km (0.6 mi).

Cautionary Notes: Animals, road crossing.

Cellphone Reception: Excellent.

Further Information: www.canadas capital.gc.ca/data/2/rec_docs/3414_ SummerTrailMap.pdf; paper copy of map available for purchase.

Lusk Cave

Length: 13.5 km (8.4 mi) return
Hiking Time: 4-6 hrs
Type of Trail: crushed stone, natural surface
Uses: walking, biking*, snowshoeing*, cross-country skiing*
Facilities: barbeque pits, beach, benches, bike racks, garbage cans, interpretive panels, outhouses, picnic tables, playgrounds, shelter, water
Gov't Topo Map: 031G12
Rating (1-5): 5 [distance, elevation change]
Trailhead GPS: N 45° 36' 17.9" W 76° 00' 37.0"

Access Information: From the Macdonald-Cartier Bridge, follow Highway 5 for 22 km (13.75 mi) to end at a lighted intersection. Turn left onto Highway 105 and continue for 5.5 km (3.5 mi) to the next street lights. From the lights, continue straight on Highway 5 for 1.2 km (0.75 mi) and turn left onto Highway 366. Follow for 7 km (4.4 mi), turning left onto Chemin du Lac Philippe. Park at the Plage Parent (Parent Beach) lot.

Introduction: Caves are rare in the Canadian Shield, but in the Gatineau Valley there are pockets of marble, a rock that can be dissolved by water. Lusk Cave is one of these and is a popular destination at all times of the year.

Being a frugal hiker, I object to paying a $9 admission fee to the beach, so I park instead at the entrance kiosk. From here, it is a pleasant stroll along the grass verge, and as soon as you reach Lac Philippe, it is possible to follow the lakeshore. In the fall, or early in the day before it gets busy, consider starting at the entrance kiosk. Choosing this option will add 4 km (2.5 mi).

The route distance listed includes the side trip to Lusk Cabin.

Route Description: This trail officially begins at the southwest corner of the Plage Parent parking lot, where a sign notifies you that the caverns are 5 km (3.1 mi) distant. The wide path heads away from the water, immediately branching right at a junction and heading downhill. The surface

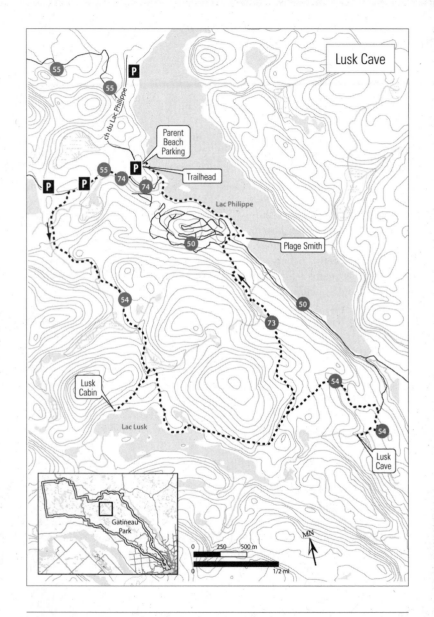

Lusk Cave

Parent Beach Parking

Trailhead

Lac Philippe

Plage Smith

Lusk Cabin

Lac Lusk

Lusk Cave

ch du Lac Philippe

Gatineau Park

MN

0   250   500 m

0   1/2 mi

is gravelled or sandy, and bikers use this path extensively.

At about 500 m/yd, you return to the road and encounter another junction. Although a sign says that the caverns are to your left, instead cross the road and follow it toward Lac Taylor. Paved at first, it soon shifts to dirt, and you pass campground areas, a dam, and Little Renaud Lake on your left. Continue on this, Trail 55, until you reach the junction with Trail 54; turn left onto that trail. The sign says that Lusk Cabin is 3 km (1.9 mi) away.

This is a lovely route, wide and with a good treadway. Robust, healthy trees shade you. Pines line the hillside as you climb, once you cross a little creek at 300 m/yd. Although not too steep, Trail 54 rises more than 50 m/yd, following and crossing another tiny stream a couple of times. As you roam through the forest, you will pass numerous wet areas, meadows, and occasional ponds, depending upon how wet it has been. When you reach a larger pool, garnished with a beaver lodge, you have only a further few hundred metres/yards before you reach the next junction, 3.5 km (2.2 mi) from Plage Parent.

Turn right to take the 500 m/yd side trail to Lusk Cabin, which I recommend. Lusk Cabin may be booked for overnight stays only during the winter but is a wonderful destination any time of year. Recently rebuilt, it sits on a gentle grass slope facing Lac Lusk and features benches, a picnic table, and an outhouse. On a sunny day, after a noon meal, it is easy to fall asleep and lose hours of walking time. Total return trip from/to Plage Parent: 8 km (5 mi).

Return to the main path. Trail 54 narrows from the width of a wood road into a footpath, and biking is no longer permitted. It quickly descends to Lac Lusk, although far from the cabin, and works its way along the edge of the water for several hundred metres/yards under a soothing pine canopy. Once Trail 54 turns away from Lac Lusk, you return to some fairly steady climbing. At 600 m/yd from the lake, it turns 90° left, then drops fairly steeply, entering a glade of towering maples bordered by a steep hill to your left. Another 400 m/yd and you reach another junction (you might notice that all the trails here are 54).

Continuing straight, the route is generally downhill and quite rugged, crossing wet areas, many with boardwalks. After 1 km (0.6 mi), you hit the junction to Lusk Cave, where you turn right and find the first interpretive panel. This path is wider, and stairs assist in the climb. Your route continues to the cave area, about 500 m/yd. The network

of paths, signs, and cave entrances is a bit too complicated to describe. However, you will probably have lots of company so are unlikely to become misplaced. Once you have explored the cave, it is time to return.

Easier option: If you are getting tired, retrace the 500 m/yd to the main trail. Turn right, down the hill to connect with Trail 50 at the tip of Lac Philippe. Turn left and follow this nearly level path, which you will share with cyclists, back to Plage Parent: 13 km (8 mi), including Lusk Cabin.

Challenging option: Those still energetic should turn left at the main trail and return the 1 km (0.6 mi) back to the next junction, which is the Sentier de la Caverne. Bear right; the signpost says 2 km (1.25 mi) to the Lac Philippe campground. Although initially it climbs underneath a hardwood canopy, the route soon descends, rapidly and steeply. It skirts a small wet area 500 m/yd later then passes beneath some massive pine. You cross a tiny outflow then continue to descend until you cross a little bridge and reach Trail 50 opposite campsite 339. Including Lusk Cabin, you have walked 12 km (7.5 mi), with 1.5 km (0.9 mi) remaining to the trailhead.

You have several options, but I recommend heading to nearby Plage Smith and following the scenic shoreline path the remainder of the way back to Plage Parent. Sentier de la Caverne might be only 500 m/yd longer than returning by Trail 50 from Lusk Cave but is far more difficult.

Cautionary Notes: Animals, poison ivy, cave.

Cellphone Reception: Undependable. Coverage likely at Lusk Cave and high on the Sentier de la Caverne but not at Plage Parent nor Lusk Cabin or most of Trail 54.

Further Information: www.canadas capital.gc.ca/data/2/rec_docs/3414_ SummerTrailMap.pdf; paper copy of map available for purchase. Also: www.canadascapital.gc.ca/bins/ ncc_web_content_page.asp?cid= 16297-16299-10170-49685-49721-4 9726&lang=1&bhcp=1.

Luskville Falls

Length: 5 km (3.1 mi) return
Hiking Time: 2-4 hrs
Type of Trail: compacted earth, natural surface, rocks
Uses: walking [closed in winter]
Facilities: benches, interpretive panels, outhouses, picnic tables
Gov't Topo Map: 031F09, 031G12
Rating (1-5): 4 [steep climbs, elevation change, rugged terrain]
Trailhead GPS: N 45° 31' 58.3" W 75° 59' 36.8"

Access Information: From the Macdonald-Cartier Bridge, take Exit 1/ Boulevard Maisonneuve for 1 km (0.6 mi) toward Centre-Ville. Turn right onto Boulevard des Allumettières. Follow des Allumettières for 13.5 km (8.4 mi) to its end, turning right onto Highway 148/Chemin Eardley. Drive on Highway 148 for 18 km (11.25 mi), turning right onto Chemin de Hôtel-de-Ville. Watch for park signage. Continue on Chemin de Hôtel-de-Ville for 800 m/yd, turning left into the parking area at about 350 m/yd.

Introduction: This trail is for those who like to climb — or who enjoy gasping for breath and speaking in very short sentences. In barely 2.5 km (1.6 mi), this path rises 270 m/yd, much of it over rocky, jagged terrain, and passes one of the prettiest waterfalls in Gatineau Park. No other climb in this book is so steep or so rugged. It is definitely not for everyone, but I loved it!

For those who do not wish to make the steep climb to the fire tower, the trailhead has a lovely picnic area with plenty of shade and open play space for children. The waterfall is only 350 m/yd away and does not require any serious effort to reach.

Route Description: The trail begins near the entrance to the picnic area, where there is an interpretive panel and signpost. Heading down a set of stairs, crossing a small bridge, and up another set of stairs on the far side, the path to the base of the falls is quite short and not at all challenging. The easy part, however, is over.

From here, the trail climbs steeply and immediately and is very rocky and rugged, the route signed either by blue on the trees or white arrows painted on the rocks. For the next 350 m/yd — although it will seem like miles and miles — the trail separates from the stream, passes massive rock faces, and reaches open rocks overlooking the farmland around Luskville. Many continue no farther, content to rest and snack, tall hardwoods providing shade. At 700 m/yd from the start, the route rejoins the stream, where there is a junction. Keep right; a signpost indicates that the Pontiac Lookout is a further 500 m/yd and the fire tower 1.8 km (1.1 mi).

For another 100 m/yd, your route parallels the creek, then turns away to climb the steepest section yet. Fortunately, many stone steps assist your ascent. As you climb, increasing numbers of large pine may be found, sprouting between the oak on the slope's thin soil. An interpretive panel at the lookout, once you eventually drag yourself there, explains both the succession of tree species and the namesake of this lookout. You are not likely to be alone here contemplating the view.

Within sight of the panel is another signpost, informing you that you have managed to hike only 1.5 km (0.9 mi) but neglecting to say

that you have climbed 200 m/yd. Only 1 km (0.6 mi) remains to the fire tower. And you even get a little bit of a break, as the trail turns left and descends toward the stream. For several hundred metres/yards, you follow the brook, now quite narrow, through the thick vegetation, climbing almost gently by comparison with your earlier exertions. When you cross the brook, without a bridge, 600 m/yd remain.

At least 50 m/yd of climbing awaits you, steep at first but not too difficult as there are many rocks for steps. As you progress into woods increasingly dominated by pine, the rocks become covered with pine needles and the path widens as it almost levels. You pass a junction at 300 m/yd. Continue straight, and as you approach the summit, jack pine appear and the path starts crossing large, flat rocks.

The final 50 m/yd is up a small hill, where you will come out into the open to find the fire tower and connect to the end of the Ridge Road, Trail 1. The signpost indicates that the McKinstry Shelter is 2.5 km (1.6 mi) away. If you have the energy, this is an easy walk along wide Trail 1. You will find tables and a wood stove inside the Shelter and an outhouse.

Most, however, will be content to return, after a suitable rest. Retrace

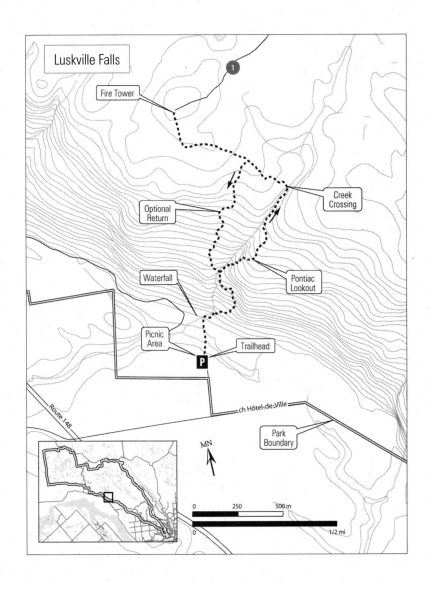

Luskville Falls

Fire Tower

Creek Crossing

Optional Return

Waterfall

Pontiac Lookout

Picnic Area

Trailhead

P

Route 148

ch Hôtel-de-Ville

Park Boundary

MN

0   250   500 m

0   1/2 mi

the descent as you did during the climb. The total walk is either 4.5 km (2.8 mi) or 5 km (3.1 mi) if you return along your original route.

Cautionary Notes: Animals, cliffs, rocky, steep climbs.

Cellphone Reception: Excellent at the summit and lookout; dead zones near the brook and beneath rock faces.

Further Information: www.canadas capital.gc.ca/data/2/rec_docs/3414_SummerTrailMap.pdf; paper copy of map available for purchase.

your route, and at 300 m/yd, when you reach the first junction, you could turn right. This path is 500 m/yd shorter, and it works down the hillside on the west side of the creek, descending constantly, rejoining the other route at the first junction 700 m/yd from the Luskville parking area. It features no grand lookout like the Pontiac, but there are a few viewing areas along the way. A wider crossing of the stream is required here, something potentially challenging in the spring or after a rainfall.

Whichever route you choose, you will probably find the downhill portion difficult on your knees. Be prepared to rest as often during

Hypothermia

Teeth chattering? Shivering uncontrollably? Hands numb? You may be entering Stage 1 Hypothermia, and are in danger. Hypothermia is a condition in which an organism's temperature drops below that required for normal metabolism and bodily functions, and it can happen in spring and fall as well as winter. If you experience these symptoms, end your hike immediately. If you are far away from help, a mildly hypothermic person can be effectively rewarmed through close body contact and by drinking warm, sweet liquids.

Pink Lake

Length: 2.5 km (1.6 mi) return
Hiking Time: 1 hr
Type of Trail: boardwalks, natural surface
Uses: walking [closed in winter]
Facilities: benches, interpretive panels, outhouses, picnic tables
Gov't Topo Map: 031G12
Rating (1-5): 1
Trailhead GPS: N 45° 28' 08.3"
   W 75° 48' 43.4"

Access Information: From the Macdonald-Cartier Bridge, take Exit 1/Boulevard Maisonneuve for 1 km (0.6 mi) toward Centre-Ville. Turn right onto Boulevard des Allumettières. Follow des Allumettières for 3 km (1.9 mi), then turn onto the exit ramp for Gatineau Park. After 300 m/yd, turn left onto Promenade de la Gatineau and follow for 8 km (5 mi), turning right into the Pink Lake parking area.

Introduction: Pink Lake is one of the most popular trails in Gatineau Park. Its short distance makes it appealing to the most casual walker, and within its scenic boundaries

is crammed an amazing variety of interpretive experiences. In order to provide ease of access around its often rugged shores, this trail offers some of the park's most elaborate walkway constructions.

Lac Pink (Pink Lake) is, to properly employ an overused term, unique. For example, it is home to a tiny saltwater fish trapped when the Atlantic Ocean retreated from the region thousands of years ago — one found nowhere else. Because of the lake's special characteristics, desalination took long enough for the little devils to adapt to living in fresh water.

In the depths of the lake there lives a prehistoric anaerobic pink photosynthetic bacterium that uses sulphur instead of oxygen when it transforms sunlight into energy. In addition, Lac Pink is "meromictic," that is, its waters do not mix like most lakes, and its deepest 7 m/yd remain without oxygen — lifeless (except for our prehistoric bacterium, of course).

Finally, the water is not even pink. It is green due to pollution. Lac Pink received its name because the original

settlers who tried to farm here in 1826 were from Ireland and were named . . . the Pinks.

Sadly, none of this, except the green water, is visible from the trail, but it is all explained in enthusiastic and copious detail on the many interpretive panels found along the route. Fortunately, Pink Lake is a very pretty walk, so even if the thought of sulphur-breathing bacteria does not particularly excite you, you should enjoy yourself.

Route Description: From the trailhead, and the first interpretive panel, 100 m/yd of boardwalk and stairs take you to the first viewing platform above the lakeshore and additional interpretive panels. Turn left, descending more stairs to a viewing platform at lake level. The trail traces the shore only a few metres/yards before reaching an elaborate stairwell that takes you over and around a rocky outcropping.

At 250 m/yd, you cross one of the little streams that are the main source of renewal for Lac Pink and then climb another set of wooden stairs to more viewing platforms set on the steep hill above the water. There are benches available for those tired by the climb. This is a wonderful place to spend a few contemplative moments. The view is lovely, and the hillside you are on is smooth, rounded rock dotted with majestic white pine and dusted with their long, brown needles.

After another 200 m/yd along the hilltop, the path turns left, away from the lake and skirts a series of pits created by mica mining that took place between 1903 and 1906. These are deep and dangerous and surrounded by fencing. Their story is also explained by some interpretive panels.

Once past the pits, another long series of stairs returns you to the lake, about 800 m/yd from the start. For the next several hundred metres/yards, you walk east along the shore of the lake, reaching a diminutive concrete dam at its far tip and crossing on a bridge behind it. Once across, you begin your return journey, hugging the steep-sided lakeshore on a narrow footpath mostly at water level. You do climb

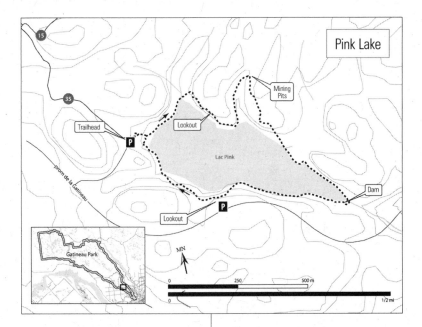

Pink Lake

once more, passing no more than 5 m/yd beneath the lake's roadside lookout on Promenade de la Gatineau, your presence probably unnoticed by the viewers above.

For the next 200 m/yd, the trail has been chopped right into the steep hillside, with rock on both sides. Hemlock shades you. In the final 150 m/yd, you descend another set of stairs to lake level a final time, skirt another steep hill, and reach the last set of stairs which connects you to the start of the loop.

Cautionary Notes: Animals.

Cellphone Reception: Excellent.

Further Information: www.canadas capital.gc.ca/data/2/rec_docs/3414_ SummerTrailMap.pdf;paper copy of map available for purchase. Also: www.canadascapital.gc.ca/bins/ ncc_web_content_page.asp?cid= 16297-16299-10170-49685-49721-4 9724&lang=1&bhcp=1.

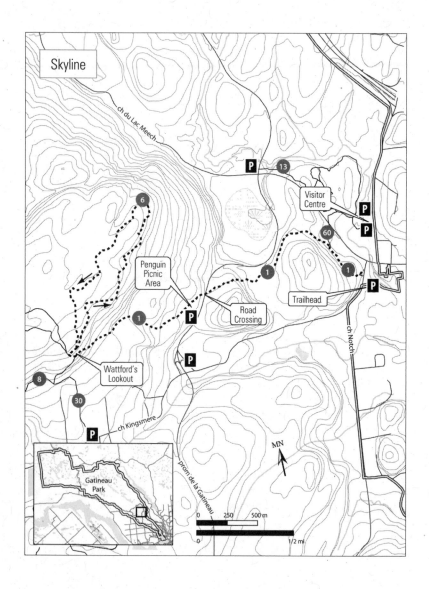

Skyline

ch du Lac Meech

P 13

Visitor Centre

6

60

Penguin Picnic Area

1

1

P

Road Crossing

Trailhead

P

1

P

Wattford's Lookout

ch Notch

8

30

P

ch Kingsmere

MN

P

prom de la Gatineau

Gatineau Park

0   250   500 m

0   1/2 ml

Skyline

Length: 9 km (5.6 mi) return
Hiking Time: 2-4 hrs
Type of Trail: compacted earth, grass, natural surface
Uses: walking, biking*, cross-country skiing
Facilities: benches, bicycle racks, garbage cans, interpretive panels, outhouses, picnic tables
Gov't Topo Map: 031G12
Rating (1-5): 3
Trailhead GPS: N 45° 30' 05.9" W 75° 48' 44.5"

Access Information: From the Macdonald-Cartier Bridge, follow Highway 5 for 12 km (7.5 mi) to Exit 12/Chemin Old Chelsea. Turn left onto Old Chelsea and continue straight through the community of the same name. After 1.1 km (0.7 mi), turn left onto Chemin Kingsmere and left again in 200 m/yd into the Old Chelsea picnic area.

Introduction: Few Canadian trails have a history as long as the Skyline, which was developed in 1938 as part of a Depression-era relief project immediately after the creation of Gatineau Park. This hike features superb views to the east and visits two large picnic grounds. Although there is considerable climbing required, most of it is undertaken in the first third of the walk, when you are relatively fresh.

Those wishing a shorter approach walk to Skyline should begin at P7 in Kingsmere and follow Trail 30. It is little more than 1 km (0.6 km) to Wattford's Lookout and requires less than half the climb. As for myself, I enjoy the hills and the physical exertion they demand!

Route Description: The trail begins across the busy, narrow road opposite the picnic area. Signs inform you that Trail 1, Ridge Road, is a section of both the Trans Canada Trail and the National Hiking Trail. Directional signs point out the Penguin picnic area, which is on your route, 2.5 km (1.6 mi) away. The path climbs immediately, although only briefly, and is fairly narrow and surprisingly rocky. At 500 m/yd, you reach a signposted junction; the Visitor's Centre is 700 m/yd right, but you keep left. Keep in mind that Trail 1 is the main corridor into Gatineau Park and is very popular with mountain bikers. As you climb toward Skyline, expect bikers to come flying — almost literally — down the hillside. Wise walkers will keep far to the side and resist the urge to walk side by side.

From the junction, the trail lifts up and around a knoll, and you should sight the Gatineau Parkway on your right through the hardwoods. You cross it at 1.5 km (0.9 mi), shortly after negotiating two short, steep, rocky hills. About 100 m/yd before the road, there is a huge glacial boulder to your left. Once over the road, you reach the Penguin picnic ground after only a few hundred metres/yards. This is a pretty spot, with tables, outhouses, and even a mounted trail map. You have already climbed about 90 m/yd from Old Chelsea; you might want a brief rest.

From Penguin, Trail 1 looks like a road, wide with a compacted surface. You might be looking at the ground quite a bit over the next 1.5 km (0.9 mi), as you ascend the steepest portion of the hike, climbing another 100 m/yd. If your head is up, you might notice a small cabin, privately owned, on your right about 700 m/yd from Penguin.

Eventually you arrive at a junction. You will find a bench — probably needed — overlooking a surprising panorama that includes both Gatineau Park and some of the taller buildings of Ottawa/Gatineau. Wattford's Lookout, as an interpretive panel explains, has long been a popular viewing point. In 2007, I watched Ottawa's New Year's Eve fireworks from this spot, the lights spectacularly visible but without sound. Wattford's Lookout is also a major trail junction. Directly ahead is Trail 30, which descends to P7. Trail 1 turns right and climbs another 10 m/yd. Skyline, Trail 6, diverts to your right; stay on it.

A loop, Trail 6 splits almost immediately; keep right as the path continues to climb gradually for the next 500 m/yd. This is an attractive setting; Skyline works around the hillside, hugging its contours with the ridge sloping away steeply on your right. Your route meanders into little gullies, requiring hopping on rocks over wet areas and tiny brooks, and projects onto small spurs, where glimpses of the fine view are available. Occasionally, where the vegetation is thinner, the view is magnificent. At 1.1 km (0.7 mi), you reach a bench, where an interpretive panel outlines the history of the Skyline Trail.

Luskville Falls,
Western Québec–Gatineau Park

Pink Lake, Western Québec–Gatineau Park

Western Shelter, Western Québec–Gatineau Park

Trail 62 (Wolf Trail/Sentier des loups), Western Québec–Gatineau Park

Wakefield, Québec

Trail 6, King Mountain, Western Québec - Gatineau Park

Cardinal

Golden Corydalis,
more commonly known
as Dutchman's Breeches

Very soon afterwards, about 150 m/yd later, Skyline begins its turn left and away from the views. You also soon come across frequent informal side trails branching to your right. These have been created by mountain bikers, who are not officially permitted on Trail 6, but because of its proximity to the mountain bike centre of Camp Fortune, often may be encountered here. The return trip is easier walking than the ridge side, even though many roots and rocks protrude into your path, and it is also much wetter. There are no views, but the trees, including some areas of beech and hemlock, are outstanding. You return to Wattford's Lookout having walked 6 km (3.75 mi). Return to the Old Chelsea via Ridge Road, a walk of 3 km (1.9 mi) that is mostly downhill.

Cautionary Notes: Animals, frequently fast mountain bikers, road crossings.

Cellphone Reception: Excellent.

Further Information: www.canadas capital.gc.ca/data/2/rec_docs/3414_ SummerTrailMap.pdf; paper copy of map available for purchase.

 ## Eastern Grey Squirrel

One companion you are likely to encounter during your hike is the eastern grey squirrel. Expect to hear them scampering through the trees overhead and to be on the receiving end of their scolding: a raucous *kuk-kuk-kuk* if you startle them. The eastern grey is the largest tree squirrel found in eastern Canada and is predominantly a nut-eating species. It is common to find gnawed husks and shells where they have enjoyed a meal littering the ground around the base of a tree or on an elevated spot along the trail.

Any black squirrel you sight is actually the same species; the eastern grey has two colour phases.

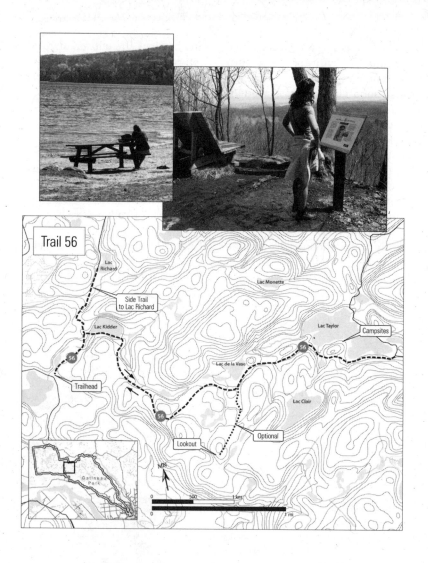

Trail 56

Length: 12 km (7.5 mi) return
Hiking Time: 4 hrs
Type of Trail: compacted surface
Uses: walking, biking, cross-
   country skiing
Facilities: benches, campsites,
   garbage cans, outhouses, picnic
   tables
Gov't Topo Map: 031F09
Rating (1-5): 4 [steep hills]
Trailhead GPS: N 45° 35' 57.9"
   W 76° 05' 48.6"

Access Information: From Ottawa, cross the Macdonald-Cartier Bridge and turn left at the second set of street lights onto Chemin d'Aylmer/ Highway 148. Follow it for 6.5 km (4.1 mi) into Aylmer, where the road turns into Chemin Eardley, and you must turn right at a street light. Continue on Highway 148 for 27 km (16.8 mi) to the village of Eardley. Turn right onto the Chemin Eardley-Masham and follow for 6 km (3.75 mi); watch for a small, unnumbered parking area on your right opposite Lac Ramsay. The pavement ends at 2.8 km (1.75 mi),

and the road up the escarpment is quite steep.

Introduction: Gatineau Park is enormously popular, and the trails closest to the cities are often far busier than I prefer. Trail 56, with its remote access up a dirt road, really is a "back door" into the park's trail system. Even so, always expect to meet others on your walk. If you want solitude, pick weekdays and/ or early mornings; I should add that I have never encountered anyone on the Lac Richard side trip.

Trail conditions are generally very good, as most of the track is former road with a compacted surface. However, its several steep climbs will make this a significant challenge for anyone not very fit. Expect to require extra water in the summer. Carry a filter if you can, as you will have many opportunities to refill.

Route Description: Past the gate that separates the roadside parking from the trail, your route is a wide, natural-surfaced former road flecked with a fair amount of grass. It starts level, mostly through softwoods, with a small wet area encountered about 350 m/yd from the start. At 650 m/yd, winter Trail 56 splits north; follow the main trail right toward Sector Philippe, which the signpost says is 11 km (6.9 mi) away.

Lac Kidder, hugged by high, rocky, pine-covered hills, appears on your left less than 100 m/yd later. Expect to find fishers at any time of year. At the far end of the lake, 500 m/yd later, the trail curves right and immediately begins to steeply climb. This continues, with a few short breaks, until about 2.5 km (1.6 mi), where you reach the highest point. If there are no leaves on the hardwoods that dominate on the hilltop, you might be able to sight the Ottawa River on your right.

You descend now, on a wide, sandy path. At 3.6 km (2.25 mi), you reach a sign-posted junction, with the right fork leading to a lookout. Continue straight; the trail becomes a wide gravelled road, with small Lac de la Vase on your left 200 m/yd later. There is an attractive open area on the shore of the lake; a good place for a stop.

The descent becomes quite steep now, continuing almost to the west end of Lac Taylor, where a set of gates blocks the road, about 4.7 km (2.9 mi) from the start. You will find some picnic tables, an outhouse, and camping pads on the lake side of your route. In another 300 m/yd, the narrow footpath to Lac Clair heads off to the right, and on the left 200 m/yd further downhill a sign indicates the location of campsites 22-31.

Having dropped to lake level again, the trail hugs the shore of Lac Taylor. If you look across the water you might sight people on Trail 55 and the yurt used for winter camping. You reach the end of Trail 56 at its junction with Trail 55 at the east end of the lake at 5.9 km (3.7 mi). There are picnic tables, a park trail map, a signpost, and more camping sites. This is a great place for a picnic. Return and retrace your path to the trailhead on the Eardley-Masham Road.

You may add a pleasant little 1.2 km (0.75 mi) return side trip, up to Lac Clair on a narrow footpath that follows the tiny creek flowing out of the pond. The small lake is gorgeous, sheltered by high, pine-covered hills, and you have a large bare rock on which to sit — maybe have a swim — on a hot summer day.

Another side trip could be made to the lookout, although I frankly do not find the view there particularly special. After a 1 km (0.6 mi) uphill hike, there is a bench on a bit of bare

Cardinal

Instantly recognizable, this brilliantly red, crested male resident of the region's forest is one of the most popular birds to sight, especially in winter. As with many birds, the female is duller in colour, a rosey brown. Cardinals reside mostly in areas with shrubs and small trees, including forest edges, hedgerows, and suburbs, where it eats seeds, fruits, and insects.

Unlike many bird species, the cardinal's population density and range have increased over the last 200 years, largely because of habitat changes made by people. Cardinals benefit from park-like urban habitats and the presence of bird feeders.

rock, with the view partly obscured by vegetation.

On the other hand, the 2-4 km (1.25-2.5 mi) return trip up winter Trail 56 to Lac Richard is quite lovely. About half the width of the main route, this path continues to narrow the further you hike. The first 800 m/yd is through mostly softwoods, opening into a swampy area. You will cross two good bridges and need to make one more climb before the trail descends to Lac Richard. Your side trip ends at a stream crossing, where the winter campsite is found. A signpost indicates that Camp Gatineau is a further 3.5 km (2.2 mi) and that it is 13 km (8.1 mi) to Sector Philippe. This is another very attractive location, with lots of rock, pine trees, a beaver dam, flowing water, and a very swimmable lake.

Cautionary Notes: Animals, remote.

Cellphone Reception: No reception at trailhead, Lac Taylor, or at any low points of the trail. Reception is available only at the top of the highest hills.

Further Information: www.canadas capital.gc.ca/data/2/rec_docs/3414_ SummerTrailMap.pdf; paper copy of map available for purchase.

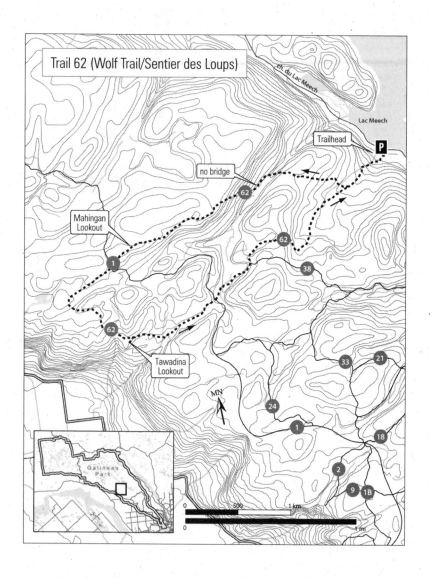

Trail 62 (Wolf Trail/Sentier des Loups)

ch. du Lac Meech

Lac Meech

Trailhead

P

no bridge

62

62

Mahingan
Lookout

1

38

62

Tawadina
Lookout

33

21

MN

24

1

18

2

9 1B

Gatineau
Park

0   500   1 km

0   1 mi

Trail 62 (Wolf Trail/Sentier des Loups)

Length: 9 km (5.6 mi) return
Hiking Time: 3-5 hrs
Type of Trail: natural surface
Uses: walking, snowshoeing
Facilities: benches, garbage cans, interpretive panels, outhouses, picnic tables
Gov't Topo Map: 031G12
Rating (1-5): 4 [steep slopes, elevation change]
Trailhead GPS: N 45° 32' 36.8" W 75° 54' 37.7"

Access Information: From the Macdonald-Cartier Bridge, follow Highway 5 for 12 km (7.5 mi) to Exit 12/Chemin Old Chelsea. Turn left onto Old Chelsea and continue straight through the community of the same name. Once in Gatineau Park, Chemin Old Chelsea becomes Chemin du Lac-Meech. Continue for 10.5 km (6.6 mi); look for P13 on your left.

Introduction: Climbing 380 m/yd in elevation, Trail 62, known to many as either the Sentier des Loups or the Wolf Trail, is one of the most challenging and most respected paths in Gatineau Park. From its start on the shores of Lac Meech to the promontory of the Tawadina Lookout, this trail is worthwhile. Even in the harshest winter weather, at -35°C (-31°F), I have met snowshoers here at all times of day. However, expect some of the steepest climbs in the park. This is definitely a trail for which you will want to pack sufficient food and water before you begin.

Route Description: Starting from the not very large P13, Trail 62 climbs immediately. Its wide path is quite rugged, deeply rutted with grassless surface but surrounded by a lush forest of magnificent maple and oak. Only 100 m/yd from the parking area, by a little bridge, you encounter an interpretive panel about the Blanchet Farm, which once stood on this spot.

Your climb continues up the slope beneath tall hardwoods creating a high canopy, and 400 m/yd in, you cross the stream again on a bridge of rocks. At 500 m/yd, you reach a signed junction; keep right, re-crossing the

brook one last time but with no bridge. The trail narrows, becoming a rocky, well-travelled footpath. Immediately across the stream, you climb very steeply uphill, quickly gaining 60 m/yd. Your route levels briefly then descends more than 30 m/yd to cross a major creek — again with no bridge — 900 m/yd beyond the junction.

For perhaps 100 m/yd, the path parallels the brook, reaching a small meadow. Immediately afterwards it leaves this wet, grassy area and ascends steeply. Watch for circular baby-blue markers centred with a white snowshoer; these are the most common trail indicators. After ascending for 300 m/yd, you reach an area of bare rock, where you will gain a view of a meadow. After 700 m/yd, you reach another open area of rock with a rather more extensive vista that includes a hint of the

Ottawa River. The path momentarily turns away from the hill crest, descending briefly into a shallow fold, then levels, and after about 400 m/yd, there is a short, steep ascent to another area of bare rock and another lookout. On a busy weekend, expect this area littered with hikers enjoying a snack. But finally, about 3.2 km (2 mi) from your start, you reach the Mahingan Lookout, where there is a bench on which to rest.

Almost as soon as you leave Mahingan, the trail descends, and 300 m/yd later, you arrive at a junction with Trail 1, the Ridge Road, where you find another bench and a signpost. Continue straight on the natural-surfaced footpath toward the Tawadina Lookout, 1.5 km (0.9 mi) distant. Your route once again crosses large, bare rocks with minimal signage. At 200 m/yd, you should notice a small pond on your right, and at 600 m/yd, the footpath turns sharply left and descends precipitously, dropping into a small ravine between ridges. It quickly climbs again but not so steeply.

You will probably see the Tawadina Lookout on your right before you reach the turnoff to it. The trail is descending, crossing a tiny stream at the lowest point. If you look carefully through the trees, you should sight the bare rock of the lookout. Turn right at the junction, climb up to the dome of the lookout, and enjoy the excellent panorama of the Ottawa River Valley.

The next 1 km (0.6 mi) is through a lovely little valley where the trail was upgraded in 2009 to make for drier walking. This path is wide enough for two to walk side by side, and numerous small bridges have been installed over the worst wet areas. For much of this section, there is a hillside rising to your right, with the route turning away from the escarpment and heading back toward Lac Meech.

When you cross the Ridge Road again, the sign indicates that it is 1 km (0.6 mi) back to Tawadina and 6 km (3.75 mi) west along Trail 1 to the McKinstry Shelter. Continue on Trail 62, which now descends, following a brook until that empties into a small pond. The trail works

right, around the open area, and you might spot hikers on the ridge opposite; they are on the Trail 62 where you had been earlier. About 700 m/yd from Trail 1, you reach a junction with Trail 38, which separates right. The newly improved trail ends. Continue straight, as the path works around a hill, which is on your right, and has wet areas on the left.

Perhaps 500 m/yd later, the view opens up as you move away from surrounding hills and into a little valley. The trail still descends but somewhat gently. Magnificent hardwoods envelop you, their canopy high overhead. For the next 1 km (0.6 mi), you pass through the most attractive forest of the walk, as the wide pathway drops toward the lake. Shortly after crossing a fairly substantial brook, you reach the junction that closes the loop; your final 500 m/yd is along the path you first climbed from P13.

Cautionary Notes: Animals, cliffs, steep climbs.

Cellphone Reception: Adequate reception only at higher elevation and south facing trail areas.

Further Information: www.canadas capital.gc.ca/data/2/rec_docs/3414_ SummerTrailMap.pdf; paper copy of map available for purchase.

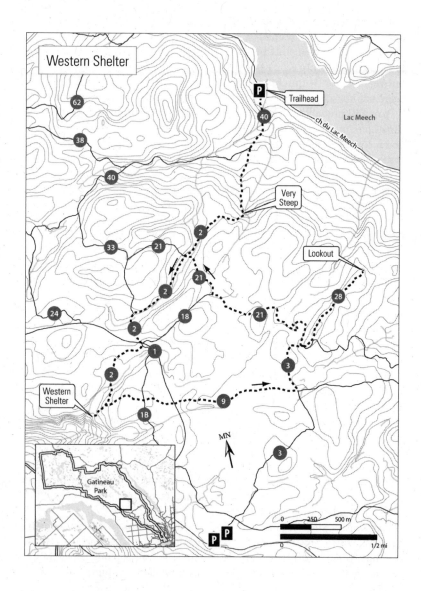

Western Shelter

Trailhead

Lac Meech

ch du Lac Meech

Very Steep

Lookout

Western Shelter

MN

Gatineau Park

0   250   500 m

0   1/2 mi

Western Shelter

Length: 10.5 km (6.6 mi) return

Hiking Time: 4-5 hrs

Type of Trail: compacted earth, natural surface

Uses: walking, biking*, cross-country skiing

Facilities: benches, interpretive panels, outhouses, picnic tables, shelter

Gov't Topo Map: 031G12

Rating (1-5): 5 [steep climb, navigation]

Trailhead GPS: N 45° 32' 12.9" W 75° 53' 58.4"

Access Information: From the Macdonald-Cartier Bridge, follow Highway 5 for 12 km (7.5 mi) to Exit 12/Chemin Old Chelsea. Turn left onto Old Chelsea and continue straight through the community of the same name. Once in Gatineau Park, Chemin Old Chelsea becomes Chemin du Lac-Meech. Continue for 9.2 km (5.75 mi); look for P12 on your left.

Introduction: The various Shelters in Gatineau Park are among its most popular features, all seasons of the year. With their wood stoves and picnic tables, they provide a defined destination and a cosy refuge in inclement weather. Of these, Western Shelter offers the most scenic view, and because of its proximity to Champlain Lookout, it is also one of the busiest. The route I have selected requires a challenging climb from Lac Meech and returns via several little-visited interior hiking paths.

I rated this route a "5" for two reasons. First, it contains nearly 300 m/yd of climb, which will challenge most weekend walkers. Second, you will encounter a dozen trail intersections, and although they are usually well signed, it is always possible to take the wrong turn and end up adding extra kilometres/miles.

Route Description: Hidden under the hardwoods canopy, the trail presents you with its greatest challenge, a grinding trudge up the escarpment. Trail 40, which you share with bicycles, is wide and flanked on the left by a cheerful brook that you cross on a bridge at 200 m/yd. The path has lifted itself almost

70 m/yd by the time it reaches the junction with Trail 2 at 500 m/yd. At the speed you are likely going, you will not miss this. Turn left onto Trail 2, the McCloskey Road, which is for walking only.

The footing becomes rougher, with more exposed rock, and the climb is even steeper as the trail approaches another lively brook on your left. At 1.1 km (0.7 mi), the path turns right and, within 100 m/yd, virtually levels, much to your relief. The total climb so far is 150 m/yd. Your route makes another curve left, and you pass a tiny pond, on your right, about 200 m/yd later. Now almost level, wide, and grass-covered, Trail 2 meanders pleasantly to a junction with Trail 21 at 1.5 km (0.9 mi). Here you will find a bench, which might have been more helpful halfway up the slope, and a sign that tells you Western Shelter is 2 km (1.25 mi) further. There is also an interpretive panel telling about the McCloskey Farm, the last on Ridge Road to be abandoned.

It is quite restful walking here; the path is wide with abundant shade, and the remains of former fields are evident around you. Continue straight on Trail 2 for 600 m/yd to the next junction. You turn left on Trail 33, passing through open areas, even climbing again briefly before dropping down to intersect with

Trail 1, Ridge Road, 2.5 km (1.6 mi) from P12. There is a bench and a signpost festooned with almost too many directions.

Continue on Trail 2, which once again is shared with cyclists, as it descends toward the Shelter and the edge of the escarpment. This wider, more gravelled path squeezes in one more tiny uphill section before connecting with Trail 9 and reaching Western Shelter at 3.2 km (2 mi). The view here is not outstanding but still attractive. There is a bench and picnic tables outside and in, if the bugs are bothersome. An outhouse is nearby, and there is a goodly supply of wood for the shelter's stove. Expect to find numbers of other hikers and families enjoying a lunch before their return hike.

To return quickly, retrace your approach route. Otherwise, veer right at Trail 9, 100 m/yd from Western Shelter. This is a true footpath, with protruding rocks and roots. Bicycles are not permitted. As it crosses Trail 1B, 300 m/yd along, there is an interpretive panel explaining the origins of this particular route. And 300 m/yd further, you cross Ridge Road, Trail 1. As it moves away from the escarpment, Trail 9 becomes easier walking, with smaller rocks. About 1.1 km (0.7 mi) from Western Shelter, Trail 9 reaches and skirts a tiny pond or a meadow, depending

on the time of year. In the thick vegetation, the junction with winter Trail 20 appears suddenly and could easily be missed. Keep straight.

You do not want to pass the next junction, with Trail 3, the Huron Trail, about 2 km (1.25 mi) from Western Shelter. If you do, you might continue all the way to the Lac Fortune Parkway, a long way from P12. Turn left onto Trail 3, which is a wide track and drier than Trail 9.

Within 400 m/yd, Trail 21 will branch to the left. Continue a few metres/yards further on Trail 3. Trail 28 branches left too; this is where we want to go. Trail 28 is my favourite part of the hike, a narrow footpath that crosses a number of substantial rock features finally emerging onto a bare rock with a bench and interpretive panel, 800 m/yd from Trail 3, 3.2 km (2 mi) from Western Shelter. The view here is back toward Lac Meech, and it is splendid in the fall. Best of all, you can see no human habitation.

Retrace the 800 m/yd back to Trail 3, and now turn right onto Trail 21, having hiked about 7.2 km (4.5 mi) so far. Trail 21 wanders around considerably, avoiding wet areas. While so engaged, for about 800 m/yd, you reach the junction with Trail 20, where a sign tells you that it is 4 km (2.5 mi) to Lac Meech. Do not despair; your route is much shorter. Suddenly you are passing through a field — a particularly attractive spot. When you sight a small pond, 200 m/yd later, expect the junction with Trail 18, where you will keep right on Trail 21. A lovely grassy treadway conducts you, with one major wet interlude, 500 m/yd back to the junction with Trail 2.

You have completed your loop and so far walked approximately 9 km (5.6 mi). The sign says that Lac Meech is 3.5 km (2.2 mi) straight ahead, but you know if you turn right, you have only 1.5 km (0.9 mi), which is mostly downhill. Enjoy!

Cautionary Notes: Animals, complicated trail network.

Cellphone Reception: Strong throughout.

Further Information: www.canadas capital.gc.ca/data/2/rec_docs/3414_SummerTrailMap.pdf.; paper copy of map available for purchase.

Poison Ivy

This nasty little bush is found throughout the National Capital Region, and if you brush into it you might end up in the emergency room. Despite its typical three-leafed appearance, poison ivy can be difficult to recognize, as it can creep along the ground, grow as a bush, or even climb like a vine. Usually found near the edges of fields and forests, if you come into contact, you have less than 30 minutes to thoroughly wash the affected skin with cold water.

Otherwise, expect a very itchy rash, which, depending on severity, may require medical attention.

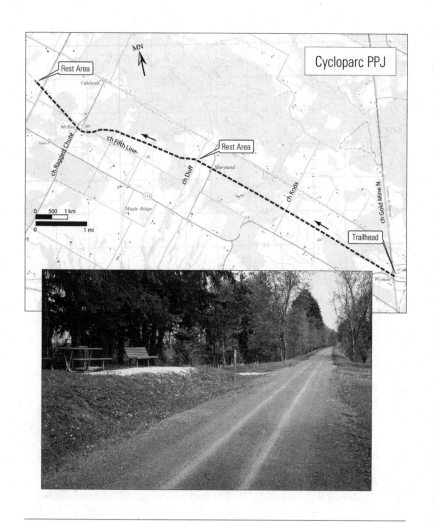

Rest Area

Caldwell

MN

Cycloparc PPJ

McKee

ch Ragged Chute

ch Fifth Line.

Rest Area

ch Duff

Maryland

ch Knox

ch Gold Mine N

148

Maple Ridge

0 500 1 km
0 1 mi

Trailhead

Wyman

Cycloparc PPJ

Length: 26 km (16.25 mi) return
Hiking Time: 6-8 hrs
Type of Trail: crushed stone
Uses: walking, biking, snow-
mobiling
Facilities: benches, bike rack,
garbage cans, interpretive
panels, outhouses, picnic tables
Gov't Topo Map: 031F09
Rating (1-5): 5 [distance]
Trailhead GPS: N 45° 32' 07.1"
W 76° 18' 00.1"

Access Information: From the
Macdonald-Cartier Bridge, take Exit 1/
Boulevard Maisonneuve for 1 km
(0.6 mi) toward Centre-Ville. Turn
right onto Boulevard des Allumettières. Follow des Allumettières
for 13.5 km (8.4 mi), turning right
onto Highway 148/Chemin Eardley.
Drive on Highway 148 for 45 km
(28 mi), turning right onto Chemin
de Wyman for 1.3 km (0.8 mi).
At the junction with Chemin
Gold Mine, turn left and park at the
trailhead.

Introduction: Cycloparc PPJ is a
92 km (57.5 mi) recreational trail

located entirely within the Pontiac
Regional County Municipality. This
essentially rural community, fewer
than 15,000 people spread over an
area of 13,848 km², has developed
a tremendous off-road walking and
cycling resource. The Cycloparc
follows the route of the abandoned
Pontiac Pacific Junction Railway —
known affectionately as the "Push,
Pull, and Jerk."

The Cycloparc may have been
designed with cycling in mind, but
its gentle path and pastoral setting
make it ideal for those who wish a
brisk ramble without encountering
any calf-burning, knee-destroying
hills.

Route Description: This former rail
bed is raised and dry and usually
tree lined. Markers each kilometre
indicate your progress along a trail
that is as straight as the railway
could make it over the low, level
ground. Although you do spend considerable time passing through forest
in the initial 2.5 km (1.6 mi), over-
all this route is very pastoral. And
even though occasional snowmobile

and 500 m/yd later, you traverse your first brook on an embankment, a small meadow to your right. At 6.5 km (4.1 mi), the Cycloparc comes out of the trees and crosses Chemin de Maryland.

A dirt road, Chemin Duff, now parallels to your left, while farmland opens up on the right. Just 100 m/yd from Chemin Knox, you reach a rest area that includes a picnic table, bench, bike rack, outhouse, and garbage can. Unfortunately, this has been located immediately opposite someone's house, so it might appear as if you will be lunching under direct observation. At this point, returning to the trailhead would result in a 13 km (8.1 mi) hike, a good day's amble. Those feeling energetic, or who find the walking easy and are in no hurry to end their exploration, may wish to continue to the next rest area.

After a furtive snack under the watchful eye of the local residents, you will cross Chemin Duff at 7 km (4.4 mi), where the trail enters a sweeping curve to the left, quickly followed by another to the right, as you pass through a forested area. There is even a detectable, but gentle, elevation change here, although by 8 km (5 mi) the Cycloparc has returned to being level and almost straight. Within 500 m/yd, you are once again flanked by cultivated

routes intersect in the forest, there is never any confusion about the direction you should follow.

Once you emerge from the first long stretch of woods, you should be able to sight Highway 148 to your left about 750 m/yd distant across the fields. At 3.8 km (2.4 mi), you reach your first road crossing, Chemin Knox, where gates restrict vehicle access to the trail, a feature repeated on all road crossings.

The Cycloparc returns into a forested area, with larch dominating in the wet ditch areas. Some larger, quite mature trees are set further back. At 5 km (3.1 mi), a very broad snowmobile trail crosses the trail, fields on both sides, which continue until the 9.5 km (6 mi) point, when you pass through an area of sandy soil that supports some magnificent stands of red pine.

For the next 800 m/yd, the trail wiggles just a little, curving left and right more sharply than elsewhere, while passing through more attractive woodlands. At 10.3 km (6.4 mi), you cross the dirt-covered Chemin Fifth Line and, 500 m/yd further, the paved Chemin Ragged Chute. Chemin Fifth Line must be crossed again at 11.4 km (7.1 mi). The trail straightens, now occasionally bordered by areas of swamp and marsh. At 12.4 km (7.7 mi), you cross the dirt-covered Chemin de Bristol-Clarendon, and right at the 13 km (8.1 mi) marker, you reach a very attractive rest area, with its bench and picnic table raised above the trail and nestled beneath some stately spruce. It practically calls out for you to sit and stay awhile.

The community of Shawville, with restaurants, grocery stores, and other services, is only 4 km (2.5 mi) further, but that would result in a return trip back to Wyman of 34 km (21.25 mi), a very ambitious day's walking. Even returning from the rest area at Kilometre 13 rest area demands a 26 km (16.25 mi) trek. However, the Cycloparc is level, excellently surfaced, and practically without hills. You just might find that once your feet start moving, they'll never want to stop. More reasonably, as this is an "out-and-back" route, you can choose to turn back whenever you like, knowing exactly how far you have to return.

Cautionary Notes: Animals, road crossings.

Cellphone Reception: Reasonable everywhere.

Further Information: cycloparcppj. org. National Capital Commission Brochure: Biking Country.

Rain Gear

Choose fabrics that are highly breathable. Completely waterproof clothing traps perspiration, resulting in becoming wet from the inside out. If possible, have two sets, one for summer and something heavier for spring/fall. On longer hikes, especially, I always carry mine.

Forêt-la-Blanche

Length: 3 km (1.9 mi) return
Hiking Time: 1 hr
Type of Trail: crushed stone,
   boardwalks, natural surface
Uses: walking, cross-country
   skiing, snowshoeing
Facilities: benches, interpretive
   centre, interpretive panels,
   outhouses, picnic tables
Gov't Topo Map: 031G11
Rating (1-5): 2
Trailhead GPS: N 45° 42' 35.8"
   W 75° 17' 31.6"

Access Information: From the Macdonald Cartier Bridge, follow Highway 5 for 2 km (1.25 mi) to Exit 2 and turn right onto Highway 50. Follow Highway 50 for 37 km (23 mi) to its end at Exit 174. Turn left onto Chemin Doherty, Highway 309. At the roundabout, 800 m/yd on, turn right onto Highway 315. Follow for 15.5 km (9.7 mi) to Saddler Road; watch for the Ecological Reserve sign. Turn right and follow for 2 km (1.25 mi) to the parking lot. Trails begin by the Interpretation Centre.

Introduction: The Forêt-la-Blanche Ecological Reserve was officially established in 2008 to protect the great diversity of plant life found in the Outaouais region. Within its 2,052 hectares (5,070 acres), several rare stands of old-growth forests and a number of endangered plants, such as ginseng, may be found. It also features more than 20 km (12.5 mi) of trails that explore the reserve's rugged, outstanding landscape. Forêt-la-Blanche is appropriate for novices and families yet worthwhile for more experienced trekkers. Trails are open daily from 10:00 to 17:00.

Route Description: From the parking lot, a signed path leads to the Interpretation Centre, where you pay your entry fees. Next to this building is an elaborate trailhead pavilion, which includes a map of the path network, as well as a number of picnic tables among the surrounding trees, should you wish to snack before you hike. You begin your walk on Trail 4, "Le cendré." From the pavilion, turn left, passing under a wooden gateway labelled

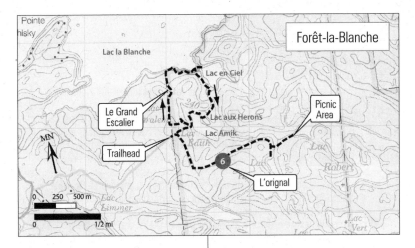

Forêt-la-Blanche

"Depart des Sentiers" and keeping to the left-hand route on the wide, crushed-stone trail. Immediately you pass a bench and the first of many interpretive panels: Eastern White Pine. Within 10 m/yd, you reach a second trail junction, where the sign directs you left. Soon the treadway becomes a natural, packed-earth surface, and it quickly becomes apparent that, in this hilly area, the route will almost always be going up or down. In addition to the many text panels, you will occasionally sight numbered posts. Also interpretive in purpose, these are explained by a brochure available at the centre.

Trail 4 descends in 250 m/yd to a viewing platform overlooking a significant wet area. Lush hardwoods cloak the path as it winds over small bridges and reaches another junction; keep left. You face a short 100 m/yd climb, then the trail steeply descends toward Lac la Blanche, which may already be visible through the vegetation. Several elaborate stair systems make the descent easier, including the appropriately named "Le Grand Escalier," which has benches partway down. On wet days, you will appreciate the slip-proof metal mesh topping each step.

At you approach the bottom of the hill, where the air temperature is often several degrees lower, the hardwoods give way to a high canopy of hemlocks, cedars, and other softwoods. You descend another staircase, cross several more little bridges, and at 1 km (0.6 mi), you reach the lookout on the shore of

Beaver

The many small lakes and wetlands of the Canadian Shield are ideal habitat for beaver, and their dams, lodges, and trail of felled trees may be found throughout the Ottawa region. This largest North American rodent creates dams as protection against predators and to provide easy access to food during winter. Beavers always work at night and are prolific builders, each gnawing through an average of 216 trees per year.

Hunted almost to extinction during the peak of the fur trade era, some 200,000 pelts a year were sold to the European market. Because of recent conservation measures, numbers have increased tremendously, and they have returned to many sites where they had disappeared.

the lake, where there is a picnic table, bench, map, and interpretive signage all under a thick softwood canopy — a very tranquil spot.

From here, the trail moves slightly away from the lake, climbing perhaps 100 m/yd to the junction with Trail 5, "La prucheraie." Turn left onto Trail 5, keeping Lac la Blanche visible on your left. Climbing 100 m/yd, there is another little viewing platform, then the trail drops all the way down to a tiny creek draining into Lac la Blanche, so close you can dip your toes. At 1.5 km (0.9 mi), divert left to a lookout over hill-enclosed Lac en Ciel. Trail 5 becomes more challenging, narrowing and climbing for the next 400 m/yd before dropping down to cross a creek, after which you follow it upstream. At 2 km (1.25 mi), after a short, steep climb, you reach another junction, where you once again keep left, now on Trail 3, "Le ouaouaron," toward Lac Amik. Visit the small waterfall to your right, about 25 m/yd.

The path follows the creek on your right uphill past an interpretive panel, before crossing on a sturdy railed bridge. You hike past one beaver dam then another beside the Lac aux Hérons sign at the start of a 150-m/yd-long boardwalk tracing the edge of the lake. After a short curving section in the forest, you emerge onto the shores of Lac Amik, where the trail works its way on the right shore, including along another section of elevated boardwalk, until it reaches a final lookout at slightly more than 2.5 km (1.6 mi). The final 500 m/yd is almost all climb, as the trail switches back and forth up the hillside, with frequent assists from stairs and occasional benches for resting, until it completes the loop back at the Depart des Sentiers gateway.

For most, this 3 km (1.9 mi) loop will be sufficient. For others, the 4 km (2.5 mi) Trail 6, "L'orignal," might be an interesting addition. This begins in the opposite direction of the other walk, keeping left at the two junctions found in the first 250 m/yd. After the last junction, the trail soon changes character, and a sign at 350 m/yd warns that this is an un-maintained backcountry trail. This means that the vegetation grows thickly in the path, and there are few bridges and boardwalks. There is very little signage, but you are on the remains of an old forest road so it should be easy to follow. The trail continues about 2.9 km (1.8 mi), passing numerous interpretive panels at a picnic table and platform perched above the shore of Lac Robert. There is also a 200 m/yd side trip available to Lac Howard, where there is another wooden platform supporting a bench.

Cautionary Notes: Animals.

Cellphone Reception: None.

Further Information: www.lablanche.ca; map brochure available on site.

Vaseline

Prone to blisters? My grandfather taught me to thickly smear my feet, especially between my toes, with Vaseline. He told me that if I did so, I would never get a blister, no matter how far I walked: I never have, even when I ran marathons.

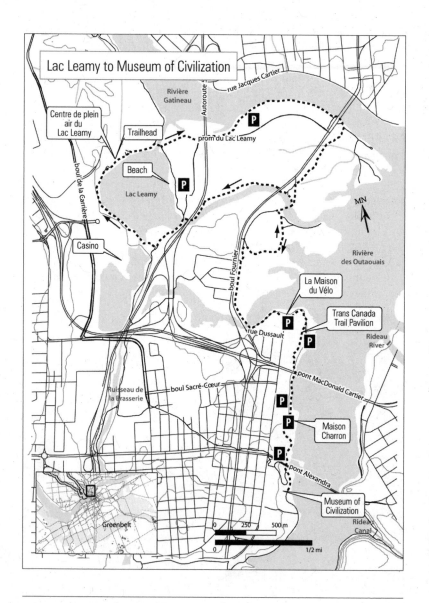

Lac Leamy to Museum of Civilization

Centre de plein air du Lac Leamy

Rivière Gatineau

Autoroute

rue Jacques Cartier

Trailhead

prom du Lac Leamy

P

Beach

P

Lac Leamy

boul de la Carrière

Casino

MN

boul Fournier

Rivière des Outaouais

La Maison du Vélo

Trans Canada Trail Pavilion

P

rue Dussault

P

Rideau River

pont MacDonald Cartier

Ruisseau de la brasserie

boul Sacré-Cœur

P

P

Maison Charron

P

pont Alexandra

Museum of Civilization

Greenbelt

Rideau Canal

0   250   500 m

0   1/2 mi

Lac Leamy to Museum of Civilization

Length: 13 km (8.2 mi) return
Hiking Time: 4 hrs
Type of Trail: crushed stone,
    asphalt
Uses: walking, biking, in-line
    skating, snowshoeing, cross-
    country skiing
Facilities: benches, covered picnic
    tables, garbage cans, interpretive
    panels, museum, outhouses,
    picnic tables, playgrounds,
    restaurants
Gov't Topo Map: 031G05
Rating (1-5): 3
Trailhead GPS: N 45° 27' 08.7"
    W 75° 43' 31.3"

Access Information: From the Macdonald-Cartier Bridge, follow Highway 5 for 3 km (1.9 mi) to Exit 3 and turn right onto Boulevard du Casino. After 100 m/yd, turn left onto Boulevard de la Carrière. Drive 300 m/yd, and turn right onto Chemin du Lac Leamy, turning right into the parking area in 400 m/yd. The trail starts at the lakeshore.

Société de transport de l'Outaouais routes 5, 6, 20, 21, and 27 take you to the intersection of Boulevard de la Carrière and Chemin du Lac Leamy.

Introduction: This walk offers something for almost everyone, with the probable exception of the backcountry enthusiast. Your route passes next to picnic grounds, restaurants, and a swimmable lake; provides scenic views of the Ottawa and Gatineau rivers; offers inviting side trips; and is of a sufficient length that you will feel as though you've truly exercised. There are numerous pleasant locations en route for rest breaks and the opportunity to include a visit to the celebrated Museum of Civilization.

This is an ideal choice for visitors to the National Capital Region, those who rely on public transportation, those new to the outdoors who wish to hike but are uncomfortable in wilderness environments, or anyone who wishes a gentle, scenic — but lengthy — stroll.

Route Description: Start at the southwest corner of the parking lot, next to the Centre de plein air du Lac Leamy, or go inside and have a snack first. At the lake, turn left on the paved pathway, keeping right of the yellow line. The trail skirts the edge of the water for 500 m/yd, passing numerous benches, until it reaches a large pedestrian/bike bridge. Cross and on the far side, turn left where the sign says "Parliament 6.3 km." (Or sneak 300 m/yd right to the beach for a quick swim!)

You are now on the Gatineau River Pathway, which meanders through the usually deserted fields of the Parc Écologique du Lac Leamy; the Promenade du Lac Leamy and its vast parking lots are to your right, the Gatineau River to your left. You cross beneath the busy (and shockingly noisy) Highway 50 about 400 m/yd from the pedestrian bridge then beneath Boulevard Fournier at 2 km (1.25 mi). Just before the bridge, there is a trail junction; keep left.

Beyond the bridges, you get fine views of the community on the opposite bank of the Gatineau, and if you look south, you should be able to see the magnificent residence of the American ambassador perched high above the Ottawa River. Almost immediately, you reach another trail junction. To the left is the first of many footpaths that meander into the flood-prone sections of the park.

When dry, they take you to the bank of the Ottawa River and fine views of the Prime Minister's residence, the Rideau Falls, and the city's skyline. I cannot recommend them, however, because they are unsigned, confusing to follow, and too frequently underwater.

The path continues straight, with a sign indicating that Parliament is 5.5 km (3.4 mi) distant and that you are now on the Voyageur Pathway. For the next 600 m/yd, the trail parallels Boulevard Fournier, peeking in and out of the forest, until crossing a quiet road and, 100 m/yd later, reaching another junction. Again, keep left, and in 100 m/yd you cross a former road bridge that is now used for the trail.

Once across, turn left onto an unpaved path. This leads you, in about 250 m/yd, to the edge of the Ottawa River directly opposite the Rideau River waterfall, an attractive view. Your route continues along the edge of the woods, reconnecting with the paved trail at 3.8 km (2.4 mi). This nudges toward Boulevard Fournier, with connecting branches to city sidewalks. Our route parallels the road closely for 700 m/yd, only diverging after crossing a major bridge at 4.5 km (2.8 mi).

You have now entered Parc Jacques-Cartier. Keeping left, with the water on your left and large apartment buildings to the right, you continue through the park, reaching this route's first climb 250 m/yd later. The trail curves sharply right, and at the top, you will find a charming stone building which houses "La Maison du vélo." This offers washrooms, tourist information, and bike rentals and service. The trail is now elevated above the river and follows its bank, providing fine views.

Barely 200 m/yd beyond "La Maison," you pass a Trans Canada Trail Pavilion, which sits at the edge of a large, grassy

Trans Canada Trail

The most ambitious trail project ever attempted, the Trans Canada Trail has a goal to be a 21,500 km (13,360 mi) recreational trail winding through every province and territory, connecting the Atlantic, Pacific, and Arctic oceans. The Trans Canada Trail promotes five core uses: walking, bicycling, cross-country skiing, horseback riding, and snowmobiling, although individual sections vary what is permitted.

In the Ottawa area, significant portions of the trail exist, including sections through Gatineau Park and along the National Capital pathways. There are also several major gaps, notably between Wakefield and Low and Carleton Place and Smiths Falls.

field, with more excellent views of Ottawa across the river. The trail traverses the field, crosses a park road, then drops to river level to pass beneath the huge Macdonald-Cartier Bridge at 5.5 km (3.4 mi).

On its far side, you are rewarded with superb views of the National Gallery of Canada and other buildings, particularly the recently renovated Library of Parliament. You also move onto a highly structured steel bridge, perched at the bottom of the steep river bank. This elaborate, but essential, 300 m/yd link delivers you to Maison Charron, a heritage building now integrated into the park. The grounds here are thick with interpretive panels, benches, and every other service required by its many visitors. In the middle of Gatineau and directly opposite Parliament Hill, this park is always busy.

Follow the paved path through the park, beneath the Alexandra Bridge, and you are delivered to the doorstep of the Museum of Civilization, 6.6 km (4.1 mi) from your start. The Museum's attractive picnic grounds make it a suitable stopping point.

To return, retrace your route 3.7 km (2.3 mi) back to the trail junction after the converted road bridge. You will find a sign that indicates that Lac Leamy is 1.3 km (0.8 mi) straight ahead; follow this, the Leamy Lake Pathway. Immediately, you pass beneath Boulevard Fournier — with a clearance of only 1.8 m (5 ft 9 in), a great opportunity for tall people to practise their (probably) neglected limbo skills.

In the next 700 m/yd, you actually pass several Trans Canada Trail interpretive panels, a small stream to your left, forest to the right, and busy highways ahead and behind. You pass underneath Highway 50, and 1 km (0.6 mi) from the previous junction, you reach Lac Leamy. A sign here indicates that the beach is 300 m/yd right, but you head left toward the Outdoor Centre.

Only 1.2 km (0.75 mi) remains, with the trail working its way around both the lake — keep right at the junction in 300 m/yd — and the Hilton Hotel, crossing two bridges, and emerging from the forest back by the Centre de plein air.

Cautionary Notes: Road crossings.

Cellphone Reception: Ex-cellent.

Further Information: www.canadascapital.gc.ca/bins/ncc_web_content_page.asp?cid=16297-16299-9970&lang=1; Free paper trail map available.

Parc du Lac Beauchamp

Length: 4.5 km (2.8 mi) return
Hiking Time: 1 hr
Type of Trail: compacted earth
Uses: walking, snowshoeing, cross-country skiing
Facilities: beach, outhouse, picnic tables
Gov't Topo Map: 031G05
Rating (1-5): 1
Trailhead GPS: N 45° 29' 31.1"
  W 75° 37' 21.5"

Access Information: From the Macdonald-Cartier Bridge, follow Highway 5 for 2 km (1.25 mi) to Exit 2 and turn right onto Highway 50. Follow Highway 50 for 3.5 km (2.2 mi) to Exit 139, turning right onto Boulevard Maloney. Follow this for 7.5 km (4.7 mi), turning left onto Chemin du Lac Beauchamp. Drive 1.2 km (0.75 mi) to the upper parking lot, P1. The trail begins at the southeast corner of the lot.

Société de transport de l'Outaouais routes 74 and 96 stop on Boulevard Maloney.

Introduction: What do you do with the site of an abandoned mine? You make it a park, of course! And that is what happened with the City of Gatineau's Parc du Lac Beauchamp. Between 1927 and 1959, a number of firms extracted mica and silicates from this land, gouging a huge pit in the process. When the mines were abandoned as no longer profitable, the pit filled with water and the scarred landscape slowly began to reforest.

In the 1970s, a not-for-profit organization developed a park beside the small 9 hectare (22 acre) lake, and in 1987, the City of Gatineau assumed operation of the site. It now boasts a popular beach and a 14 km (8.75 mi) designated trail network that is probably more busy in the winter, when 8 km (5 mi) are groomed for cross-country skiing, than in the summer.

Parc du Lac Beauchamp is an ideal location for those who wish to begin hiking but are particularly nervous about wild animals or getting lost. Surrounded by recent housing developments, the park is a sweet pocket of natural space in a rapidly expanding urban centre.

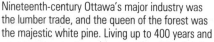

White Pine

Nineteenth-century Ottawa's major industry was the lumber trade, and the queen of the forest was the majestic white pine. Living up to 400 years and towering more than 50 m/yd, the white pine was highly desired for its use in ship's masts, and this region's forests, adjacent to the Ottawa River, were a rich source.

White pines prefer well-drained soil and cool, humid climates, but can also grow in boggy areas and rocky highlands. They are one of three pine species native to the region, and can be distinguished by their bundle of five needles together. They retain their needles and green colour throughout the year.

If you take a wrong turn, you need only walk for about five minutes in any direction before you reach a house.

Route Description: There are two start paths in the southeast corner; take the easternmost, although they soon connect. This wide trail heads through the trees for barely 75 m/yd before being joined on the right by another path. Within 50 m/yd, you reach the railway tracks; immediately before them, you turn left and continue for perhaps 250 m/yd, with the tracks on your right and a substantial wet area on the left. The walking here will probably be soggy.

The trail veers slightly left, climbs a little hill, then continues for barely 100 m/yd before turning left up a startlingly muscular knoll. Some 50 m/yd further, you reach your first signed junction. Turn right; you are on the Boucle Quest ski route, indicated by a white "O" in a blue circle.

This is delightful, rolling terrain with the path working up and down the plentiful rocky knolls. There are too many side paths, so follow the quite wide "O" route as it roams

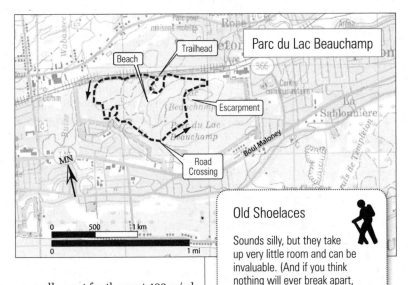

Parc du Lac Beauchamp

Beach · Trailhead · Escarpment · Road Crossing · MN

0   500   1 km
0   1 mi

> **Old Shoelaces**
>
> Sounds silly, but they take up very little room and can be invaluable. (And if you think nothing will ever break apart, good luck.) If you carry a small tarp, you can quickly erect a shelter by tying it between trees using the old laces.

generally west for the next 400 m/yd before it makes an unambiguous left turn and climbs the largest hill so far encountered.

After 200 m/yd, you reach another junction, where you keep left. But less than 100 m/yd later, you reach the junction with "T1," the Traverse de la Mine, where you turn right. You have travelled barely 1.2 km (0.75 mi).

T1 is much more level, initially at least, heading south for 150 m/yd before turning sharply left and heading northeast for nearly 200 m/yd. The woods here are quite attractive, and the path is wide and makes for easy walking. T1 makes another tight turn, this time right, as it attempts to avoid wet areas. It wends its way

over a knoll, turning left again at the bottom.

At 1.9 km (1.2 mi), T1 crosses a major path; continue straight up the longest climb thus far, an interesting rock face to your right. At the top of this hill, the appearance of the forest changes dramatically. Now there is only scattered vegetation clinging thinly to rocky soil and large open areas. For the first time you will notice a considerable amount of pine.

Keep straight, ignoring frequent minor side paths. You reach, and cross, the Chemin du Lac Beauchamp at 2.2 km (1.4 mi), where vehicle access to the trail is prevented by metal gates. As you climb into a considerable open area of flat, treeless rock, it might be difficult to distinguish the route, but if you keep to the left in this open area, you should see a concrete pillar ahead of you and a sign for trail "E," the Boucle Est.

"E" now crosses over bare rock, bordered by red and white pine, for about 300 m/yd before reaching a Y junction. Keep left on "E," which soon works its way to the edge of a cliff that overlooks Lac Beauchamp, climbing gradually as you leave the bare rock behind. High trees growing at lower levels block your view.

At 3 km (1.9 mi), "E" comes almost to the edge of the rock face, where a piece of the cliff has split away but has not fallen into the low area. Unfortunately, very little view is available. The trail follows the cliff, curving right, and reaches the next important junction 200 m/yd later.

"E" heads left and meanders over the ridge in a large loop before returning to the concrete pillar and reconnecting with T1. Returning this way will provide a walk of 5.8 km (3.6 mi). Those not afraid of wet feet should turn left, and follow the unsigned path down the hillside to the shore of Lac Beauchamp. However, unless conditions are ideal, much of this last 800 m/yd will be a boggy morass where it will be impossible to pick a dry path. Should you do so, you return to the picnic area and beach below P1 and the park building, where you can enjoy a snack or even a swim on a warm summer day.

Cautionary Notes: Road crossing.

Cellphone Reception: Excellent.

Further Information: www.ville. gatineau.qc.ca/page.asp?a=culture &c=en-CA&p=quoi_faire/nature_ plein_air/parc_lac_beauchamp.

Forêt-la-Blanche,
Western Québec – Beyond Gatineau Park

Parc national de Plaisance – Sentier des Outaouais, Western Québec – Beyond Gatineau Park

Parc national de Plaisance–Sentier des Outaouais, Western Québec–Beyond Gatineau Park

Parcours Louis-Joseph-Papineau,
Western Québec – Beyond Gatineau Park

Water lilies in Gatineau Park

Wakefield, Western Québec–Beyond Gatineau Park

Moccasin Flower, or pink Lady's Slipper, a wild orchid.

Wakefield, Western Québec–Beyond Gatineau Park

Parc linéaire de la Vallée-de-la-Gatineau

Length: 19.5 km (12.2 mi) return
Hiking Time: 5-6 hrs
Type of Trail: crushed stone
Uses: walking, biking,
    snowmobiling
Facilities: benches, covered tables,
    garbage cans, outhouses, picnic
    tables
Gov't Topo Map: 031G13/031F16
Rating (1-5): 4 [distance]
Trailhead GPS: N 45° 48' 39.8"
    W 75° 57' 10.4"

Access Information: From the Macdonald-Cartier Bridge, follow Highway 5 for 22 km (13.75 mi) to end at a lighted intersection. Turn left onto Highway 105 and continue for 5.5 km (3.5 mi) to the next street lights. Turn right into Wakefield on Chemin Valley for 1.2 km (0.75 mi) then left on Chemin Riverside for 2.1 km (1.3 mi). Resume on Highway 105, continuing for 21 km (13 mi) to the community of Low. The trail is visible on the left; turn left opposite Chemin Principale and park.

Introduction: The Parc linéaire de la Vallée-de-la-Gatineau is an 80 km

(50 mi) section of abandoned rail line that has been converted into a recreational corridor. The trail follows the route of the abandoned Canadian Pacific Railway line between Hull and Maniwaki that was completed in 1904. The last regular passenger service was in 1963, and regular freight runs were discontinued in 1968. A portion of the line still exists between Hull and Wakefield and is serviced by the summer excursion stream train.

This is a relatively gentle walk with almost no elevation change. You also get to enjoy the convenience of formal picnic areas every 5 km (3.1 mi). These make excellent decision points for when you should turn around and return.

Route Description: You begin at a pavilion in the centre of the village of Low, not quite at the very beginning of the trail, because there is better parking available as well as picnic tables and other amenities. Head north, away from Ottawa. You will immediately notice that this is a well-maintained route, surfaced

with crushed stone, 3 m/yd wide, and well signed. In fact, 200 m/yd after you begin, you cross Chemin de Fieldville, which is signed on the trail, and where gates limit access for motorized vehicles. On the opposite side of the road, you pass the 4 km (2.5 mi) marker and an indicator that this path is also a designated part of the Trans Canada Trail.

Within 300 m/yd, you have left the houses of Low behind and moved into an area of cultivated fields among rolling hills. At 1 km (0.6 mi), a sign, facing in the other direction, indicates the shelter's proximity. (One kilometre; haven't you been paying attention?) About here, you move into a forested area, even perceptibly climbing. When you pass

the 5 km (3.1 mi) marker, there are more fields. Through this section the route is rarely straight for long; frequent shorts turns are required to avoid the worst of the hills.

At 2 km (1.25 mi), you pass through quite a large reconstructed rail cut. The trail then opens up on the left into a large farmed area. Shortly afterward, at about the 6 km (3.75 mi) marker, the trees are largely replaced by cleared land on both sides of your route, and you will pass close to some farm buildings. Respect the many "No Trespassing" signs. Continue thus, crossing Chemin McCrank at 3.5 km (2.2 mi), where the trail is again gated. Immediately across Chemin McCrank, which is bordered by

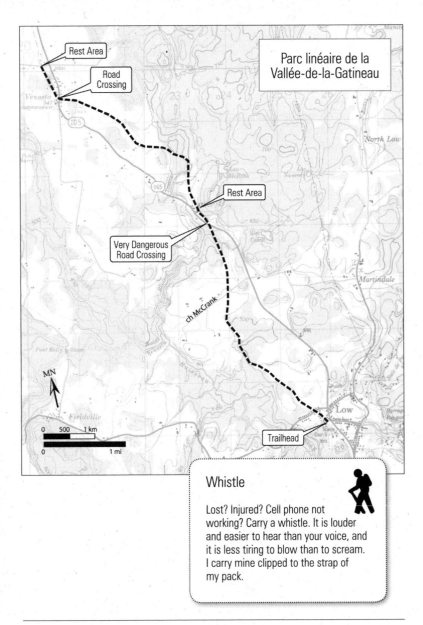

Rest Area

Road Crossing

Venosta

Parc linéaire de la Vallée-de-la-Gatineau

North Low

Rest Area

Very Dangerous Road Crossing

Martindale

ch McCrank

MN

Fieldville

0   500   1 km

0   1 mi

Low

Trailhead

Whistle

Lost? Injured? Cell phone not working? Carry a whistle. It is louder and easier to hear than your voice, and it is less tiring to blow than to scream. I carry mine clipped to the strap of my pack.

open fields, the trail begins a fairly significant (for an abandoned rail line) descent. A sign indicates that there is a picnic spot coming up in 1 km (0.6 mi).

At 4.6 km (2.9 mi), the trail crosses very busy Highway 105, where the speed limit is 90 kph (55 mph). Be extremely cautious. Just across the road a sign tells you that Venosta is 5 km (3.1 km) away. There is then a gate and, immediately beyond that, a picnic area featuring a table, bench, garbage can, and outhouse. It is set in a picturesque little hollow and would be an ideal spot for an extended break if it was not situated so close to the noisy highway.

From here, you can decide whether to end your hike and return to Low, for a 9.5 km (5.9 mi) total walk, or continue to the next picnic site, which just happens to be in Venosta, 5 km (3.1 mi) distant. If you continue, you should enjoy the next section of the trail. For perhaps 300 m/yd, it parallels Highway 105 but then separates, moving into thick forest along a river gorge. The terrain here is quite hilly, so sometimes you are perched on an embankment and other times travelling through a cut. This has a quite remote feel for almost 1.5 km (0.9 mi), though mature, brooding spruce.

Quite suddenly, a landowner's road crosses the trail, and you re-enter an area of cleared field lining both sides of the route. It will continue this way for the remainder of the walk, gradually straightening as it moves out of the ravine. The fields are flat as well, except for one interesting-looking hill on your right that, alas, is on private property. Surprisingly quickly, you reach a sign saying that the picnic ground is only 1 km (0.6 mi) further. Of course, if you have been counting the kilometre markers, you know that we have already passed 12 km (7.5 mi).

The final kilometre (0.6 mi) contains numerous landmarks. There is a signpost for the next community: Kazabazua, 10 km (6.25 mi). You must cross Highway 105 again, negotiating the gates, and the traffic. Since the crossing is immediately opposite Our Lady of Sorrows Church, it is permissible to pray for your safety. You pass the 13 km (8.1 mi) marker and 300 m/yd after the road, will pass the former train station, which is now a private residence. Do not confuse it with the picnic grounds. There is another set of gates, located seemingly at random in the middle of the community. Finally, you reach the rest area, located just before Chemin Burrough. This contains a bench, table, garbage can, and outhouse, and there is a large parking lot adjacent.

This should be far enough for even the most avid hikers. To return to your vehicle at Low will result in a total walk of 19.5 km (12.2 mi). The Parc linéaire, of course, continues all the way to Maniwaki, more than 65 km (40.5 mi) distant. Perhaps that can wait for another day. Enjoy a snack and retrace your path.

Cautionary Notes: Animals, poison ivy, road crossings.

Cellphone Reception: Undependable. Good in some open areas but often poor in forests.

Further Information: National Capital Commission Brochure: Biking Country.

 Groundhog

Members of the squirrel family, groundhogs are common residents near pastures, croplands, back-yards, and wooded areas. It is common to see one or more motionless individuals standing erect watching for danger, then when they see it, dashing toward their burrows to escape your approach. The typical adult may be more than 50 cm (20 in) long and weigh up to 5 kg (11 lb). They live in complex burrows that have multiple entrances.

Groundhogs are natural inhabitants of forested areas, but they have adapted to close proximity to humans and are frequently found alongside abandoned rail lines converted to trails and in parks.

Canada Goose

Ottawa sits on one of North America's main migratory flyways, and every spring and fall the region's watercourses and farmers' fields are dimpled with tens of thousands of these often unwelcome visitors.

Canada geese are easy to identify — large, plump birds with black heads and necks and contrasting white throats. They are noisy, constantly making low honking sounds that rise in volume considerably when they become airborne. Their long V-formations, often heard before seen, always evoke a sense of awe and wonder.

On trails near water, geese are frequently a hazard, either because of their violent territorial defence when approached — they show little fear of humans — or their extravagant and lush droppings (bikers beware!).

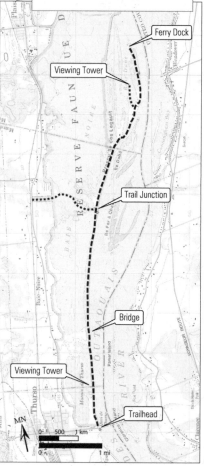

Parc national de Plaisance – Sentier des Outaouais

Ferry Dock

Viewing Tower

Trail Junction

Bridge

Viewing Tower

Trailhead

MN

0   500   1 km

0   1 mi

Parc national de Plaisance – Sentier des Outaouais

Length: 21 km (13 mi) return
Hiking Time: 5-6 hrs
Type of Trail: crushed stone
Uses: walking, biking, snow-
shoeing, cross-country skiing
Facilities: boat launch, garbage
cans, outhouses, picnic tables,
viewing platforms
Gov't Topo Map: 031G11
Rating (1-5): 4 [distance]
Trailhead GPS: N 45° 35' 20.2"
W 75° 14' 29.7"

Access Information: From the
Macdonald-Cartier Bridge, follow
Highway 5 for 2 km (1.25 mi) to
Exit 2 and turn right onto Highway
50. Follow Highway 50 for 30 km
(18.75 mi) to Exit 166. Turn left 600
m/yd after the exit at the junction
with Highway 315. Drive 500 m/yd
to the street light and junction with
Highway 148. Continue straight,
then veer left, following Highway
148 for 16 km (10 mi) to the community of Thurso and the junction
with Highway 317/Rue Galipeau.
Turn right and follow for 800 m/yd;
the parking lot is on the left.

Introduction: Parc national de
Plaisance is situated on narrow
strips of land running parallel to the
Ottawa River but separated from the
Outaouais plain by extensive bays
and wetlands. These rolling ridges
are remnants of the path cut in the
land when all of this area was part
of the glacier-fed Champlain Sea
more than 10,000 years ago.

In the spring, more than 100,000
Canada geese visit the bays and
marshes of Parc national de Plaisance.
The Sentier des Outaouais takes you
past much of their resting area, and
its two observation towers provide
excellent viewing opportunities.
But this is an enjoyable trail at any
time of the year. It is always close
to water, flat, well surfaced, and
features frequent amenities such
as picnic tables. Its forests are impressive, with mature hardwoods
towering high overhead.

Tackling the entire length of the
Sentier des Outaouais will require
a 21 km (13 mi) hike, which might
be a bit of a challenge for many.
However, the kilometre markers,
measured from the Thurso trailhead

at Maison Galipeau, will permit you to easily choose when you wish to turn back.

Parc national de Plaisance is divided into two parts separated by water. However, during the summer months the park operates a pontoon boat ferry connecting the two, which leaves from the end of the Sentier des Outaouais. This could enable you to hike in from Thurso, take the ferry to the campgrounds in the Presqu'île sector, and return the following day.

Route Description: At the Thurso park entrance, the trailhead is well defined, with informative signage, fences, and services such as garbage cans, picnic tables, and even a boat launch — just in case you brought your canoe. The crushed-stone trail immediately provides excellent views of the Ottawa River as it traverses the thin spit of dry ground separating the main flow on your right from the wetlands on the left.

Although not completely straight, like an abandoned rail line, the trail is 3.5 m/yd wide and initially offers very little tree cover. And because this is such a low-lying area, there is very little off the path that is dry. You will notice that the trail is conveniently built slightly higher than the surrounding lands.

At 500 m/yd, you reach a picnic table, on the right, and a tall observation tower 25 m/yd to your left. This overlooks the Marais Perras, which is often packed with waterfowl, especially migrating Canada geese. Once past the tower, the dry strip narrows, although there is some sheltering shrubbery. You pass picnic tables at 1.2 km (0.75 mi), and again at 1.9 km (1.2 mi). You should also notice kilometre markers along your route. At 2.3 km (1.4 mi), you cross a surprisingly steep wooden bridge over the little Rivière Petite Blanche.

Now the trail narrows slightly, with an occasional strip of green in its centre. Immediately across the bridge, the trail turns sharply right before resuming its route alongside the river. You enter the first truly forested area 500 m/yd later, with quite high trees and thick vegetation. To your left, when you can sight it, is the Baie Noire Ouest. The tree canopy here will provide welcome protection from both summer sun and fall winds.

You continue in this forest, with the river never more than 10 m/yd on your right and the Baie Noire Ouest creeping ever closer on your left, until, at 5.6 km (3.5 mi), you reach the signed junction with the Sentier la Baie Noire, which joins from the left. For many this will be a good spot to turn around and return to the Thurso trailhead. Those who wish to continue should note that the sign indicates that the Sentier des Outaouais continues another 5 km (3 mi).

Your route is now more like a country lane, with an open field area on the left, although the trail itself remains under tree cover. It isn't until near the 7 km (4.4 mi) mark that you first sight Baie Noire Est on your left. About 400 m/yd further, the trail makes a quirky little turn and you pass a picnic area, including an outhouse. At 8.2 km (5.1 mi), you pass the remains of two old barns, and the trail turns away from the river briefly, where a side trail leads to another tall observation platform overlooking Baie Dubé.

The final 2 km (1.25 mi) continues much the same initially, with the river close to your right. At the 9 km (5.6 mi) marker, you should sight the church steeple at Wendover on the far side of the Ottawa River. But during the last 1 km (0.6 mi), the path turns away from the Ottawa, continuing beneath the beautiful high canopy, though passing a few fields, until it literally runs out of land, reaching the landing for the pontoon boat connecting the park's two sectors. Your choice here is either to wait for a ride to the camping areas on the Presqu'île side, or to retrace your route back to Thurso. Fortunately, there is a picnic table so you can rest for a moment and have some lunch before you decide.

Cautionary Notes: Poison ivy.

Cellphone Reception: Excellent.

Further Information: www.sepaq. com/pq/pla/en. Brochure available at park entrance.

Blue Jeans

Great at home; not so good in the outdoors. Not only are blue jeans constricting, but when they get wet they can triple in weight! And they take forever to dry. Choose something else for your hike, for your own safety.

Parcours Louis-Joseph-Papineau

Length: 20.5 km (12.8 mi) return
Hiking Time: 5-7 hrs
Type of Trail: crushed stone, compacted earth
Uses: walking, biking, snowshoeing, cross-country skiing
Facilities: artwork, benches, bike racks, picnic tables
Gov't Topo Map: 031G11
Rating (1-5): 5 [distance, elevation change]
Trailhead GPS: N 45° 43' 13.1" W 75° 03' 28.8"

Access Information: From the Macdonald-Cartier Bridge, follow Highway 5 for 2 km (1.25 mi) to Exit 2 and turn right onto Highway 50. Follow Highway 50 for 30 km (18.75 mi) to Exit 166. Turn left at the junction with Highway 315, 600 m/yd after the exit. Drive 500 m/yd to street light and junction with Highway 148. Continue straight then left, following Highway 148 for 33 km (20.6 mi) to the community of Papineauville and the junction with Highway 321. Turn left and continue for 13 km (8.1 mi) to Saint-André-Avellin. The entrance to the parking area is a dirt lane on the left immediately past the Bar Chez Max and opposite the Dépanneur du Village, 39 rue Principale. The trailhead is 50 m/yd back from the road.

Introduction: How often can you hike and view artwork? Not that often around Ottawa, so for that reason, this trail is almost unique. The Municipalité Régionale de Comté de Papineau is to be applauded for demonstrating that a trail can be so much more than just an unadorned path through the forest. If you explore any trail in this book, make it this one.

The Parcours Louis-Joseph-Papineau is one of my favourite hikes, particularly in the fall. However, it is extremely easy to miss the trailhead, so allow yourself a little extra time to ask for directions.

Route Description: The path begins at the welcome centre for the Montagnes Blanches Ski de Fond, where there are picnic tables. The trail is wide and covered in crushed stone and numerous signs, including

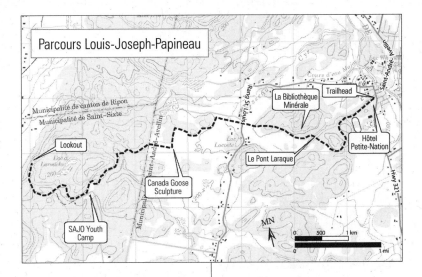

Parcours Louis-Joseph-Papineau

a map, provide details of the route (these are all in French). At about 150 m/yd, you reach an area with the first sculptures, including a large drum, under a canopy of hemlocks. Each piece of artwork is explained by a detailed interpretive panel.

For the next few hundred metres/ yards numerous side trails branch off, part of the cross-country ski network, but the main route is easy to follow as it climbs steadily until it reaches the 1 km (0.6 mi) sign-post, near Le Métronome Organique sculpture. Gently descending, the trail passes a gazebo, at 200 m/yd, and several more sculptures before passing through a gate at 1.3 km (0.8 mi). An ATV trail is on the other side, but continue straight while your path works its way around a thickly forested hillside.

At 2 km (1.25 mi), the trail emerges from the forest to overlook a small field on the left, with a bench and bicycle rack opposite. You head back downhill and into the woods, dropping gradually until you cross a bridge 400 m/yd later. The path climbs again, and a long field opens up on the left. For the next 800 m/ yd, your route is wide and flat, forest on the right, pasture left. At 3.2 km (2 mi), you reach the foot of a quite steep hill. But about 25 m/ yd up, you will find on the right my favourite artwork, La Bibliothèque Minérale, a library made up of the various rock types found in the re-

gion. There is also a bench, making this a great spot for a rest.

The hill climbs another 100 m/yd then steeply descends the opposite side, soon emerging from the trees into open land — bordered on your left by an electrified fence! (Resist the urge to test it; you will not like the outcome.) You reach Rang Saint-Louis at 4 km (2.5 mi). Gates define the trail entrance on both sides of the road, and there are lots of signs. There is also an interesting sculpture at the side of the road made up of rocks, bicycle fragments, and a big tree stump. You will need to decide for yourself what it looks like.

Across Rang Saint-Louis, the trail passes between fields toward a wooded hilltop, 500 m/yd away,

where a fanciful windmill sits. The trail turns left just before the trees and skirts around the hill at the edge of the cleared land. For the next several hundred metres/yards, there are a number of artworks placed among the trees on your right as the path meanders along the edge of the forest. Turning right to climb a short hill, you will find the 5 km (3.1 mi) signpost. Shortly after, a gravel pit forces a wide circle to the left, and at 5.5 km (3.4 mi), you cross the pit entrance; look on your left for a sculpture of large Canada geese.

Another large field must be crossed, and about 100 m/yd short of the trees, where there is a bench, you will pass the 6 km (3.75 mi) signpost. For most of the next kilo-metre (0.6 mi), you pass through an area of very young trees. At 6.8 km (4.25 mi), a snowmobile trail crosses and on your right, is a small trailer used as a clubhouse. It becomes much hillier now, and just past the 7 km (4.4 mi) point, there is an interesting artwork on the right. For the next kilometre (0.6 mi), the trail passes through some stunning hardwoods as it works round a cliff, and quite abruptly, you emerge from the forest at the edge of a sports field. You have arrived at the SAJO youth camp.

At the far end of the field, you will find a trail map mounted on a utility pole, and just beyond that, you will reach the 8 km (5 mi) signpost. On your right is a variety of obstacle course equipment, if you are in the mood to play. This might be a good place to head back, but should you wish to continue, the trail skirts the camp at the edge of the forest before turning away and beginning its most challenging section. About 600 m/yd beyond the camp, you encounter a steep 150 m/yd climb. At the top, the trail turns almost 180° and quickly drops, passing the 9 km (5.6 mi) mark, then, 100 m/yd later, there is a dirt road where you might notice a "trail under construction" sign.

At the top of a small hill, 100 m/yd later, you will find a small sculpture at a junction; turn right and climb again. About 400 m/yd later, you reach another junction, with a belvedere (lookout) to the left. The main trail continues straight, becoming progressively more rugged. The crushed stone has disappeared, replaced by loose, irregular rocks. Some artwork may still be found but without the interesting interpretive signs. The ascent is steeper and almost continuous; you will reach the 10 km (6.25 mi) signpost at the base of yet another climb. However, only 200 m/yd later, you reach your destination — a sheltered lookout

with a scenic view of the adjacent river valley and next range of hills. Thankfully, there is a bench here, so you can relax and rest before you negotiate the return hike.

The path continues, but around 250 m/yd past the lookout, there is a barrier across the trail with a sign stating that it is under construction. Eventually, the route will be connected to Highway 317. However, it is unclear when, or if, this will be completed.

Cautionary Notes: Road crossings, animals.

Cellphone Reception: Strong throughout.

Further Information: None.

Sugar Maple

Although more than one dozen varieties of maple grow around Ottawa, none is valued more than the sugar maple, which makes up much of the hardwoods of the region. Growing as high as 35 m/yd and festooned with its iconic pointed leaves, the sugar maple is one of the most colourful trees in the fall, and in the spring, it is the major source of sap for making maple syrup.

A long-lived tree common in mature forests, extensive sugar maple stands are found in many of the region's parks and protected areas whenever soil conditions permit. Québec is the maple syrup capital of Canada

Sentier des Montagnes Noires

Length: 9.5 km (6 mi) return
Hiking Time: 3-4 hrs
Type of Trail: grass, natural
  surface, packed earth
Uses: walking, biking*, snow-
  shoeing, cross-country skiing
Facilities: benches, cabin, garbage
  cans, outhouses, picnic tables,
  shelters, wood stove
Gov't Topo Map: 031G14
Rating (1-5): 3
Trailhead GPS: N 45° 48' 32.4"
  W 75° 08' 49.8"

Access Information: From the
Macdonald-Cartier Bridge follow
Highway 5 for 2 km (1.25 mi) to
Exit 2 and turn right onto Highway
50. Follow Highway 50 for 30 km
(18.75 mi) to Exit 166. Turn left at
the junction with Highway 315, 600
m/yd after the exit. Drive 500 m/
yd to a street light and the junction with Highway 148. Continue
straight, then veer left, following
Highway 148 for 15 km (9.4 mi) to
the community of Thurso and the
junction with Highway 317. Turn
left and continue for 28 km (17.5 mi)
to the community of Ripon. At a
T-junction, turn left onto Route de
Montpelier and follow for 4.8 km
(3 mi) to the junction with Highway
315. Turn left then immediately left
again into Stationnement P1.

Introduction: This delightful system
of trails is well signed, well maintained, and should be enjoyable for
a day hike and picnic either for lone
hikers or for a family. It features an
expansive view of the hills north
and east; on a clear day you can
easily pick out the ski hill of Mont
Tremblant, more than 70 km (44 mi)
distant.

Route Description: The first thing
you will notice is how well labelled
everything is. On the large map dis-
played in P1, you will see that every
trail segment is numbered and that
points of interest are letter-coded.
The uses permitted on each trail
segment are listed as is the distance
and difficulty rating. On the opposite side of the parking lot, the
trail begins beneath a large gateway
mounting signs giving trail numbers
and distances to various features.

The hike begins in an open field, reaching a signed junction 15 m/yd from the trailhead. Turn right, following Trail 1. The route starts wide enough for two, crossing Chemin de la Montaigne Noire beneath gateways 300 m/yd from the start, paralleled by an ATV trail. The first short climb begins, passing 100 m/yd through a meadow before entering the forest, but after 300 m/yd you descend to reach and cross Chemin Amyot at 1 km (0.6 mi). You may notice P6 and a toboggan hill to your right.

Trail 1 re-enters the woods, climbing gently but keeping the pine-covered summit to the left. Only 300 m/yd from Chemin Amyot, you reach the junction with Trail 2. Keep straight, crossing a small brook and climbing. The path is a former wood road, wide enough for two, and without rocks or roots. At almost 2 km (1.25 mi), you cross a small, sturdy bridge, labelled "N," which has a bench. Continue another 100 m/yd to site "M," where there is a cabin with a wood stove and a picnic table, a great spot for a rest, especially in winter.

From here, the path begins to curve back. Site "L," a beaver pond and lodge, is on your left 100 m/yd later, and 300 m/yd further you reach an open area where you turn sharply left. The path parallels a road as it is passes through areas that appear to be old fields that are reforesting. You should notice Site

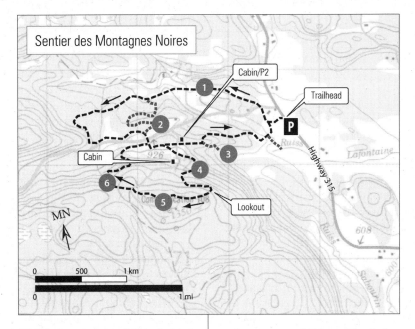

Sentier des Montagnes Noires

"K," former sugar cabins, through the trees on your left at about 500 m/yd. Immediately after, 3 km (1.9 mi) into your hike, you reach a second, different junction with Trail 2.

The next short distance does not appear to match up with the trail map, which shows three choices when in fact you have four. Simply turn right, following the sign that directs you 200 m/yd to the "?" You immediately cross the road, traverse a small unrailed bridge, and follow the path to P2 and its shelter. This is a major junction, with a large open parking area, an outhouse, picnic tables, wood stove, garbage can, and interpretive/information panels.

From here, you begin your climb to the lookout. Pass under the gateway for Trail 4, as the trail ascends Mont Grand Pic with increasing steepness. The dirt road to P4, located near the summit, is on your right. At first wide, once the trail makes its first turn left, it narrows, becoming rocky and rugged and more challenging. Fortunately, after another 250 m/yd, it returns to an old wood road, grassy and wider. It keeps climbing, however, and does so with a few breaks all the way until you reach Site "B," an interpretive panel next to a glacial erratic boulder. You will be teased by hints of the view to come as you climb, and you might even be able to sight your vehicle below at P1. When you actually descend, you know you are almost there, and you quickly arrive at a junction with Trail 5. P4 is to your left, where there is an outhouse. On your right is the impressive structure at the lookout, including a covered table, three other picnic tables, a garbage can, and several excellent interpretive panels. You have hiked almost 5 km (3.1 mi); this is the finest location for a break.

From the lookout, turn right onto Trail 5, following it as it meanders along the hillside through the forest; it soon narrows to a footpath with a natural surface. At 450 m/yd, there is a set of stairs to descend, several small stairs about 300 m/yd later, and a larger staircase — 30 to 40 steps — with a good view. At its bottom, you will find Site "F" then more stairs. Some 200 m/yd later, Trail 5 ends at P3 on the Chemin du Mont Grand Pic, where there is another map.

Trail 6 might be difficult to locate because there is no gateway to mark it. If you search behind the map post, you should sight a small blue rectangular sign with a white hiker and a number 6 bolted to a tree. This is the most rugged section of the hike, a barely cleared track without improvements. Some might prefer to return to P2 along the road. Trail 6 meanders over and down the hillside for more than 1.5 km (0.9 mi), twice crossing an ATV trail, and in many ways, it offers some of the most enjoyable walking. Once you cross a small creek that has no bridge — it can be quite muddy here — you enter an area of red spruce where it is easy to lose the path. Trail 6 joins Trail 1 quite unannounced; turn right, and in 200 m/yd, you again reach the shelter at P2.

From here, follow Trail 3 downhill on a wide, grassy surface. About 150 m/yd along, Trail 9 joins; keep left. Then 100 m/yd later, the two routes split; continue left, following Trail 9. You soon cross a series of bridges then reach Site "G," where there is some old farming equipment and a bench. Your route descends, gradually emerging from the trees to reach another junction with Trail 3, where you will turn left again. You should be able to see your car, with only 400 m/yd remaining.

Cautionary Notes: Animals, ATVs, road crossings.

Cellphone Reception: Excellent.

Further Information: Trail map brochure available at trailhead.

Sentiers L'Escapade

Length: 20 km (12.5 mi) return
Hiking Time: 5-8 hrs
Type of Trail: crushed stone,
natural surface, compacted earth
Uses: walking, horseback riding,
cross-country skiing
Facilities: barbeque pits, benches,
map and interpretive panels,
outhouses, picnic tables,
playgrounds, shelters, water
Gov't Topo Map: 031G08
Rating (1-5): 5 [distance, elevation
change]
Trailhead GPS: N 45° 28' 34.7"
W 74° 17' 45.7"

Access Information: From the Highway 174/417 split, follow Highway
417 west for 114 km (71 mi) to
the Québec border. Continue on
Highway 40 for 9 km (5.6 mi) to Exit
9. Turn right onto Highway 342/
Rue Saint-Jean-Baptiste and follow
for 2 km (1.25 mi). Turn right onto
Rue Pagé; the parking area for Parc
Chartier de Lotbinière is 400 m/yd
further. The trailhead is on the opposite side of the playground.

Introduction: The small community
of Rigaud has created an impressive
and extensive trail network on the
wooded hills bordering the town.
Mont Rigaud dominates the southern horizon, cresting more than 150
m/yd above. Look forward to a surprisingly challenging day-long hike.

This is also one of the few places
where you can cross-country ski to a
traditional "sucrerie" or maple sugar
camp. La Sucrerie de la Montagne
is a popular spot during the spring.
The smells from its busy kitchen
might be impossible to resist, so do
not forget your wallet!

Route Description: A large signpost at the trailhead lists the many
regulations and features a map of
the 25 km (15.6 mi)+ network. The
first part of your route is on "La
Clé des bois," where you begin by
climbing the slope of a gentle hill
on a wide path under a high canopy of gorgeous maples. Numerous
interpretive panels are found in the
first 400 m/yd and another two as
the trail exits the forest, crosses a
quiet road, and enters a field. The

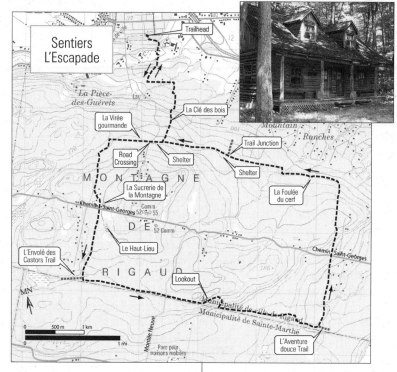

Sentiers
L'Escapade

Trailhead

La Pièce-
des-Guérets

La Clé des bois

La Virée
gourmande

Trail Junction

Road
Crossing

Shelter

Mountain

Ranches

Shelter

M O N T A G N E

La Sucrerie de
la Montagne

La Foulée
du cerf

Chemin Saint-Georges

D E

Le Haut-Lieu

L'Envolé des
Castors Trail

Chemin Saint-Georges

R I G A U D

Lookout

MN

Municipalité de ville de Rigaud

Municipalité de Sainte-Marthe

0   500 m   1 km

0   1 mi

Parc pour
maisons mobiles

L'Aventure
douce Trail

route jogs around the edge of this
field then follows a wood road past
a small pond and back into forest.
Frequent directional signs ensure
you will easily follow the correct
path.

Once back in the forest, the trail
climbs for the next several hundred metres/yards, until it reaches
and crosses the dirt road that is
the entrance to the Arbraska aerial
adventure camp. The trail turns
sharply left, paralleling the road

until past the camp's parking area,
when it continues alone for another
200 m/yd before turning right and
gently climbing to intersect with "La
Montée-Neuve" ATV trail, 1.8 km
(1.1 mi) from the start.

The next section is a little confusing and not well signed, but you
should find a signpost that will direct you steeply uphill on what looks
like a rocky, eroded forest road with
the ATV trail to your left. These
woods suffered badly from a wind

storm, so occasionally they are quite open. You should notice some of the aerial wires in the trees above you. In the next kilometre (0.6 mi), you climb about 90 m/yd, although the incline becomes more gradual in the final few hundred metres/yards. When you notice a paved road to your right, you are just about to reach the end of La Clé des bois.

You arrive at a junction, where there is a shelter, map, and directional sign. Turn right; it is 2.2 km (1.4 mi) to La Sucrerie de la Montagne. Your path, now "La Virée gourmande," soon crosses the paved road, the trail framed by high gateways with metal gates. It wends through attractive woods, more or less level, for 900 m/yd before turning 90° left, about 100 m/yd after crossing a dirt road, where there was a map. The path soon reconnects to the dirt road, following it for 200 m/yd before separating to the left and resuming its climb through the forest. The building of the extensive Sucrerie de la Montagne appears surprisingly soon, 1.6 km (1 mi) from the junction. Another excellent interpretive panel — these are all in French — tells you about the trilliums you might see in spring.

The trail passes among the buildings of La Sucrerie and is not well signed. You need to continue more or less straight until you reach the

paved Chemin Saint-Georges, which you cross. La Virée gourmande ends, and you continue along "Le Haut-Lieu." You start along the west edge of a field, and there is a map and interpretive panel located just before you re-enter the forest. The trail takes you through attractive high-canopied hardwoods, offering possible occasional glimpses of nearby farms and houses on the right. At 1 km (0.6 mi), there is an interpretive panel next to a massive tree split into three separate sections.

About 100 m/yd later, there is a short steep climb and at the top, is the junction with the "L'Envolée du Castor" trail. Turn left and keep on your route. The next 1.5 km (0.9 mi) is fairly nondescript, being essentially in thick forest with no views. You pass another interpretive panel and immediately reach a dirt road crossing, the "Montée Neuve," 8 km (5 mi) from the trailhead.

Across the road, the trail narrows

and becomes rockier as you head toward the best viewing area of the hike, 750 m/yd from the road. You can see for a considerable distance, all the way to the United States. About 100 m/yd past this lookout, the trail descends rather sharply on a narrow, rocky, badly eroded section that is fortunately quite short. You drop about 50 m/yd, and then the route improves, returning to a wider path under a high leafy canopy. It is nearly straight and gently heads to the junction with "L'Aventure douce" at 10.8 km (6.75 mi).

Turn left, following the blue markers, as the trail passes a series of small beaver ponds initially, then quite close to a number of houses before reaching the paved Chemin Saint-Georges after an easy 1.3 km (0.8 mi). Gates frame the trail entrance on both sides of the road, and once across, you are now on the red-marked "La Foulée du cerf." This climbs gently at first, some houses visible on the right. At 200 m/yd, it curves left, making a short, steep climb, then narrowing to a footpath. The climb continues for about 650 m/yd before it begins to drop again and turns gradually to the left. You should find a picnic table at 1.25 km (0.75 mi) and a map, seemingly in the middle of nowhere, at 1.7 km (1.1 mi). The trail works roughly parallel to the ridge, reaching a small beaver pond at 2 km (1.25 mi), where there is a bench and another table.

La Foulée du cerf works around the pond then gently begins to climb. Houses appear to your right through the trees, although one home owner has cleared almost to the edge of the trail. Only 200 m/yd later, you reach another junction, where there is a shelter. La Foulée du cerf turns right; you will head left, returning to La Virée gourmande, although a different section than previously. You have now walked 15.3 km (9.6 mi).

The trail continues to parallel the ridge, linking to the ATV trail in 400 m/yd, where you turn right. Now like a backcountry road, this is extremely wide for the final 1.2 km (0.75 mi), until it reaches the junction with La Clé des bois. To complete your hike, turn right, and retrace the first 3 km (1.9 mi) route you hiked.

Cautionary Notes: Animals, poison ivy, road crossings, ATVs.

Cellphone Reception: Excellent on north and east sides of the hill; limited or no reception facing south and west.

Further Information: None.

Wakefield to Lac Brown

Length: 9.5 km (6 mi) return
Hiking Time: 3-4 hrs
Type of Trail: dirt road, grass,
 natural surface, packed earth
Uses: walking, biking*, snow-
 shoeing*, cross-country skiing*
Facilities: benches, bike rack,
 garbage cans, outhouses, picnic
 tables
Gov't Topo Map: 031G12
Rating (1-5): 3
Trailhead GPS: N 45° 48' 32.4"
 W 75° 08' 49.8"

Access Information: From the
Macdonald-Cartier Bridge, follow
Highway 5 for 22 km (13.75 mi) to
the end at a lighted intersection.
Turn left onto Highway 105 and
continue for 5.5 km (3.5 mi) to the
next street lights. Turn right onto
Chemin Valley and continue for
1.2 km (0.75 mi) to the intersection
with Chemin Riverside; turn left.
Continue through Wakefield for 900
m/yd to a parking area on the right.

Introduction: I admit that I am cheat-
ing somewhat not listing this trail
as part of Gatineau Park, because

more than half its distance is within
its boundaries. However, it begins
and ends outside, and the section
through Wakefield, straddling the
Gatineau River, is sufficiently attractive to warrant inclusion, and
few hikes will lead you past the
grave of one of Canada's prime ministers. Lester Pearson may be found
in a modest resting place among his
Wakefield neighbours.

Those interested in creative car-
free camping might wish to consider
riding the steam train from Hull to
Wakefield. You could ride up on a
Saturday, hike to the cabin at Lac
Brown, and return the next day to
catch the train back to the city. The
truly ambitious could also choose to
use the park's trails to hike all the

way back to Ottawa — but leave that for a long weekend.

Wakefield is a fascinating community, rustic in appearance yet a popular tourist destination. Its Black Sheep Inn is nationally known for its outstanding evening musical offerings. (Don't be deceived by its rough appearance, outside or in.) This hike provides you with the opportunity to combine the outdoors with history, culture, and fine dining.

Users should note that the Wakefield trails are for walking and snowshoeing only, while Trails 52 and 57 permit biking in the warm months but only cross-country skiing in the winter (no snowshoeing). There is a snowshoe trail to Lac Brown from P17 that follows a different route than the one I have profiled.

Route Description: From the parking lot, turn right and follow the railway tracks, which parallel the Gatineau River, for 300 m/yd. You will reach a lookout facing the lake, where there is a sign profiling Wakefield's trails. This is an attractive, shaded spot where there is a bike rack, a garbage can, and an outhouse.

Turn right, cross Chemin Riverside, and climb up Chemin School House, passing the medical centre, which will be on your left. Chemin School House comes to a dead end in only 100 m/yd, but a footpath

cuts through the narrow strip of trees to connect with the parking lot of the school. You should notice a trail sign pointing back the way you came toward the Black Sheep.

Continue straight past the school, across the playground, and enter the woods on the path opposite. You immediately will reach Wakefield Trail Junction J, which heads left toward the Wakefield Mill. Continue straight, continuously climbing another 50 m/yd to Junction I, where you continue heading toward the summit. The trail quickly becomes very steep and narrow up the rocky hillside. Expect to need to stop briefly and recover either breath or quivering calf muscles. Red foot symbols, labelled with a "W," sign your route.

When you finally arrive at the summit, you are rewarded by finding a bench; you may need to sit, even though you have hiked barely 700 m/yd. There is also a tremendous view of the Gatineau River and the surrounding countryside. The trail meanders around rocks and trees, revealing other views of the land below. Too soon it begins to descend, dropping rapidly to emerge from the forest onto a large open area and trail junction G 300 m/yd later. To your left is the MacLaren Cemetery, resting place of Prime

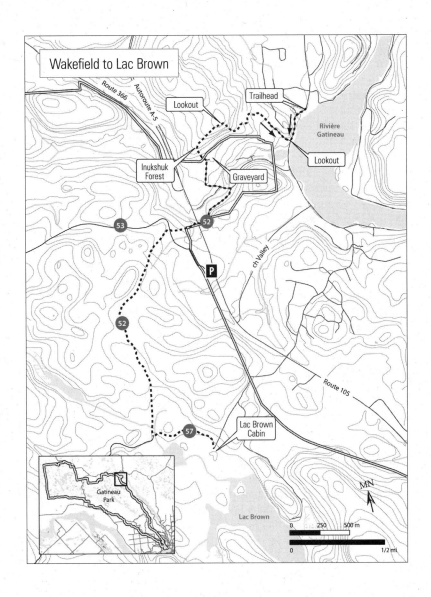

Wakefield to Lac Brown

Route 366
Autoroute A-5
Lookout
Trailhead
Rivière Gatineau
Lookout
Inukshuk Forest
Graveyard
53
52
P
ch Valley
52
Route 105
57
Lac Brown Cabin
Gatineau Park
Lac Brown
0   250   500 m
0   1/2 mi
MN

Minister Lester B. Pearson, where you might wish to explore.

From the cemetery, follow the dirt road downhill for about 400 m/yd, passing the MacLaren House and crossing over a dam to reach a junction beside the picturesque Wakefield Mill. There will be some benches at the dam overlooking the cascade beside the mill. At the mill, turn right and follow Chemin Mill, keeping the La Pêche River on your right. You should notice Trail D heading into the woods to your left; ignore it. The sign for Trail E points toward Gatineau Park. In about 500 m/yd, the road turns into a foot and bicycle path and crosses underneath busy Highway 5. It soon enters the forest and climbs to a 4-way signed junction with Chemin Kennedy, 900 m/yd from the mill.

Continue straight on wide Trail 52 beneath a shading canopy of hardwoods as it climbs, at times steeply, for another 500 m/yd. As you ascend, the vegetation will gradually change to spruce and pine. For the next few hundred metres/yards, the climb is less steep, and there are even a few short descents. Trail 52, reasonably well signed, will make a distinct turn to the left. Watch for the remains of an old stone fence on your right about 900 m/yd from Chemin Kennedy. The path even makes a few little twists and turns, descending gradually until you cross a little brook 1.6 km (1 mi) past Chemin Kennedy. Shortly afterwards, you come out into a somewhat more open area, climbing gradually until, 2 km (1.25 mi) from Chemin Kennedy, you reach a signed junction between Trails 52 and 57.

Turn left. From the junction, Trail 57 is wide and easy to follow. You continue, mostly without shade, only 500 m/yd before emerging into an open field bordering a small lake and housing two large cabins. This is your destination, and there is an outhouse and picnic tables available where you may relax before you return along the route you hiked in.

Cautionary Notes: Animals, cliffs, poison ivy.

Cellphone Reception: Excellent.

Further Information: Some of the route may be found on the Gatineau Park map: www.canadascapital. gc.ca/data/2/rec_docs/3414_Summer TrailMap.pdf; paper copy of map available for purchase.

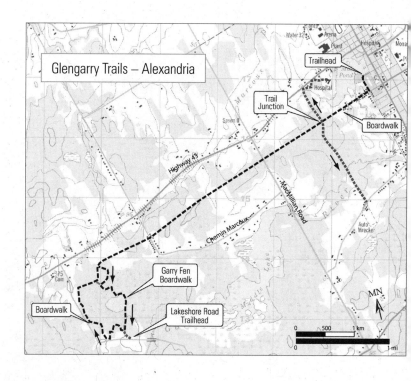

Glengarry Trails – Alexandria

Trailhead

Trail Junction

Boardwalk

Highway 43

Chemin Marcoux

MacMillian Road

Garry Fen Boardwalk

Boardwalk

Lakeshore Road Trailhead

Hospital

MN

0   500   1 km

0   1 mi

Glengarry Trails – Alexandria

Length: 15 km (9.4 mi) return
Hiking Time: 4 hrs
Type of Trail: asphalt, crushed stone, natural surface
Uses: walking, biking, snowshoeing, cross-country skiing, snowmobiling*
Facilities: garbage cans, outhouses, picnic tables, playground
Gov't Topo Map: 031G07
Rating (1-5): 3
Trailhead GPS: N 45° 18' 22.9" W 74° 38' 10.5"

Access Information: From the Highway 174/417 split, follow Highway 417 east for 80 km (50 mi) to Exit 35. Turn right onto McCrimmon Road and follow it for 1.5 km (0.9 mi), turning right onto County Road 34. Continue for 15 km (9.5 mi) into Alexandria to Derby Street. Turn right and drive 100 m/yd to the parking area for Island Park. Start the walk at the southwest corner of the lot.

No parking is permitted on Lochiel Street West.

Introduction: East of Ottawa between the Ottawa and St. Lawrence rivers, the terrain is almost as flat as the prairies. Covered by the waters of the Champlain Sea only 10,000 years ago, this vast plain, dotted with woodlands and boggy marshes, is now mostly farmland. The Glengarry Trails are located here, in the predominantly rural Township of North Glengarry. Its largest community, Alexandria, where our walk begins, comprises fewer than 3,500 people.

This trail system was developed and is maintained by a volunteer organization, the Friends of Glengarry Trails Association. Nearly 15 km (9.4 mi) of paths are available for year-round use, all located in the low-lying, often boggy lands of the Garry River watershed. The trails are easy to walk, but waterproof footwear is strongly recommended.

Route Description: From Island Park, walk 300 m/yd up West Boundary Road to Lochiel Street West. Turn right and follow the road to its end, 500 m/yd later. Here you will find

a trailhead sign with a map and a garbage can, as the path crosses a large wetland on a long boardwalk. When you reach the forest on its far side, you will have covered 1 km (0.6 mi).

The wide path, called the Red Trail, is surfaced in crushed stone; it begins in an area of mostly hardwoods and climbs a slight rise. After 250 m/yd, you reach a signed junction with another trail map. Continue straight; you are now on the Green Road Trail, and the forest has changed to thick cedar.

After barely 100 m/yd, you reach a cabin belonging to the Glengarry Snowmobile Club. This is a major junction with snowmobile trails heading left and right, and these trails also now share the Green Road Trail. Once past the cabin, the ground around you becomes very wet, with the trail acting as a causeway through the swamp. At about 300 m/yd, there is a small washout.

Green Road is wide and straight and, with the exception of a small rise, remains bordered by swampy ground until you reach Auld Mac-Millan Road, at 2.4 km (1.5 mi). Metal gates block the trail. Cross the road; the trail continues on the other side, where you find more wet areas. In fact, just 100 m/yd from the road, on your left, you should sight a large beaver lodge, home to the cause of all the surrounding flooding. After 400 m/yd, you might notice a sign for cross-country skiers, which directs them onto a separate track, parallel to Green Road.

Also, at about this point, there begin to be a few minor bends in the trail and even some gentle climbs. Cedars dominate to the left; on the right are quite open hardwoods. At 3.4 km (2.1 mi), at the top of a small hill, there is a tiny shelter, used in winter by skiers as a warming hut. Just past here, you cross a large open area, with a massive beaver dam to the left. Around 400 m/yd past the warming hut, there is an old field to your right. You might notice an old stone fence bordering the left side of the road, probably made up of the stones removed from the field.

The next 400 m/yd feature the most attractive forest, including, for the first time, large numbers of pine. You abruptly emerge into a freshly cleared area, a house visible near the trail on the right. Less than 300 m/yd later, you will sight more homes and yards to your left, and 100 m/yd later ,you reach and cross Marcoux Road at 4.8 km (3 mi). Again, signed gates block the trail, and there is a map.

On the far side of Marcoux Road, the trail descends down to another large scraggly, boggy area, crossing a stream 400 m/yd later. You should be able to see County Road 43 to your right. Once over the stream, you climb again,and are now surrounded

by former fields. Watch for a huge rock, on the left, at 5.5 km (3.4 mi). Continue straight, and 1 km (0.6 mi) after crossing Marcoux Road, you reach the end of the Green Road Trail at its junction with the Garry Fen Trail.

There are several picnic tables at the junction, right in the southeast corner of a field. Houses are visible to your right. Turn left, following the orange rectangle and cross-country skier symbols. There are several other unsigned pathways here, so be attentive and stay on the correct one. Within 100 m/yd, you reach a signed junction; turn left in the direction of the boardwalk, 1.1 km (0.7 mi) distant.

You are no longer on a former road but a narrow footpath meandering through the forest. Again, watch the signs closely, because, in 300 m/yd, you reach a junction where a sign identifies "Garry Fen Boardwalk" to the right, which you take. You immediately encounter another junction where you must go left, then another in less than 50 m/yd where you turn left again. If you have stayed on the correct route, you will enjoy a pleasant amble through the thick forest, guided by directional arrows, until you reach the boardwalk.

This is the highlight of the walk, as, for the next 600 m/yd, the trail works around the idyllic Garry Fen. This long boardwalk features numerous interpretive panels — the text is mostly faded, unfortunately — and several benches. It is a perfect location to stop and spend a few peaceful moments.

Leaving the fen, the path continues another 300 m/yd, passing several additional interpretive panels — these ones legible — to a junction, where there is a bench. To complete the loop, turn right; continue straight to arrive at the trailhead on Lakeshore Road.

For the next 2 km (1.25 mi), your route snakes confusedly through the forest as it vainly attempts to stay on dry ground. Twice the trail skirts Lakeshore Road, once paralleling it on a 200 m/yd boardwalk. After this boardwalk, your route curves right; a sign tells you that it is 1.1 km (0.7 mi) to the south entrance.

Continue following the old wood road, moving beneath mostly softwoods, although there are a few large white birches. Traverse a small boardwalk 300 m/yd later and, 100 m/yd further, cross a small bridge. In another 100 m/yd, you reach a junction; turn left, where the sign says "Bonnie Glen — 500 m". You gradually climb back to the junction with the Green Road Trail. Once there, retrace the 5.7 km (3.6 mi) back to Island Park in Alexandria.

Cautionary Notes: Animals, hunting season, poison ivy, road crossings.

Cellphone Reception: Excellent throughout.

Further Information: www.glengarry trails.com.

Trout Lily

Sentiers l'Escapade,
Western Québec–Beyond Gatineau Park

Macnamara Nature Trail,
Eastern Ontario–Beyond Greenbelt

Manitou Mountain, Eastern Ontario–Beyond Greenbelt

Marlborough Forest,
Eastern Ontario – Beyond Greenbelt

Prescott-Russell Recreational Trail,
Eastern Ontario–Beyond Greenbelt

St. Lawrence Recreational Path, Eastern Ontario – Beyond Greenbelt

Bullfrog

K&P Trail – Calabogie

Length: 13 km (8.2 mi) return
Hiking Time: 4 hrs
Type of Trail: compacted earth
Uses: walking, biking, horseback riding, ATVing, snowshoeing, cross-country skiing, snowmobiling
Facilities: interpretive panels, outhouses
Gov't Topo Map: 031F07
Rating (1-5): 3
Trailhead GPS: N 45° 17' 54.2" W 76° 43' 03.7"

Access Information: From the Highway 416/417 split, drive west on Highway 417 for 63 km (39 mi) to Calabogie Road/County Road 508. Turn left and follow it for 23 km (14.5 mi), turning left onto Lanark Road/County Road 511. Continue on CR511 for 1.5 km (0.9 mi), crossing the Madawaska River and turning right into the Tourist Information Centre parking lot. The trail begins on the opposite side of the road.

Introduction: Renfrew County sits on the boundary between southern and northern Ontario, and that borderline makeup shows in its geography, which features productive farmland near the Ottawa River and forested Canadian Shield hills in its interior. The section of the K&P Trail between Calabogie and Ashdad touches both facets of the region, providing glimpses of the rugged nature of the Shield in the many rock cuts near the Madawaska River, while finishing alongside the cultivated fields around Ashdad.

This trail follows the route of the Kingston & Pembroke Railway, the "Old K&P," or, as it was ruefully known, the "Kick & Push." It never did reach Pembroke, stopping at Renfrew in 1884. In 1913, it was absorbed into the Canadian Pacific system and was abandoned in the 1970s. The County of Renfrew opened the former rail line as a shared-use trail in 2005.

Route Description: From the Tourism Information parking lot, cross CR511 and head to the trailhead pavilion located at the turnoff to Generating Station Lane. This pavilion features a map, trail regulations,

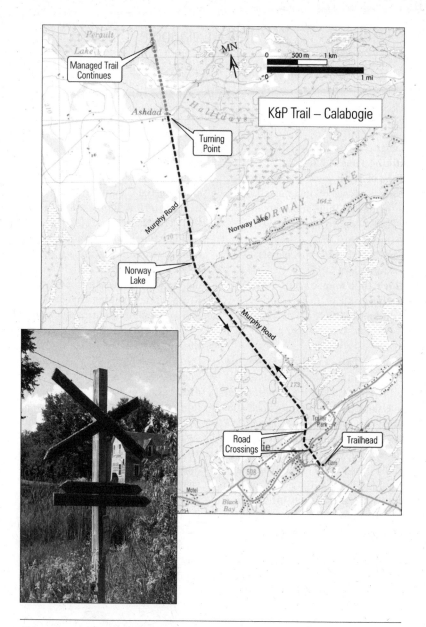

Managed Trail
Continues

Perault
Lake

MN

0 500 m 1 km
0 1 mi

K&P Trail – Calabogie

Ashdad

Turning
Point

Halliday's

NORWAY LAKE
164±

Murphy Road

Norway Lake

Norway
Lake

Murphy Road

Road
Crossings

Trailhead

508

Motel

Black
Bay

and historical background information. Turn left and immediately cross a narrow bridge over the lively outflow from the nearby dam. High fences block your view, unfortunately.

As an abandoned rail line, the treadway is compacted earth, the original base for the rails. This is wide and usually free from potholes, although motorized use has created occasional furrows. The first 750 m/yd pass through the village of Calabogie, requiring the crossing of CR511 and CR508. There are several gates in between, and 400 m/yd from the start, you will cross another bridge, this one over the original course of the Madawaska, which provides a better view. The 250 m/yd between the first and second road crossings will probably be the wettest of your walk, because the trail passes through a rock cut and then climbs, so any water drains right down the middle of the path.

Once across CR508, the trail leaves houses behind. Once again, you pass through a deep cut lined by cedars, which considerably shade and cool the trail. This gate is set back from the road, after the cut, where there is also a small pond to your right. The trail begins a long sweeping curve to the left, straightening at 1.1 km (0.7 mi). The forest, mostly softwood, is fairly thick, and a layer of fresh gravel surfaces the trail. You can also detect a definite climb, although it is very gentle.

At 1.6 km (1 mi), the rail bed acts as a causeway crossing an open wetland on both sides of the trail, then settles in for 900 m/yd of unbroken forest, disturbed only by evidence of a recent logging operation. At 2.5 km (1.6 mi), a major wood road crosses the trail; be cautious, in case logging is going on. And 400 m/yd further, there is another wetland, with a beaver lodge visible on the right.

The first gated and signed road is crossed at 3.3 km (2.1 mi): Murphy Road. Immediately afterward, the character of the forest begins to change, with more rocks intruding from the soil and pine beginning to crown the small hills. Cuts and wet areas alternate. Unexpectedly, at 3.9 km (2.4 mi), you will find a civic address sign, #8612, at the entrance to a driveway on your right. This informs you that some landowners may use the trail for vehicle access to their property. Only 100 m/yd later, you will reach a flat, open area on your right that leads from the trail into the clear waters of Norway Lake. This is an excellent location to picnic and possibly to turn back to Calabogie afterwards.

For those wanting to stretch their legs a little more, continue as the K&P curves right round the lake, settles into another straightaway, passes another driveway, and crosses another attractive pond 400 m/yd later. Beaver are very active through here, as you will notice 300 m/yd later, where they are attempting to create a dam that would flood the trail. This pattern of cuts and wetlands continues until you cross another dirt road — actually also Murphy Road, although you might notice a sign for Appel Lane at 5.2 km (3.25 mi).

For the first time, there are houses near the trail, and to your left, there are cultivated fields. As with all the road crossings, there are metal gates and numerous regulatory and informational signs, usually for snowmobiles. Now the terrain becomes much gentler, with fewer softwoods, no more wetlands, and nearly level walking. To the left, for the remainder of the walk, pasture land will be visible through the vegetation lining the K&P. There is even a cluster of abandoned farm buildings, and 1 km (0.6 mi) from Murphy Road, trail and field converge where a farm lane crosses to connect with another field on the right.

At this point, several buildings, including some attractive old brick farmhouses, dot the far edge of the fields. The K&P noticeably descends, dropping until it reaches an intersection with the Ashdad Road at 6.5 km (4.1 mi), beside several homes. Although the K&P continues, it is time to turn about and return to Calabogie.

Cautionary Notes: Animals, motorized use, road crossings.

Cellphone Reception: Excellent.

Further Information: None.

Macnamara Nature Trail

Length: 4.5 km (2.8 mi) return
Hiking Time: 1 hr
Type of Trail: boardwalk, natural
surface, wood chips
Uses: walking, snowshoeing, cross-
country skiing
Facilities: benches, interpretive
sites with guide, picnic tables
Gov't Topo Map: 031F08
Rating (1-5): 1
Trailhead GPS: N 45° 26' 18.0"
W 76° 20' 11.0"

Access Information: From the Highway 416/417 split, follow Highway 417 west for 48 km (30 mi) to Exit 180. Turn right onto Regional Road 29 and follow it for 1.2 km (0.75 mi) to the junction with Highway 17/Madawaska Boulevard. Turn left onto Highway 17, following it for 1.9 km (1.2 mi), then turn right onto McNab Street. Continue on McNab for 800 m/yd; an unsigned parking area is on the right.

Introduction: Few trails are found on corporate property, but the Macnamara Nature Trail, created and maintained entirely by volunteers, wends through land owned by Nylene Canada Incorporated, whose plant is nearby. This is also part of the Nopiming Game Preserve, one of the few in Ontario on private land. The trail is named after Charles Macnamara, an ardent field naturalist, who, in the early 20th century, documented wild orchids, birds, beavers, and the natural history of the Arnprior area.

His trail passes through some of the lands he lovingly explored, including 19 numbered interpretive stops of features explained in a trail guide that is available at the trail kiosk. Boardwalks, benches, and viewing platforms make this short route accessible to almost anyone, and it is a wonderful location for an exploration of the natural world of the lower Ottawa River valley. Remember to bring along some sunflower seeds for the many bird feeders along the trail.

Route Description: At the parking lot, a small kiosk contains trail guides and features a map of the route. The wood-chip-covered path leads into

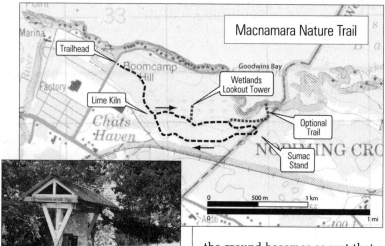

Macnamara Nature Trail

the nearby forest, with the first interpretive spot visible from the kiosk. As soon as you get under the forest canopy, the wood chips mostly disappear, replaced by a well-defined natural treadway. The trail quickly becomes a narrow lane, meandering over the natural shape of the terrain, which gently slopes toward the Ottawa River.

Numerous side trails join in, but watch for hiker markers — blue diamonds attached to trees. About 200 m/yd along, you reach interpretive site #2 on your left, and through the mixed hardwoods and softwoods, you will probably see a factory on your right. By 400 m/yd,

the ground becomes so wet that a boardwalk is required, but the path attempts to stay on slightly elevated land whenever possible. This requires no great climb but rather a pleasant up-and-down hike.

At 500 m/yd, there is a major boardwalk, extending perhaps 100 m/yd, then the trail is again natural and covered with wood chips. Site #5, 60 m/yd further off to your right, is the ruins of a lime kiln. The stone foundations remain, and a wooden deck is provided for observation. White cedars shelter the area, and fences frame it. Off to the side is the quarried marble outcropping.

Just past the kiln, you reach a bench surrounded by a number of bird feeders, a good place to relax. The path crosses a tiny stream and meanders uphill through mostly birch and maple. Site #6, a side trip to the left, takes you to an exposed outcropping of marble. The main trail climbs to the top of an oak-covered ridge, where it continues until about 1.2 km (0.75 mi), where the side trail to the wetlands lookout tower separates. This is about 250 m/yd down off the ridge.

The main trail continues to follow the ridge with the Ottawa River on the left; the walking here is dry and comfortable. At site #8, there is a bench, where, in the fall, you can listen to the patter of falling acorns. Just after reaching site #9, the path works gradually down the hillside, passing beneath some quite tall birch to cross a small stream on a boardwalk at 1.6 km (1 mi), where you will find site #10.

Across the boardwalk is what the trail guide refers to as an "optional trail," and this is not recommended for everyone. This is a much more primitive route with rickety, rotting bridges, signed only with flagging tape and fading splashes of paint, which leads to the banks of the Ottawa River in 750 m/yd. If you make this sometimes wet walk, your reward will be a small bit of sand and some rocks by the water's edge, where you can sit and relax.

From site #10, the main route climbs back uphill alongside a deeply eroding gorge until you reach the crest of the ridge, where there is a little bench, and cross a wood road at 150 m/yd. It turns left when confronted by a small limestone ridge, following that past sites #11 and #12. Immediately past site #12, a stand of sumac, the trail turns right and climbs the escarpment, turning right again 50 m/yd later on the crest.

After 200 m/yd, the footpath connects to an old wood road under a canopy of maple and becomes wide enough for two. You soon cross a small bridge, and 200 m/yd past that, you turn off the wide road onto a footpath to your right that heads down the slope. There is quite a bit of signage, so you should have no problems. About 200 m/yd down the path, there is another bench next to site #17, which is beside to another gorge. A boardwalk conducts you across a small stream, which the path follows past sites #18 and #19 for the remaining few hundred metres/yards until you complete the loop near the lime kiln.

To return to the trailhead, turn left and retrace your route.

Cautionary Notes: None.

Cellphone Reception: Excellent.

Further Information: www.mfnc.ca, interpretive trail guide available at trailhead.

Manitou Mountain

Length: 11.5 km (7.2 mi) return
Hiking Time: 4-5 hrs
Type of Trail: natural surface
Uses: walking, snowshoeing
Facilities: none
Gov't Topo Map: 031F07
Rating (1-5): 5 [navigation, steep
   climbs]
Trailhead GPS: N 45° 15' 26.2"
   W 76° 45' 53.0"

Access Information: From the Highway 416/417 split, drive west on Highway 417 for 63 km (39 mi) to Calabogie Road/County Road 508. Turn left and follow it for 30 km (18.75 mi), turning left onto Barrett Chute Road (Calabogie Peaks Resort). Drive for 3.8 km (2.4 mi). Watch for a blue sign on the right marking the trailhead; park on the road.

Introduction: This trail officially opened in June 2009, but it has quickly become known as one of the most admired local options for hiking enthusiasts. Climbing to the top of Dickson Mountain, the summit of the Calabogie Peaks Resort's downhill ski trails, this challenging trek features steep climbs, several expansive vistas, and a first-rate workout for anyone who undertakes it.

   This is most definitely not a hike for beginners. Signage is minimal, the cleared treadway is sometimes virtually indistinguishable from the surrounding forest, and you are far from easy assistance. Map and compass are essential for this route.

Route Description: A small sign indicates the trailhead, and the path is marked by small blue vertical paint flashes on trees. The slender footpath climbs immediately, cresting a small hill topped with a cairn containing a brass survey marker. Soon the path turns left, following a ridge until, at 300 m/yd, you reach and pass under a power line. For the next 400 m/yd, the path meanders up and down the hillside, almost describing circles, until you reach a moss-covered rock where cairns mark the trail. From here, you follow a ridge line briefly, before dropping down to cross a usually dry creek bed about 1 km (0.6 mi) from your start.

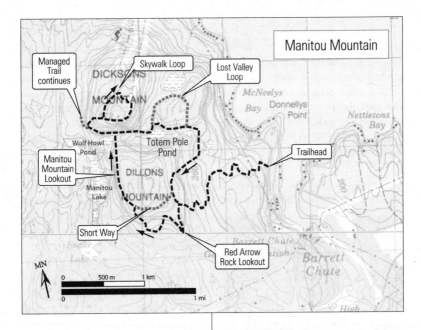

Once across, you gradually ascend on a former wood road, with beautiful hardwood-covered ridges on either side. After 450 m/yd, the path narrows and steepens, squeezing between rocky knolls. However, after 50 m/yd, your route returns to gentle climbing, at least for the next 300 m/yd. But as you continue, the slope becomes steeper, and the trail twists back and forth to negotiate it. After one particularly sharp right turn, you enter into the steepest 200 m/yd, climbing 30 m/yd.

As you puff through a left turn near the top, watch carefully, because you are reaching a junction, and there is only a cairn of rocks to indicate it. Turn left onto what is called the "Long Way," which is marked by red flashes. Within 350 m/yd of walking along the ridge line, you emerge at Red Arrow Rock Lookout, an exposed rocky spur that descends thereafter, with an impressive view of virtually undisturbed forests.

After you have enjoyed the view, turn back as if heading toward the junction but immediately turn left — a difficult-to-see red flash indicates the turn — to follow the Long Way as it works lower down the ridge on a quite indistinct path.

This is much more difficult walking at first, as it curves left after 200 m/yd and descends a lovely hardwood-covered slope. After another 200 m/yd, the trail curves right and climbs the mountain again, rising almost 65 m/yd over the next 600 m/yd. Your route parallels a large rock face for much of this section.

You connect to the main trail with little warning, only the blue flashes on the trees. Turn left and follow

this more distinguishable route as it works its way along the slope of the mountain, with increasingly better views available to your left. After 500 m/yd, you reach the Manitou Mountain Lookout, perched high above Manitou Lake, overlooking the lower ridge line opposite. This is a wonderful view, with almost no evidence of human habitation to be seen. You might notice a painted zigzag pattern on a rock at ground level, or a small First Nation's totem hanging on a branch; these are the only markers for the lookout.

Continuing further, the trail quickly descends through a pine slope to Wolf Howl Pond and the well-signed junction with the Indian Pass junction, about 500 m/yd from the lookout and 4.5 km (2.8 mi) from the start. Now turn left, and scramble carefully along the steep slope path for about 200 m/yd to the junction with the ominously named "Ascent Trail," marked by orange flashes.

Turn right; here you must work, struggling up 50 m/yd of elevation in only 150 m/yd of distance. Ropes are provided for assistance. A brief level spot provides resting space, then you must climb an additional 25 m/yd over the next 250 m/yd of trail to the extremely well-marked junction with the Skywalk Loop.

Keep left, and follow the distinct path, marked by plastic blue

diamonds and yellow arrows (it is a cross-country ski trail in the winter). Thankfully, the path gently descends for a time. You will begin to pass numbered interpretive sites, plastic-covered text nailed to trees. You should notice site #9 first. After 300 m/yd, the trail turns sharply right and begins to climb again and is now even signed with hiker symbols.

After a meandering 600 m/yd, you reach a junction. A sign indicates "Return to Chair Lift" to the right, so turn right. You emerge onto an amazing view, an open area on the top of Dickson Mountain with views of Calabogie Lake and the countryside far to the north and east. This is definitely an adequate

reward for your exertions, and you will likely spend some time with your binoculars.

Skywalk Loop continues another 400 m/yd around the crest of the steep hillside, providing more views, this time of Wolf Howl Pond, Manitou Lake, and the pristine lands behind Dickson Mountain. The interpretive panels also continue, beginning from site #4. Once you return to the junction with the Ascent Trail, you now get to descend the steep slope, almost as challenging, and return to the Indian Pass junction, having walked 2.7 km (1.7 mi) since you first reached that point.

Turn left, onto the orange-flashed Indian Pass. This path descends gently for 500 m/yd to small Totem Pole Pond, the imposing cliff of Dickson Mountain visible through the trees on your left. At the pond, Indian Pass turns left and makes a short, ugly 100 m/yd climb, the most difficult of the hike. This delivers you to the well-signed junction with the Lost Valley Loop, beside tiny Medicine Pine Pond. Turn right and follow the trail as it passes between the ponds and over rolling terrain for the next 400 m/yd, until it becomes an old wood road. The stream that empties Totem Pole Pond is to your right.

There is another junction with the Lost Valley Loop here; this trail branches left, but the junction is poorly signed and very easy to miss. Once past that point, you are hiking the Wendigo Way, which continues on the old road another 200 m/yd, then turns right over the small stream and soon begins a long and unrelenting climb through the thick forest. For the next 900 m/yd, marked mostly by flagging tape and only occasional orange paint flashes, the very indistinct track works uphill 95 m/yd. As it finally levels, you reach the junction with the Manitou Mountain main trail. Turn left, and in 150 m/yd, you reach the junction with the Long Way path. Turn left and retrace your first 2 km (1.25 mi) back down to the trailhead.

Cautionary Notes: Animals, cliffs, poison ivy.

Cellphone Reception: Excellent on hilltops and east-facing slopes. Poor or no reception in gullies.

Further Information: www.somuch more.ca/Manitoumtncopy.html.

Wolf

If you camp overnight in the Ottawa area, you might be surprised and awestruck to hear the mournful howl of a wolf pack. Howl back, if you dare; wolves often howl spontaneously when the pack meets, and they apparently enjoy it. They might howl back in response.

Once resident across all North America, Ottawa now sits near the southern limit of their range. Wolves' chief prey is large mammals such as deer and moose, and despite their ferocious reputation, there are almost no records of attacks against humans. They fear humans, so although you might hear them, it is unlikely you will ever see them.

Indian pipe. It has no chlorophyll and feeds on decaying material in the soil.

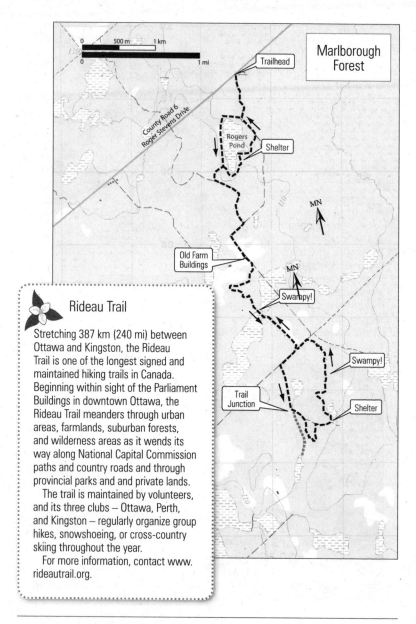

Marlborough
Forest

Trailhead

County Road 6
Roger Stevens Drive

Rogers
Pond

Shelter

MN

Old Farm
Buildings

MN

Swampy!

Swampy!

Trail
Junction

Shelter

Rideau Trail

Stretching 387 km (240 mi) between
Ottawa and Kingston, the Rideau
Trail is one of the longest signed and
maintained hiking trails in Canada.
Beginning within sight of the Parliament
Buildings in downtown Ottawa, the
Rideau Trail meanders through urban
areas, farmlands, suburban forests,
and wilderness areas as it wends its
way along National Capital Commission
paths and country roads and through
provincial parks and and private lands.

The trail is maintained by volunteers,
and its three clubs — Ottawa, Perth,
and Kingston — regularly organize group
hikes, snowshoeing, or cross-country
skiing throughout the year.

For more information, contact www.
rideautrail.org.

Marlborough Forest

Length: 14 km (8.75 mi) return
Hiking Time: 4 hrs
Type of Trail: gravel, natural
  surface
Uses: walking, biking*, horseback
  riding*, ATVing*, snowshoeing,
  cross-country skiing,
  snowmobiling*
Facilities: garbage cans, shelters
Gov't Topo Map: 031G04
Rating (1-5): 5 [navigation]
Trailhead GPS: N 45° 04' 18.9"
  W 75° 49' 10.4"

Access Information: From the Highway 416/417 split, take Highway
416 south for 27 km (17 mi) to Exit
49. Turn right onto County Road 6/
Roger Stevens Drive and continue
for 13.5 km (8 mi). The parking area
E3 is on the left.

Introduction: Encompassing more
than 12,000 hectares (29,500 acres),
the Marlborough Forest is the
third-largest municipally owned
woodland in Ontario — even larger than the Larose Forest east of
Ottawa. Ownership is split evenly
between private and public, with

management of the public portions
being undertaken by the Ontario
Ministry of Natural Resources.

The land area of the forest consists entirely of fragile wetlands
and thin-soiled woodlands and is
a diverse blend of mixed conifer
and mixed hardwood forest, patchy
openings, old fields, plantations,
swamp, and bog. Commercial logging cannot work well on this
terrain, so the majority of the forest
has been left to the processes of natural succession. There is substantial
ATV and snowmobile use on the
main roads, and large game hunting
is permitted.

There are some trails that I recommend for certain times of the year
and, in the case of the Marlborough
Forest, that is fall and winter. So
much of the land area is made up
of wetlands that the forest hosts an
astonishingly large mosquito population. If you are susceptible to these
voracious bloodsuckers, a spring
and summer walk here will be an
endless — and losing — battle. In
the spring, many trails flood, and in-
appropriate ATV use on the hiking

routes churns them into a knee-deep soup. Under a blanket of snow, however, the Marlborough Forest can be a delight.

Route Description: Several large signs grace parking lot E3: one for Rogers Pond, another stating that this is the Cedar Grove Walking Trail, and an interpretive pavilion. The path is easy to distinguish: a wide dirt road barred by a thick metal gate. Just past it, you will notice a sign for the Rideau Trail, stating that the Dwyer Hill Road is 9.5 km (6 mi) distant and another sign listing numerous prohibited behaviours.

For 150 m/yd, continue straight, then follow the path through an "S"-curve. From compacted earth, the surface changes to large gravel, making walking uncomfortable for the next 450 m/yd. Fortunately, as you reach Rogers Pond, this gravel ends. Keep straight, following the Rideau Trail orange triangles, circling the pond to the right where the trail crosses a small dam and traverses an old field. Signage is limited, so keep close to the water until you reach the forest, where you should see both orange and yellow triangles marking the path.

This section is much narrower, more of a footpath, as it meanders through thick cedar close to Rogers Pond, which is on the left. After

500 m/yd, the Rideau Trail, marked by orange triangles, splits right from the Cedar Grove Trail; follow the orange. This path quickly becomes little more than an animal track through the forest, weaving its way between trees and across small pockets of stony semi-open ground. However, in only 200 m/yd, you emerge onto a dirt road, clearly used by ATVs; turn left.

Follow this road for 700 m/yd, until you reach a T-junction. Turn right, continue another 300 m/yd to another road junction, then turn left. The forest now gradually opens up, with old fields visible to your right, then left. You are gradually climbing, and in 350 m/yd, you reach the top of the rise, where on your right is the remains of a former farm.

Motorized tracks are everywhere, so watch for the orange triangles. Less than 100 m/yd past the ruins, about 3.1 km (2 mi) from the trailhead, the Rideau Trail heads right into the forest. You now need to pay attention to these orange markers, as the next section is impossible to describe and almost as difficult to see on the ground. The trail twists, winds, and slithers its way through the semi-open and often wet earth. Your route can only be described as serpentine as it performs almost acrobatic convolutions through this sometimes thick, sometimes open area. The Rideau Trail is to be commended for the excellence of its signage; without it, I could not have followed this route.

This confusing section lasts only about 1 km (0.6 mi), then the trail connects back onto another dirt road to cross an earthen dam about 300 m/yd long. On the far side, the road is gravelled, and this continues until you reach a T-junction with the ominously named Flood Road (perfectly understandable if you walk here in the spring, or after a heavy rain) at 5 km (3.1 mi). The Rideau Trail heads left. You turn right, following Flood Road for 300 m/yd before turning left at the next dirt road junction.

After 600 m/yd on this road, you reach a junction where the orange triangles resume. Turn left. This much narrower track continues straight for about 300 m/yd, and then turns into the thick forest on a much less distinct path. Once again your route roams confusedly though the forest, and you must depend upon the orange triangles. After perhaps 1.2 km (0.75 mi), if you manage not to be misdirected by the many ATV tracks, you will reach your reward, the Earth Star Shelter. This is maintained by the Rideau Trail Association and is a great spot to rest and enjoy a snack.

From the shelter, the trail roams through the brush and up and down a small ridge for another 1.3 km (0.8 mi) until it reaches Flood Road. Turn left, and in 200 m/yd, you reach the road that leads back to the earthen dam. You have hiked 7.5 km (4.7 mi) so far.

Turn right toward the dam, and retrace your route the 4 km (2.5 mi) back to Rogers Pond and the junction with the Cedar Grove Trail. Once here, turn right and follow this pleasant footpath as it circles Rogers Pond. This may be the most enjoyable portion of your walk, as this trail features several small bridges, a long boardwalk, occasional views of the pond, and even another shelter, the route well signed by yellow triangles. After less than 2 km (1.25 mi), you connect to the gravel road that takes you the remaining 600 m/yd to the trailhead.

Cautionary Notes: Animals, motorized use.

Cellphone Reception: Poor near the trailhead and Rogers Pond. Better on the Earth Star Loop.

Further Information: None.

New York Central Fitness Trail

Length: 12 km (7.5 mi) return
Hiking Time: 3 hrs
Type of Trail: asphalt
Uses: walking, biking, in-line
   skating, snowshoeing, cross-
   country skiing
Facilities: benches, garbage cans,
   outhouses, picnic tables,
   playgrounds
Gov't Topo Map: 031G06
Rating (1-5): 2
Trailhead GPS: N 45° 15' 47.3"
   W 75° 21' 34.1"

Access Information: From the Highway 174/417 split, follow Highway 417 east for 25 km (15.6 mi) to Exit 88. Turn right onto Rockdale Road/County Road 17, drive for 4 km (2.5 mi), and turn right onto Route 200. Follow it for 4 km (2.5 mi), turning left onto North Russell Road. This becomes Concession Street. At 2 km (1.25 mi) from Route 200, turn left on First Avenue, just after crossing the trail. The parking area is 100 m/yd ahead.

Introduction: Pastoral eastern Ontario might seem like an unlikely place to find a trail named the "New York Central Fitness," but between 1898 and 1957, this route was part of a railway system connecting Ottawa with New York. As air travel siphoned off passenger traffic and Northern Ontario lumber found other markets, the railway was abandoned. In 1979, the Township of Russell purchased some of this property and converted it for recreational purposes. The developed portion is currently 7.2 km (4.5 mi) long and links the villages of Embrun and Russell. Discussions are underway to extend the trail to the city of Ottawa.

If you want to see an example of how a properly managed trail can become a treasured community resource over time, you must visit the New York Central. Almost every house along the route has its own link connecting to the trail, and residents use the path constantly. This is a great community pathway.

Route Description: From the parking area, where there are regulatory signs and garbage cans, turn right onto the paved pathway. Within

100 m/yd, you slip under the canopy of the many trees growing alongside the route. Initially, except for St. Theresa's School, there will be fields to your left and houses on your right. You will immediately notice how many of the homes have connected to the trail, building bridges to span the ditch paralleling the former rail embankment. Expect company through here.

At 700 m/yd, you should notice a park on your right, where there are bike racks, covered picnic tables, and even a playground — in case you feel an irresistible urge to climb the monkey bars. And 500 m/yd later, a signed crosswalk conducts you over Eadie Road, where you leave the houses of Russell behind. For the next 1 km (0.6 mi), your route, almost as straight as an arrow, continues through a charming hardwood forest, interrupted only by a power-line corridor 250 m/yd from

Eadie Road. About 1.8 km (1.1 mi) from the start, ploughed fields crowd up to the tree line on your left, and during the next 350 m/yd, you should notice a busy road gradually getting closer. There are also more houses here, some featuring quite elaborate trail connections.

At 2.2 km (1.4 mi), the trail reaches busy County Road 3. There are benches here, in the shade. Although well signed on the highway and the trail, and marked by a crosswalk, this is an extremely dangerous intersection, where a trail user was struck by a car and killed. Proceed extra carefully.

Once across, the trail parallels the CR3 for the next 1.6 km (1 mi). Cultivated fields take over on the right. But the trail proceeds insulated somewhat inside a buffer of pleasant hardwoods, interrupted only by one farm road. There are even a few additional benches.

Red-Winged Blackbird

As you hike past a wetland or farming area, expect to hear the distinctive *oak-a-lee* song or *chek* call of the red-winged blackbird. One of the most numerous birds in North America, the all-black male often displays his bright red shoulder patches as he flits between cattails chasing insects. The striped brown female, in contrast, looks almost like a large sparrow. Migration begins in September or October, and they are among the first birds to return in the spring.

At 3.8 km (2.4 mi), CR3 must be crossed again, in equally challenging circumstances, with the road curving precisely at the trail crossing. But only 200 m/yd later, the very busy County Road 17 must be crossed. At least there is a stop sign here for traffic, but be extremely cautious.

We have reached Embrun, and although fields remain on our left, an industrial park looms on our right. Just after passing the Ontario Provincial Police station at 4.7 km (2.9 mi), a public access path crosses the deep drainage ditch bordering the path, and after this, residential buildings appear to your left. This section becomes a repeat of Russell, with almost every home having developed its individual entrance. It is quite charming. There are more benches at your next road crossing, 800 m/yd later, at sedate St. Pierre Road.

The trail is curving gently right now, and it ends 400 m/yd further at the former railway station, which is now a tourist bureau. There is a parking lot, covered area, and outhouse. You are roughly 6 km (3.75 mi) from your starting point. Retrace your route to return.

If you enjoyed this so much you wish to extend your walk, the trail continues to the left of the First Street parking area in Russell for 1.2 km (0.75 mi) and is a very attractive section of the trail. This curves to the right, connects with a substantial wooded area on the left, and ends at Forced Road.

Cautionary Notes: Dangerous road crossings (there have been fatalities), poison ivy.

Cellphone Reception: Excellent throughout.

Further Information: Brochure available at municipal tourism outlets and town hall.

Ottawa-Carleton Trailway

Length: 42 km (26.25 mi) return
Hiking Time: 10-14 hrs
Type of Trail: crushed stone, asphalt
Uses: walking, biking, horseback riding, snowshoeing, cross-country skiing, snowmobiling
Facilities: benches, bike racks, garbage cans, interpretive panels, outhouse, water
Gov't Topo Map: 031F01, 031G05, 031G04
Rating (1-5): 5 [distance]
Trailhead GPS: N 45° 15' 29.3" W 75° 55' 15.6"

Access Information: From the Highway 416/417 split, follow Highway 417 west for 12.5 km (7.8 mi). Turn left onto Carp Road/Ottawa Road 5 and continue into Stittsville. At 3 km (1.9 mi), Carp Road merges with Stittsville Main Street; keep right. Follow for 1.3 km (0.8 mi) to Abbot Street and turn left. Park at the first available space on the right. The trail begins on the opposite side of Village Square Park.

Introduction: One of the great benefits of converting abandoned rail lines to trails is the preservation of a piece of our history. The route followed by the Ottawa-Carleton Trailway is that of the long-forgotten Canadian Central Railway, which opened officially on September 15, 1870. Railways were the superhighways of their era and to have a railway connection meant prosperity for a community, connecting it to the larger world and turning it into a commercial hub. Some of the industries still active today in Carleton Place located there partly because of its rail connection.

The Canadian Central became part of the Canadian Pacific Railway system, and until 1967, cross-country passenger trains transited en route to their ocean destinations. When I am on this trail, at its most remote points, I close my eyes and try to imagine when this was part of the steel spine of the country, when goods and people flowed over its lonely distances. Sometimes, I even believe I can hear the ghost of the steam train's whistle.

Railroads

Railroads were the superhighways of the late 19th and early 20th centuries, the only practical method to move goods and people except for the rivers and canals. The lands surrounding the Ottawa River, rich in lumber and minerals, generated an explosion of rail building that crisscrossed the region and extended into many of its river valleys.

By the end of the Second World War, railroads were unmistakably in decline, and most of the region's branch lines, and even a few main routes, were abandoned. Yet their role in transportation is not over, for hundreds of kilometres have been converted to recreational trails in the past two decades.

stock.xchng.com, Benedecki

Ottawa – Carleton Trailway
West Section

Trail Shared with vehicles

Trail Ends

Extensive New Development

Carleton Place

0   500   1 km

0   1 mi

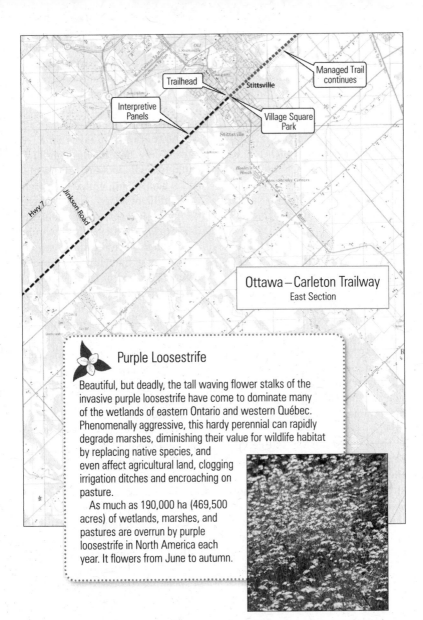

Trailhead

Managed Trail
continues

Stittsville

Interpretive
Panels

Village Square
Park

Stittsville

Henley's
Heath

Stenley Corners

Hwy 7

Jinkson Road

Ottawa – Carleton Trailway
East Section

Purple Loosestrife

Beautiful, but deadly, the tall waving flower stalks of the
invasive purple loosestrife have come to dominate many
of the wetlands of eastern Ontario and western Québec.
Phenomenally aggressive, this hardy perennial can rapidly
degrade marshes, diminishing their value for wildlife habitat
by replacing native species, and
even affect agricultural land, clogging
irrigation ditches and encroaching on
pasture.

   As much as 190,000 ha (469,500
acres) of wetlands, marshes, and
pastures are overrun by purple
loosestrife in North America each
year. It flowers from June to autumn.

This is the only trail in the book that I recommend you complete over two days, although, for some, a 40 km (25 mi) trek on essentially level terrain will be possible in one day. You can also use two cars, leaving one at the end of the route. Fortunately, because this is a linear corridor, walkers can choose to turn back at any point rather than undertake the full distance, so shorter trips are easily planned.

Route Description: There are a number of facilities at Village Square Park, including picnic tables and water. However, the trailhead is across Stittsville Main Street, where a fence blocks the wide, crushed-stone path and a large Ottawa-Carleton Trailway pavilion may be found. Take time to read the history of the path on which you will be walking, which is also a component of the Trans Canada Trail.

From Stittsville Main Street, the route begins by passing between the houses of the community, insulated by a buffer of vegetation. Community connectors join from the left at 200 m/yd and the right at 400 m/yd, and expect residents to be sharing the path through here. Other, smaller side trails branch away, although, when you cross West Ridge Drive at 800 m/yd, you

leave the houses behind. You will also notice a small park with picnic tables, garbage cans, bike racks, and a community trail to your right. There is also a Trans Canada Trail discovery panel about deer.

The trail rapidly takes on a remote feeling, heading through thick and unfriendly looking woodlands. At 1.9 km (1.2 mi), it passes through the middle of a large marsh where two more interpretive panels, on beavers and turtles, stand watch. After 300 m/yd in the open, you return to forest, though not as thick as before. The next notable feature is a power line that you pass beneath at 3.3 km (2.1 mi). About 300 m/yd later, you reach another marshy area, which, with a few breaks on occasional islands of dry land, takes 900 m/yd to cross. The route continues, without much change, until you reach Jinkinson Road, 6.4 km (4 mi) from Stittsville. There are no amenities, but there is a sign telling you that the next road crossing is 4.5 km (2.8 mi) further.

The next 3 km (1.9 mi) is much more open, with farmland occasionally visible on either side. You might even notice an adjacent golf course, and at 9.2 km (5.75 mi), a path crosses your trail connecting the two sides of the course. Beware of speeding golf carts! From there, 1.8 km (1.1 mi) remains until you reach the Dwyer Hill Road, 11 km (6.9 mi) from Stittsville. Those intending to spend only one day on this route should probably turn back no later than here.

Once across Dwyer Hill, the trail passes between open fields for 400 m/yd, though always with a wooded separation. Returning to thicker forest, your route perceptibly lowers into a huge wet area that probably covers the trail at times during the spring runoff. At your lowest point, you are 12 km (7.5 mi) from Stittsville. The path climbs again but very gradually. Even from here you can see the massive bridge carrying Highway 7 above the trail. You reach it, and pass underneath, at 13.2 km (8.2 mi).

The thick forest is left behind, and in the next 700 m/yd, you pass between several large businesses. Upon reaching the Aston Station Road a gate restricts access to the trail because, on the far side, it becomes a street for the next 750 m/yd, connecting several businesses and farms, and it is even paved for a portion. Busy Highway 7 is visible to your left barely 100 m/yd away. Once past a final driveway, the trail curves gently right and moves gradually further from the highway. Briefly in forest, the path soon sheds its trees and continues through an extended area of cultivation, passing quite close to two large farms and crossed by a number of their roads.

When you reach the Appleton Side Road, you have walked 18 km (11.2 mi) but only a short distance remains. This is an attractive pastoral area, farmland on both sides, although the land to your left is rapidly being developed. At 1.4 km (0.9 mi), you cross a small stream, where there are bike racks and a small viewing area. Only 1.3 km (0.8 mi) remains until you reach the end of the trail — a modest sign and concrete barricade blocking the end of Coleman Street in Carleton Place, — which is a rather ordinary and cheerless end to such a great long-distance community connector.

Those intending to spend the night must continue straight down Coleman Street another 1 km (0.6 mi) to reach the downtown.

Cautionary Notes: Animals, poison ivy, several road crossings, sharing portions of the route with motor vehicles.

Cellphone Reception: Excellent in Stittsville and Carleton Place but poor reception between Dwyer Hill and Jinkinson roads.

Further Information: None.

Prescott-Russell Recreational Trail: Hammond to Bourget

Length: 12 km (7.5 mi) return
Hiking Time: 3 hrs
Type of Trail: crushed stone
Uses: walking, biking, cross-country skiing, snowmobiling
Facilities: covered picnic table, garbage can, information pavilion with trail map, outhouse
Gov't Topo Map: 031G06
Rating (1-5): 2
Trailhead GPS: N 45° 26' 07.9" W 75° 14' 14.6"

Access Information: From the Highway 174/417 split, take Highway 174 (becoming Highway 17) for 26 km (16.25 mi) to Canaan Road. Turn right and follow for 2 km (1.25 mi), turning left onto Baseline Road. Continue for 2 km (1.25 mi) then turn right onto Joanisse Road/CR21. Follow CR21 for 9 km (5.6 mi) until it curves left and becomes Lacroix Road. Continue a further 1.5 km (0.9 mi) to a stop sign in Hammond. Turn right onto Gendron Road. Trail parking is on the right 700 m/yd later.

Introduction: The Prescott-Russell Recreational Trail, which traverses the rural farmlands east of Ottawa, officially opened in June 2004. It extends 72 km (45 mi), from the Québec provincial border to the city limits of Ottawa, and is constructed on the abandoned rail bed of the former Montreal-Ottawa line. This corridor reaches from Rigaud in Québec to Highway 417 at Innis Road in Ottawa.

The section between the communities of Hammond and Bourget connects two of the five pavilions constructed on the trail and is a comfortable walking distance for a day hike. Grocery stores and other amenities are available in either community and are only a short distance from the trail. This will be a pleasant amble for anyone, offering easy walking through a pastoral setting.

Route Description: The wide, crushed-stone path immediately crosses Gendron Road, almost imperceptibly descending to cross a small creek 400 m/yd from the start. The

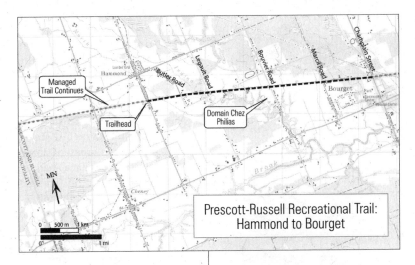

Prescott-Russell Recreational Trail:
Hammond to Bourget

land on either side is open and farm fields and initially the trail is elevated above the surrounding landscape. A lovely stand of mature cedar and spruce borders the field to your left. At 1 km (0.6 mi), you reach your first crossing, Butler Road, where there are a number of houses. Gates, intended to block trail access to ATVs and other motorized vehicles, are found at every road crossing.

The first bridge, 1.4 km (0.9 mi) into the hike, crosses small, meandering Indian Creek. You continue through forest cover for an additional 300 m/yd until you reach gates at Legault Road and Levine Road. The latter parallels your route on the right for an additional 800 m/yd until it cuts left to cross the trail. On your right, you should see a sign

for Domain Chez Philias, which provides winter accommodations and maple syrup brunches in the spring.

You cross another tiny brook about 100 m/yd later, and you should be able to see the church spires of Bourget ahead and to the right. At 3.3 km (2.1 mi), with open ground all around, you cross Bouvier Road. And only 400 m/yd later, you reach the only point on the walk where the land bordering the trail is slightly higher. This is very brief, and the ground soon slopes away again, especially on the right. This section of the trail is a very long straightaway, and you can see far ahead. To your right, the trees of the Larose Forest, eastern Ontario's second largest tree plantation, can be sighted.

more walking because, only 200 m/yd further along, you will find the former train station, now a private residence that has been attractively restored and still features the station sign. Almost since you crossed Marcil Road, fences have lined the trail on the right. There is an opening just beyond the former train station, permitting access to the community. If you continue only an additional 700 m/yd, or 6 km (3.75 mi) from Hammond, the trail reaches Champlain Street in Bourget, with sidewalks and bike lanes and a small park with a bench and interpretive panel. Businesses and amenities may be found to the right.

As you approach the next crossing, Marcil Road, about 4.7 km (2.9 mi) from the start, you will find a number of new homes. You enter trees again, but soon you will sight a paved road on your right and the Bourget trail pavilion ahead of you. You encounter the only curve in the trail as you reach the pavilion, which has been placed in the middle of the former rail bed. The trail has been routed around this structure, creating a little wiggle — almost certainly to slow snowmobilers as they enter the community.

You reach the pavilion approximately 5.2 km (3.25 mi) from the start, and you could return from here. However, I recommend a little

Retrace your route to return to Hammond.

Cautionary Notes: Several road crossings, snowmobiles permitted, with ATVs often found on the trail, poison ivy.

Cellphone Reception: Adequate reception throughout.

Further Information: www.prescott-russell.on.ca/counties.jsp?section=recreatrail.

St. Lawrence Recreational Path

Length: 18.5 km (11.5 mi) return
Hiking Time: 4-6 hrs
Type of Trail: crushed stone, asphalt
Uses: walking, biking, snow-shoeing, cross-country skiing
Facilities: benches, campgrounds, covered picnic tables, garbage cans, outhouses
Gov't Topo Maps: 031G02, 031B14
Rating (1-5): 4 [distance]
Trailhead GPS: N 44° 59' 53.1" W 74° 58' 27.4"

Access Information: From the Highway 174/417 split, follow route 417 east for 33 km (20.5 mi) to Exit 79. Turn south onto County Road 5, which will become CR12 in 8 km (5 mi). Continue an additional 30 km (18.75 mi), turning right at the junction with CR14. Follow CR14 for 14 km (8.75 mi) to the junction with Highway 2. Turn left, and 700 m/yd later, turn right onto Long Sault Parkway. Turn into the parking area immediately on the right; the trail begins in the northeast corner of the parking lot.

Introduction: The 200 km (125 mi) between Kingston and the Québec border is known as the St. Lawrence Heritage Corner and is home to a wide variety of parks and recreational sites. The "Parks of the St. Lawrence" includes, within 100 km (62.5 mi) by air of Ottawa, Upper Canada Village, Upper Canada Migratory Bird Sanctuary, Long Sault Parkway, and a number of day-use area parks, campgrounds, and recreational trails.

The St. Lawrence Recreational Trail extends for nearly 75 km (47 mi) between the communities of Lancaster and Morrisburg, although there are some sections where it follows roads. The section between the west end of the Long Sault Parkway and Upper Canada Village is excellent for families and groups — a well-maintained path with abundant facilities, including camping. It also passes through the Upper Canada Migratory Bird Sanctuary, which has its own 8 km (5 mi) network of footpaths. The full 18.5 km (11.5 mi) profiled might be too far for some, but there are frequent locations

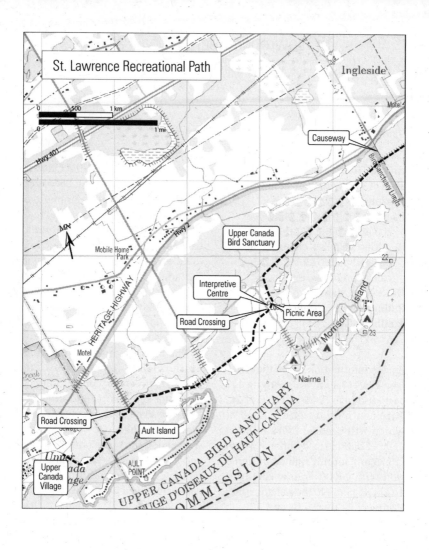

St. Lawrence Recreational Path

Ingleside

Causeway

Upper Canada
Bird Sanctuary

Interpretive
Centre

Picnic Area

Road Crossing

Morrison Island

Nairne I

Road Crossing

Ault Island

UPPER CANADA BIRD SANCTUARY
REFUGE D'OISEAUX DU HAUT-CANADA
COMMISSION

AULT
POINT

Upper
Canada
Village

Mobile Home
Park

HERITAGE HIGHWAY

Motel

Motel

Hwy 401

Hwy 2

MN

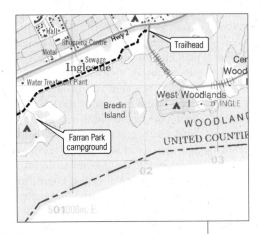

inland for 25 m/yd to follow a creek. Once across, it veers left to return to its original path, turning right again 25 m/yd later. It briefly moves away from the river, crossing a road, the entrance to the Farran Park campground, 250 m/yd later. Immediately on the other side, you pass through a narrow metal gate where there is another bench and garbage can. The water is now on your right, and there is a bronze plaque by its edge commemorating the Upper Canada Migratory Bird Sanctuary.

This next 1 km (0.6 mi) is quite lovely as the trail crosses a narrow causeway with water lapping both sides. At its far end, the trail moves into the thickly wooded grounds of the Upper Canada Bird Sanctuary, leaving open water behind. It is still very wet through here, however, with ditches on both sides of the trail filled with still water. Expect hordes of hungry mosquitoes!

For the next 1 km (0.6 mi), thick woods and wet ditches contain the path. However, shortly after, a footpath joins from the left, and the woods open up to the right, providing better views of a marshy area popular with waterfowl and amphibians. About 500 m/yd later,

along the way that are worthwhile destinations and shorter hikes.

Route Description: The wide, paved path begins by moving through tended fields as it gently meanders towards the shore of the St. Lawrence River. Initially attractive and pastoral, grass grows right to the edge of the trail and well-spaced mature trees line either side. By 600 m/yd, you are next to the water, and although your route parallels busy Highway 2, traffic noise is limited. At 1 km (0.6 mi), you reach a small parking area with benches and garbage cans. For the next 750 m/yd, the trail is virtually straight, with grassy fields extending to your right and the river less than 10 m/yd on your left.

The path heads into the mouth of a small bay, turning right sharply another footpath connects from the left.

About 5 km (3.1 mi) into your hike, the trail turns sharply left, and you pass through another narrow gate. You quickly emerge from the forest and encounter a major trail junction. If you turn right, the paved trail ends about 200 m/yd later. Instead, turn left onto the crushed gravel, where you will soon reach a large picnic ground with washrooms and covered picnic tables. The trail even passes directly across the entrance to the interpretive centre for the Bird Sanctuary. This is a great area to stop for lunch, explore the interpretive centre, and possibly even explore some of the Bird Sanctuary's 8 km (5 mi) of paths. If you return to the trailhead from here, your total walk will be 11 km (6.9 mi).

If you continue, you cross Morrison's Road 300 m/yd later, and the crushed-stone pathway becomes more windy and hilly. For the next 1.2 km (0.75 mi), you pass through abandoned farm fields that are reforesting; there is little to view through the thick brush. Quite suddenly, you reach water, crossing a dike popular with fishers, with a dirt road heading off to the right before you cross.

Once across the dike, you are actually on Ault Island. The trail here shows signs of less use, with grass growing in its centre strip. When you pass under high pines 800 m/yd later, their needles cover the treadway. One final road crossing occurs 400 m/yd further, about 8 km (5 mi) from your start. Gates frame the trail on both sides of the road. Once across this road, the path narrows, and its surface of crushed stone nearly disappears as mature forest crowds the edges. Beautiful open water soon appears on the right, and the trail comes right to its bank. At points, the trail almost becomes as rough as if it had not been maintained. However, about 1 km (0.6 mi) from the Ault Island Road, the crushed stone suddenly reappears; the path turns 90° right and crosses over a small, gated bridge.

Your route ends 200 m/yd later at a road. From here, Upper Canada Village is less than 1 km (0.6 mi) further. To return to the start, retrace your route.

Cautionary Notes: Poison ivy, road crossings, ticks.

Cellphone Reception: Adequate throughout.

Further Information: www.cornwalltourism.com/nature14.htm.

Watershield

Cataraqui Trail – Chaffey's Locks,
Eastern Ontario – Frontenac Arch

Charleston Lake Provincial Park – Tallow Rock Bay Trail,
Eastern Ontario – Frontenac Arch

Scilla

South Otter Lake, Doe Lake Trail, Frontenac Provincial Park,
Eastern Ontario–Frontenac Arch

Marble Rock, Eastern Ontario–Frontenac Arch

Cardinal flower

Foley Mountain, Rideau Trail–Westport, Eastern Ontario–Frontenac Arch

Stonebridge Trail

Length: 8 km (5 mi) return
Hiking Time: 2 hrs
Type of Trail: crushed stone
Uses: walking, biking, snowshoeing
Facilities: benches, garbage cans
Gov't Topo Map: 031G05
Rating (1-5): 2
Trailhead GPS: N 45° 15' 42.0"
    W 75° 43' 54.2"

Access Information: From the Highway 416/417 split, follow Highway 416 for 9 km (5.5 mi) to Exit 66. Turn left onto Fallowfield Road/Ottawa Road 12, turning right onto Strandherd Drive 1 km (0.6 mi) later. After 4.3 km (2.7 mi), turn right onto Greenbank Road. In 500 m/yd, turn left onto Jockvale Road. Continue 1.2 km (0.75 mi); look for a large sign on the left reading "Stonebridge Trail." The path begins at the far end of the parking area.

Introduction: This is a pleasant walk in an area that has rapidly developed into suburbia. Its two halves are quite different, with the first 2 km (1.25 mi) almost always within sight of houses, and the final 2 km (1.25 mi) at times feeling more remote than they actually are. Being so close to both the Jock and the Rideau rivers makes this a worthwhile hike for novices and families alike.

Route Description: You start on a gravel walkway, which connects immediately to a wide gravel road. Turn right, past an area of newly planted trees. Within 200 m/yd, you reach a very large open area of playgrounds, a ball diamond, and soccer fields, where the trail splits. Keep left, along the outer perimeter of W.C. Levesque Fields, while the trail works its way closer to the banks of the Jock River. A little side path leads right down to the water. After about 600 m/yd of paralleling the field, the trail splits again, with the left branch, which you should follow, heading into an area of larger, older trees.

There are many side trails, mostly leading toward the river, through this too-brief, 200 m/yd forested stretch. Then the taller trees disappear, leaving no shade, and for 300 m/yd, it is semi-open. Fortunately, you next enter an area of high cedars, which provides the best view so far of the Jock River, which is on your left. The trail meanders around a gully, a deep little river, and passes under a couple of towering maples. At 1.5 km (0.9 mi), you emerge from the forest again; on your right is a water control structure, gated, with houses behind it. The trail bends left, descends a set of stairs, then crosses a bridge level with the Jock River. For the first time, you can dip your feet from the trail.

On the other side of the bridge, there is a little lookout to the left. You then climb a little, pass through a stand of trees, and come almost into the backyard of some new residences, one of which contains an observatory — not something you expect to find in most suburbs. A side trail will take you to the street, Marwood Court, should you choose.

You finally move away from houses for a time, as the path heads back into forest. This is some of the most attractive trail so far, situated on the bank above the river, wide and surfaced with crushed stone. Yet after only a few hundred metres/ yards, you hear the sounds of heavy traffic, and on your right, the tended grounds of Capital Memorial Gardens crowd the path. The trail drops and curves, a wooden fence protecting you from hiking into the water. At 2 km (1.25 mi), you pass underneath the massive steel and concrete Prince of Wales Drive road bridge.

Just ahead of you, the Jock feeds into the Rideau River, and the trail will now follow this larger watercourse. From the bridge, the path climbs, passing into an area of spruce, and crosses a private drive 220 m/yd later, where there are gates across the trail. As your route curves right, you should be able to view the Rideau through thickening vegetation. For the first time, you feel almost as if you are somewhere remote. You cross a metal bridge 300 m/yd further over a deep gully then, 300 m/yd further, a much larger bridge over a considerably deeper ravine. Once across, the trail splits briefly; to the left, there is a bench overlooking the water, while the main trail turns right and parallels

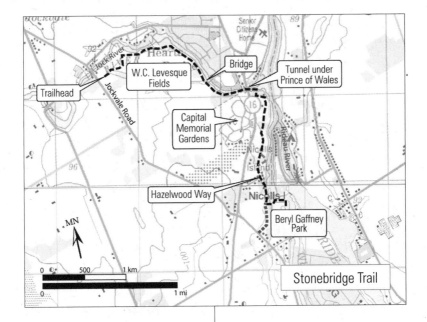

Stonebridge Trail

the ravine until it reaches a gate at the end of Hazelwood Way. The left route rejoins just before the gate at 3.2 km (2 mi).

There is no signage here, but walk the 100 m/yd to the opposite end of this street, and you will find that the trail resumes on the far side of another gate. This path looks older, with grass growing in from the edges, leaving only a centre strip of gravel. After only 100 m/yd, there is another junction; turn left and cross a small wooden bridge, where you emerge into a field. At the next junction, turn left again and continue until you reach the woods, where

you will turn left one more time. Suddenly the path descends into a little gully and, at the stream crossing at the bottom, are some very large stones that have been placed there. Once across, at 3.8 km (2.4 mi), you climb a set of stairs and walk out into another field. From here, you get an excellent view to your left of the river, Nicolls Island, and a dam that is part of the Rideau Canal system. It is a hard scramble down the steep banks to the water's edge, but if you can do so, it is a pleasant location to eat your lunch and soak your weary feet. Otherwise, only 100 m/ yd remain before the path finishes

at the end of Lockview Road, next to a sign announcing that this is Beryl Gaffney Park.

You have hiked 4 km (2.5 mi). Retrace your route to return to the trailhead.

Cautionary Notes: Poison ivy.

Cellphone Reception: Adequate throughout.

Further Information: None.

 Ticks

Ticks are small, eight-legged arachnids that attach themselves to mammals and gorge themselves on their blood. Unfed ticks are not much larger than a sesame seed, and they move around on the ground, grass, and bushes, waiting to attach themselves to any animal that brushes past.

Ticks are found throughout southern Ontario, and their range is spreading as the climate changes. Most tick bites cause only skin irritation and swelling, but a small percentage of ticks carry diseases, the most deadly of which is Lyme disease. DEET on clothes is effective at repelling ticks, but other measures are prudent. For more information on ticks, see health.gov. on.ca/english/public/pub/disease/lyme_mn.html.

Doe Lake

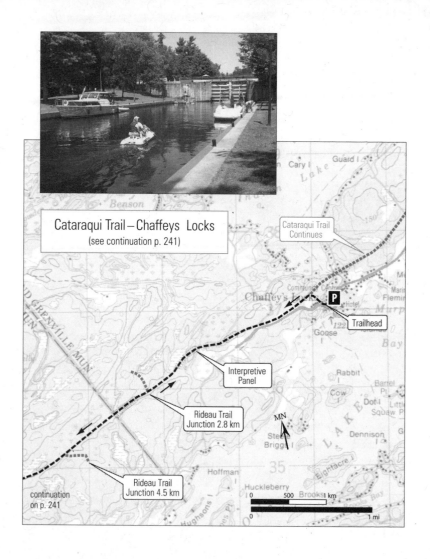

Cataraqui Trail – Chaffeys Locks
(see continuation p. 241)

Cataraqui Trail Continues

Chaffey's L...

P Trailhead

Interpretive Panel

Rideau Trail Junction 2.8 km

Rideau Trail Junction 4.5 km

continuation on p. 241

MN

0   500   1 km

0   1 mi

Cataraqui Trail – Chaffeys Locks

Length: 19 km (11.9 mi) return

Hiking Time: 5-7 hrs

Type of Trail: acphalt, compacted earth, crushed stone

Uses: walking, biking, horseback riding, snowshoeing, cross-country skiing, snowmobiling

Facilities: barbeques, benches, garbage cans, museum, outhouses, tables

Gov't Topo Map: 031C09

Rating (1-5): 5 [distance, isolation]

Trailhead GPS: N 44° 34' 44.2" W 76° 19' 11.3"

Access Information: From the Highway 416/417 split, follow Highway 417 west for 14 km (8.75 mi) to Exit 145 at Highway 7. Turn onto Highway 7 and continue for 23 km (14. mi) to Carleton Place, where you turn left onto Highway 15. Follow Highway 15 for 26 km (16.25 mi) to Smiths Falls. Continue on Highway 15 through Smiths Falls and for an additional 38 km (23.75 mi) to the junction with Chaffeys Locks Road, about 2.5 km (1.6 mi) past the tiny community of Crosby. Turn right and follow this road for 10 km (6.25 mi) to Chaffeys Lock; the parking area is near the canal.

Introduction: Few hikes will provide you with the opportunity to sample as many recreational resources as this does. You begin and end on the Rideau Canal, a UNESCO World Heritage Site. During your walk, you will be following the Cataraqui Trail, the Rideau Trail, and the Trans Canada Trail, sometimes simultaneously.

However, the principal path for most of your route is the Cataraqui Trail, a 104 km (65 mi) abandoned railway line that extends from Smiths Falls to Strathcona, near Lake Ontario. This shared-use trail, owned by the Cataraqui Region Conservation Authority, was abandoned by the Canadian National Railway in 1989 and officially opened as a recreational corridor in September 2000.

At Chaffeys Locks, the land through which the Cataraqui Trail passes changes quite dramatically. North and east, it is gentle and rolling, ideal for agricultural use. West and south, it heads into the Frontenac Arch, a southern extension of the rugged Canadian Shield. In this region, the soils are too thin to support farming, so the land is virtually empty of habitation. Wetlands and rocky outcroppings alternate, with occasional deep, clear lakes perfect for secluded swimming.

I have profiled this route from Chaffeys Locks as far as Garter Lake, a great destination but an ambitious 19 km (11.9 mi) return trip. It can be shortened by turning back at any point you choose.

Route Description: Begin your walk by crossing the bridge over Chaffeys Lock and following the paved road for 200 m/yd. Turn right onto a gravelled road marked "Private." About 100 m/yd further, turn left when the trail forks, and in 200 m/yd, you reach the Cataraqui Trail, where you head left. (If you turn right, 200 m/yd will take you to the bridge crossing the Rideau Canal. It is worth the short side trip.)

This path starts on an embankment, higher than the ground on either side, with a hard-packed natural surface. Vegetation has grown thickly on the edges of the route, with trees growing on the slope, providing no view at all. Within 500 m/yd, you will pass the remains of a railway building on your left

and an open area growing over with sumac. The Opinicon Road is also quite close on your left, and 1.3 km (0.8 mi) from the start, the trail crosses Indian Lake Road. There is a gate on the opposite side, and a sign identifying it as the Cataraqui Trail.

The surrounding terrain immediately becomes more rugged, with the trail alternating between being on an embankment or inside a narrow cut. The trees are mostly hardwood, and they crowd the fringes of the path. About 600 m/yd past Indian Lake Road, you can view a large wetland on your right; 200 m/yd further, you will find a Trans Canada Trail interpretive panel about snapping turtles posted on your left on a steep embankment high above a pond.

The path gently curves left, and 200 m/yd further, you will sight another picturesque wetland area. Although barely perceptible, the trail now swings gently right and descends. About 500 m/yd later, a signpost on the right marks where the Rideau Trail merges with the Cataraqui. Perhaps 200 m/yd later, you pass the Cataraqui Trail's 45 km (28 mi) marker, indicating your distance from Smiths Falls.

The trail now becomes a little more grown in, slightly wetter — less gravel, more dirt — as you pass through a number of narrow rock cuts. When you pass the Bedford Town-

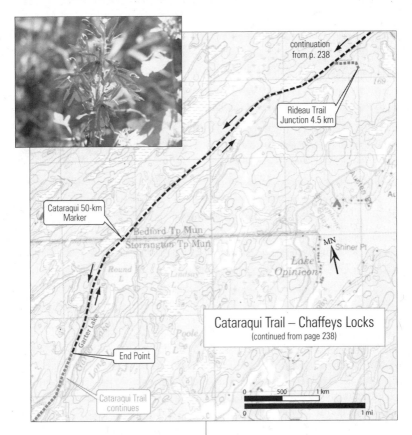

continuation from p. 238

Rideau Trail Junction 4.5 km

Cataraqui 50-km Marker

Bedford Tp Mun
Storrington Tp Mun

MN
Shiner Pt

Lake Opinicon

Round L.

Lindsay

Garter Lake

Poole L.

Cataraqui Trail – Chaffeys Locks
(continued from page 238)

End Point

Cataraqui Trail continues

0   500   1 km

0   1 mi

ship boundary sign, you have walked slightly less than 4 km (2.5 mi). For much of the next kilometre (0.6 mi), the trail is bounded on both sides by swamp, and the mosquitoes are exceptionally bad. The Rideau Trail departs to the left around 4.5 km (2.8 mi), and at 5 km (3.1 mi), you will sight another large wetland on your right but at trail level.

For the next several kilometres (miles), the trail alternates between being bordered by steep rocky outcrops and significant wet areas as the terrain becomes progressively more rugged. At times, the wet areas threaten to flood the trail and probably do each spring. However, the treadway becomes mostly grass covered, making for quite pleasant

Frontenac Arch

The Frontenac Arch is a broad and ancient granite ridge, situated between Ottawa and Kingston, that joins the Canadian Shield to the Adirondack Mountains. The topography of the region is rugged: steep, rocky slopes and ridges, typical of the Precambrian Shield and vastly different from the lowlands south of the Ottawa River near the city. Charleston Lake and Frontenac Provincial Park are both found within the Arch's boundaries.

In 2002, UNESCO designated this region as the Frontenac Arch Biosphere Reserve, one of only 13 in Canada. A biosphere reserve is defined as an area with important natural and ecological values where people live, work, and enjoy a variety of economic and recreational activities based on respect for the environment.

walking, and the trail begins to open onto some broad views. No human habitation can be sighted anywhere.

You will reach the Cataraqui 50 km (31.25 mi) sign at 8 km (5 mi), shortly after passing a large wet area retained by a beaver dam in elevation to your right, and you might sight Round Lake to your left. For the next kilometre (0.6 mi), you pass through several deep railway cuts before emerging to find yourself above a beautiful, slender 1 km (0.6 mi) long lake on your left. This is Garter Lake, your destination, a wonderful location for a picnic and a swim. At about 9.5 km (6 mi), you should find a rough footpath

scrambling down the embankment. You will need to be sure-footed, but the lake will look irresistible after a long, hot ramble.

Retrace your route to complete the hike.

Cautionary Notes: Animals, hunters, poison ivy.

Cellphone Reception: Strong at the start but weakening as the trip proceeds and disappears in sheltered areas by Round Lake.

Further Information: www.rideau-info.com/cattrail, www.cataraqui region.on.ca/lands/cattrail.htm.

Charleston Lake Provincial Park – Tallow Rock Bay Trail

Length: 10 km (6.25 mi) return
Hiking Time: 4 hrs
Type of Trail: boardwalk, natural surface
Uses: walking, snowshoeing
Facilities: campsites, outhouses, picnic tables
Gov't Topo Map: 031C09
Rating (1-5): 3
Trailhead GPS: N 44° 30' 14.3"
   W 76° 02' 19.3"

Access Information: From the Highway 416/417 split, drive 75 km (47 mi) on Highway 416 to Highway 401. Follow Highway 401 west for 62 km (38.75 mi) to Exit 659, turning right onto Reynolds Road/County Road 3. Continue 14 km (8.75 mi) through the village of Lansdowne and the hamlet of Outlet. A park sign is on the right; turn onto Woodvale Road and drive for 1.2 km (0.75 mi) to the park entrance. Turn left and follow the paved surface for 1 km (0.6 mi) to a parking area. Westside Trails trailhead pavilion is on the left; begin here.

Introduction: Charleston Lake Provincial Park comprises almost 2,500 hectares (6,100 acres) of crown land scattered across the shores and islands of large Charleston Lake. This is a phenomenally popular summer destination, and its 238 campsites are filled almost every weekend. A wide variety of hiking options are available within its boundaries, including one trail, Blue Mountain, which requires canoe travel to access the trailhead.

The Tallow Rock Bay Trail, however, is my recommendation. It is the longest trek available in the park, taking you into its most remote corners. Numerous backcountry campsites are found along its route, accessible only by foot or water, and there are several lookouts, a number of side trails, and a floating bridge. This trail passes through relatively challenging terrain in some places and, including optional side trails, exceeds 12 km (7.5 mi). Accordingly, it rates a higher difficulty level than is usual for this distance.

Route Description: Everyone will find the first 500 m/yd quite easy, as the wide, gravelled trail passes over two marshy areas on long boardwalks. Benches may be found after the first boardwalk and on a platform in the second, longer boardwalk.

The first trail junction, signed, is found at the far side of the second boardwalk. Take the left fork, which says that wheelchair travel is not recommended. The path immediately becomes rougher, with no further gravel on the treadway. About 50 m/yd further, the trail splits again, with the Quiddity Trail heading off to the right. Stay left, and left again at the canoe portage 10 m/yd later.

Crossing a small stream, the trail climbs and becomes more rugged. Pine and cedar dominate the trees here, unlike the hardwoods at the start. You might notice occasional fences on your left; this is the extreme eastern edge of the park, and the fences mark the boundary. The trail is usually quite distinct but watch for route markers attached to trees: light blue diamonds with a white hiker in the centre.

At almost 1 km (0.6 mi), you reach another junction, this one splitting the route into the Tallow Rock Bay loop, west and east. Turn left, taking the west loop, and within 10 m/yd, you will see a brown metal sign fixed about 3 m/yd above the ground that says this is 1 km (0.6 mi). Through here, the trail meanders nicely, dodging rocks and wet areas, paralleling the rocky ridges, and is often covered in pine needles.

By 1.5 km (0.9 mi), you are back into hardwoods, and the terrain is becoming easier. Look here for a massive oak with branches like tines on a fork. It is almost the only old tree in the area. The path begins to climb again, somewhat more steeply, and about 300 m/yd further, you cross an open wet area, assisted by numerous long planks. Another 200 m/yd further, the trail joins an old farm road, which is blocked by a metal gate. The 2 km (1.25 mi) marker will be sighted just beyond this point.

For about the next 400 m/yd, you pass through a fairly open area of reforesting farmland. This ends with a long hill, when you re-enter the woods. Just before the 3 km (1.9 mi) marker, the trail suddenly backtracks to cross near a small beaver dam then skirts a small pond.

For the next several hundred metres (yards), the trail runs up between two ridges, gradually climbing. Some of the cliffs beside the trail, especially on the left, are more than 20 m/yd high. During wet weather, expect a lot of water in the path. Cresting on a pine-covered ridge at about 3.5 km (2.2 mi), you now descend another 500 m/yd through

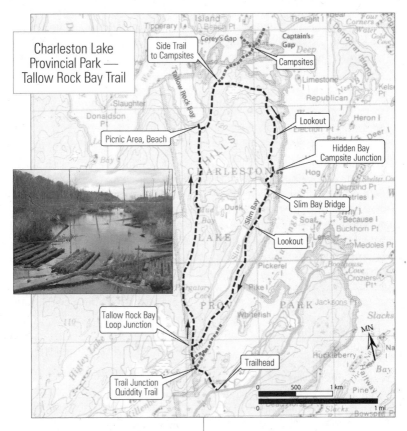

Charleston Lake
Provincial Park —
Tallow Rock Bay Trail

Side Trail
to Campsites

Campsites

Lookout

Hidden Bay
Campsite Junction

Picnic Area, Beach

Slim Bay Bridge

Lookout

Tallow Rock Bay
Loop Junction

Trailhead

Trail Junction
Quiddity Trail

MN

0   500   1 km

0   1 mi

lovely hardwood-covered slopes to Tallow Rock Bay, encountering the 4 km (2.5 mi) marker about 100 m/yd before reaching the water. The main trail turns right; you continue straight to a tiny beach nestled between two stony ridges, where you will find a picnic table.

From Tallow Rock Bay, the path becomes more challenging, following the edge of the lake but traversing several steep hills. About 200 m/yd along, you will encounter a signpost that indicates the camping areas are still ahead. Immediately afterwards, you face perhaps the toughest climb of the day — a short, steep trudge up a rocky section. At 4.5 km (2.8 mi), you reach a crest and area of open rock where pine and cedar predominate. This continues through the 5 km (3.1 mi) point, and shortly afterwards, you reach the junction with the side trail to the Covey's Gap and Captain's Gap campsites. If you decide to explore this side trail, you will add an additional 2 km (1.25 mi) to your hike.

The main path descends sharply, a goat path clinging to the steep slope as its edges around the Beaver Pond. You should get an excellent view of the elaborately crafted beaver dam. After here, several ridges must be crossed, requiring constant climbing and descending through narrow gaps in the rocky ridges. After crossing one small stream, you reach a lookout with excellent views of Charleston Lake; just beyond here, you will reach the 6 km (3.75 mi) marker.

You are heading south now, and the trail fights its way through quite challenging rocky terrain, generally descending but with frequent short climbs as well. At 6.7 km (4.2 mi), the short path to Hidden Cove campsite branches to the left. Perhaps the hike's greatest surprise occurs when the path, essentially at lake level, suddenly climbs through a narrow fissure in the rock wall. Once through, the route descends again to reach the floating Slim Bay Bridge, less than 100 m/yd past the 7 km (4.4 mi) marker.

This fascinating structure, quite long and prone to bobbing erratically in rough weather, permits the crossing of Slim Bay. On the opposite side, the trail becomes much gentler, wider, and almost free of rocks. Bob's Cove campsite is to the left, 300 m/yd later. The path climbs again and crests above Slim Bay at about 7.8 km (4.9 mi), with some of the best views of the walk. After that, the path descends again, and moves away from the water's edge. Most of the next kilometre (0.6 mi) is thick forest as you climb to the 9 km (5.5 mi) marker and the junction that marks the completion of the Tallow Rock Bay Trail. From here, you have 1 km (0.6 mi) remaining on the path you hiked in on.

Cautionary Notes: Animals, poison ivy, ticks.

Cellphone Reception: No coverage at trailhead or at lower elevations deeper in the park. Coverage can be obtained on the tops of hills, especially on bare rock.

Further Information: www.friendsof charlestonlake.ca; www.ontarioparks. com/English/char.html; brochure available at park.

Frontenac Provincial Park –
Doe Lake and Arab Gorge

Length: 4.5 km (2.7 mi) return
Hiking Time: 2 hrs
Type of Trail: boardwalk, natural
    surface
Uses: walking, snowshoeing, cross-
    country skiing
Facilities: benches, campsites,
    garbage cans, outhouses,
    parking, picnic tables, public
    telephones, vending machines,
    visitor centre
Gov't Topo Map: 031C10, 031C07
Rating (1-5): 1
Trailhead GPS: N 44° 30' 16.0"
    W 76° 33' 16.4"

Access Information: From the Highway 416/417 split, follow Highway
417 west for 14 km (8.75 mi) to Exit
145. Turn onto Highway 7 and continue to Sharbot Lake, appromate-
ly 91 km (57 mi). Turn left onto
Highway 38 and drive for 40 km
(25 mi) to County Road 19/Desert
Lake Road, where you turn left.
There is a park road sign. Continue
for 27 km (16.9 mi) to Salmon Lake
Road, turning left. The park entrance
is reached 2 km (1.25 mi) later.
Turn right toward the Park Office

and parking area. A map and day
pass can be purchased at the Visitor
Centre.

Introduction: Pick up the colourful
Doe Lake guide, $1 (2009), at the Park
Office before you start; it provides an
excellent social and natural history
that adds considerably to the experience. Although Frontenac Provincial
Park was designed specifically to
provide backcountry experiences,
there are several worthwhile hikes
near the Park Office suitable for
families and casual walkers. None
are more popular than the 1.5 km
(0.9 mi) Arab Lake Gorge, which follows an extensive boardwalk, or the
3 km (1.9 mi) Doe Lake Loop, which
visits two lakes and the site of a former mica mine. They can be hiked
together or separately.

I rated this route "1," but there
are several climbs on the backside of
the Doe Lake Trail that some might
find challenging. If climbs concern
you, restrict yourself to the Arab
Gorge or turn back after interpretive
site 5, the Trapper's Shanty, on the
Doe Lake Trail.

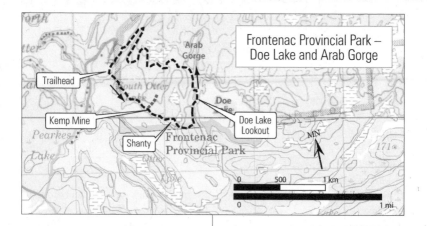

Route Description: The trailhead information kiosk for both trails may be found immediately behind the Park Office, and they share a common path down the hillside and across the mouth of Arab Gorge on a boardwalk. On the far side, turn right onto the Doe Lake Trail and follow the natural surface footpath as it borders the water, which is South Otter Lake. Watch for route markers, a blue diamond centred with a white hiker symbol.

You will immediately note the rugged terrain; rocky outcroppings bulge provocatively into the path, nearly forcing it into the lake. In the first 600 m/yd, you will cross three boardwalks over wet areas and pass interpretive sites 1-3.

At about 650 m/yd, a dead-end side trail, well signed, branches left and up the hill about for 100 m/yd to the site of the former Kemp Mine. Today this consists of a couple of distinctly unimpressive holes in the ground surrounded by fences; here the guidebook is indispensable.

The main trail continues to follow the shoreline of South Otter Lake, mostly through open forest beneath a pine canopy, and you should notice some benches just off the path by the water's edge. At around 900 m/yd, you turn inland to interpretive site 5, the remains of a trapper's shanty on the shore of a beaver pond. The trail crosses below the dam then climbs, sometimes almost steeply, until you reach the impressive lookout above Doe Lake, 1.3 km (0.8 mi) from the trailhead. The thoughtfully provided bench will be welcome, allowing you to both enjoy the view and catch your breath.

From here, the trail turns left almost 180°, following the shoreline of Doe Lake beneath a predominantly hardwood canopy as it descends the ridge. Dropping steadily, sometimes assisted with stairs, the path reaches lake level at site 7, another beaver dam, and crosses over a footbridge signed at 1.5 km (0.9 mi), the halfway point.

But you quickly turn away from the lake to traverse the most challenging portion of the walk as the trail climbs up the rocky hillside, never remaining straight or level for very long. About 700 m/yd after crossing the bridge, you will reach another major boardwalk, having passed sites 8 and 9 along the way. You should be able to sight another pond to your right, and the path flirts around it, crossing numerous small boardwalks but staying away from its banks until you climb a low, cedar-covered rocky ridge. Here, at interpretive site 10, about 2.5 km

---

Water Filtration

Finding safe drinking water while you are hiking is unlikely, and on hot, summer days you can rarely carry enough. Portable water filtration units are compact, easy to use, and should ensure that you are able to stay hydrated without running the risk of beaver fever — or worse!

(1.6 mi) from the start, you will find a bench overlooking the beaver dam and this busy rodent's handiwork, a pond studded with the dead remains of drowned trees.

From the bench, about 500 m/yd remains, with the trail descending through the forest — albeit with one more short steep ascent — back to Arab Gorge. The two trails connect at the bridge leading to the Park Office, where you turn right onto the Arab Lake Gorge trail to follow a boardwalk that passes beneath an overhanging ridge of rock. The boardwalk continues up the narrow, steep-sided gorge for at least 200 m/yd, the evidence of beaver activity everywhere apparent. You will notice more numbered posts; there is a separate interpretive guide available for this trail.

The easy walking route continues, alternating between boardwalk and natural surface covered in wood chips.

Sunscreen

Simply put, use SPF 15 or higher frequently and liberally every two hours as long as you stay in the outdoors, especially at peak times: 11:00 a.m. to 3:00 p.m. Use even on overcast days, and don't forget your ears!

It crosses over the brook on an elevated bridge, until, about 700 m/yd from the start, it turns almost 180° and begins to climb up the hillside. The remainder of the walk returns you to the Park Office, and although there is some climbing required, benches provide both resting places and views of the gorge and boardwalk beneath you.

When the surface of the path becomes covered in crushed stone, you are within 25 m/yd of the Park Office.

Cautionary Notes: Animals.

Cellphone Reception: Adequate at the trailhead but rare in most of park. Often available on hilltops but not in the ravine.

Further Information: www.ontario-parks.com/English/fron.html; Doe Lake and Arab Gorge trail guidebooks available for purchase at park entrance.

Blisters

Even the most careful hiker will get blisters. Left untreated, they can turn the shortest walk into a painful nightmare. Treat a blister like an open wound: clean with soap and water and dress with Second Skin. If your feet are dirty or sweaty, clean with an alcohol swipe to help adhesive tape adhere.

Food

I always carry something, even for short hikes. I prefer to nibble, and so carry nuts, dried fruits, and heavy breads. Anything is better than nothing, but try to stay away from chips, chocolate bars, and other "junk" foods.

Frontenac Provincial Park –
Slide Lake Loop

Length: 28 km (17.5 mi) return
Hiking Time: 8+ hrs
Type of Trail: natural footpath, rock
Uses: walking, snowshoeing
Facilities: benches, campsites, garbage cans, outhouses, parking, picnic tables, public telephones, vending machines, visitor centre
Gov't Topo Map: 031C09, 031C10
Rating (1-5): 5 [rugged terrain, distance]
Trailhead GPS: N 44° 30' 21.3" W 76° 33' 15.8"

Access Information: From the Highway 416/417 split, follow Highway 417 west for 14 km (8.75 mi) to Exit 145. Turn onto Highway 7, and continue to Sharbot Lake, approximately 91 km (57 mi). Turn left onto Highway 38, and drive for 40 km (25 mi) to County Road 19/Desert Lake Road, where you turn left. There is a park road sign. Continue for 27 km (16.9 mi) to Salmon Lake Road, turning left. The park entrance is reached 2 km (1.25 mi) later. Turn right to the Visitor Centre; the parking area is on the left. A map and day pass can be purchased at the Visitor Centre.

Introduction: Frontenac Provincial Park is an outstanding wilderness resource nestled in the most rugged of Canadian Shield terrain between Ottawa and Kingston. Relatively small compared to Gatineau Park, at only 52 km² (20 mi²), it nevertheless contains more than 160 km (100 mi) of hiking trails, oodles of canoe routes, and 48 backcountry campsites. Probably an entire book could be written about just this one park.

This rather long route is the one that I completed on my first visit to Frontenac. It uses portions of several trails, and most will prefer to approach it as a two-day experience. Or perhaps you're like me and have so much fun that you will want to walk it all at once.

Route Description: The hike begins at the north end of the parking area; follow the Corridor Trail route toward Big Salmon Lake. You will notice the orange triangle markers of the Rideau Trail, but watch for the light blue diamonds that are the park's trail markers. This is a narrow, well-worn footpath — an unimproved natural surface — initially paralleling both the Big Salmon Lake Road and the natural contour of the hilly terrain. At 1.5 km (0.9 mi), you reach the first of many junctions you will encounter today — to Doe Lake and campsite 2. Keep straight; you will no longer see the Rideau Trail symbol.

Almost immediately afterward, you will sight Arab Lake to your right and slightly lower; the junction to the West Arkon Lake Loop splits left in 300 m/yd, but continue straight. About 2 km (1.25 mi) later, you go through the Arab Lake parking area, where there is an outhouse. A few hundred metres/yards later is another junction, for the East Arkon Lake trail, but stay right as your route moves away from the road into an area of ridges and vegetation. At about 3.5 km (2.2 mi), you will sight a lovely little beaver pond on your left, with surprisingly large trees used for its impoundment. Immediately after, the trail crosses three boardwalks, and you might choose to walk over to another beaver dam — this one on your right — to view the large pond they have created.

Near 4 km (2.5 mi), you encounter

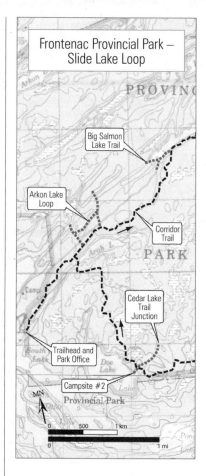

Frontenac Provincial Park –
Slide Lake Loop

another signed junction. Left is the Big Salmon Lake parking, but continue right toward campsites 4 and 5. The path now skirts slender Big Salmon Lake, alternatively descending and climbing a pine-covered ridge. About 1 km (0.6 mi)

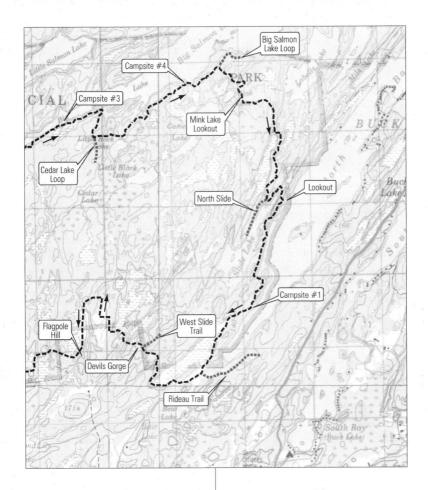

along, you should sight campsite 3 across the lake. Approximately 500 m/yd further, the trail makes a sharp right turn, heading away from the water and climbing up a rocky slope to a viewing area about 200 m/yd on your left.

The next junction, 100 m/yd further, is quite significant. If you continue straight on the Cedar Lake Loop, you shorten your hike to approximately 17 km (10.6 mi). To see Slide Lake, turn left, down the hill, and continue toward campsites 4 and 5. The next section is seasonally wet and winding, with rugged ridges and wide open areas. Campsite 4 appears quite suddenly on your left, on the shores of Big Salmon Lake. After briefly sharing space with a portage, the path turns inland, climbing and quite rugged through the pine-covered rocky areas.

Perhaps 500 m/yd later, you turn right almost 90° at the next junction, toward campsite 1 and Buck Lake. Challenging walking is ahead, as you traverse the rocky, dry, twisting path topped by the climb to the Mink Lake Lookout, one of the best in the park. Watch carefully for trail markers as you navigate across extended stretches of open rock, especially for posts and cairns. Only 500 m/yd beyond the lookout, the trail turns right again and parallels a long deep gorge for several hundred metres/yards before switchbacking down the steep slope to cross a creek on a narrow plank bridge. The tread here is almost non-existent, as the trail skirts the pond on a steep hillside, but this is nevertheless some of the best hiking so far.

After a further 1 km (0.6 mi), which features a few short steep climbs and bridge crossings, you reach the North Slide junction, where there is a map. Keep left, following blue triangle and blue diamond markers, toward campsite 1, which is 2.4 km (1.5 mi) away. You will navigate some of the most rugged and attractive terrain in eastern Ontario, the slender spine of land separating Buck Lake and Slide Lake.

Campsite 1, on the shores of Buck Lake, is a gentle spot, with benches and an outhouse. From here to a former feldspar mine, you will enjoy the easiest walking of the route, a section of which crosses a large field. At the South Slide junction, 1.3 km (0.8 mi) along, a large sign with a map informs you that you are merging with the Rideau Trail. From here, you have 10 km (6.25 mi) remaining to return to the Park Office.

Your route soon heads back into rockier terrain, and a creek crossing 1.3 km (0.8 mi) later is tricky as it is over a beaver dam. At the West Slide junction, another large sign directs you toward campsite 2, 4 km (2.5 mi) distant. Devils Gorge,

reached within a few hundred metres/ yards, is another pretty spot, crossed by a sturdy bridge. But the following few kilometres/miles to Flagpole Hill, aimlessly winding, open, rocky, and almost barren, are among the least pleasant of the route.

Campsite 2 and the Cedar Lake Trail Junction are reached above Doe Lake, about 2.5 km (1.6 mi) from Flagpole Hill. The 2.5 km (1.6 mi) from here to the junction with the Corridor Trail is quite pleasant: generally dry, without many steep climbs, and meandering between the many beaver ponds. There is even a scenic lookout on a ridge above Doe Lake. Just before you reach the final junction, you cross the southwest

end of Arab Lake. After a short 100 m/yd climb, turn left at the junction and retrace the 1.5 km (0.9 mi) back to the Park Office and your start.

Cautionary Notes: Animals, remote route, rugged terrain.

Cellphone Reception: Adequate at the trailhead but uncertain in the park's interior. Available only on hilltops, almost never in ravines.

Further Information: www.ontario parks.com/English/fron.html; trail map available at park entrance.

Mac Johnson Wildlife Area – Brockville

Length: 8.5 km (5.25 mi) return
Hiking Time: 2 hrs
Type of Trail: boardwalk, crushed stone, natural surface
Uses: walking, snowshoeing, cross-country skiing
Facilities: activity centre, benches, garbage cans, interpretive panels, outhouses, picnic tables,
Gov't Topo Map: 031B12
Rating (1-5): 1
Trailhead GPS: N 44° 37' 48.8" W 75° 43' 49.1"

Access Information: From the Highway 416/417 split, follow Highway 416 for 75 km (47 mi) to Highway 401. Turn onto Highway 401 west, driving 22.5 km (14 mi) to Exit 696. Turn right onto Stewart Boulevard/County Road 29; follow it for 5 km (3.1 mi) to the tiny community of Tincap and turn right again onto Airport/Debruge Road. Continue for 2 km (1.25 mi), turning right at the signed entrance. Drive for 600 m/yd to the parking area.

Introduction: The 532 hectares (1,315 acres) of the Mac Johnson Wildlife Area include fields, forests, and wetlands surrounding a reservoir that was once known as the Back Pond, and are a provincially significant habitat of plant, animal, and bird life. Long a popular local recreation site, the property has been developed with the addition of picnic facilities, a stacked-loop trail system, an interpretive program, and a nature centre. Perhaps its most distinctive feature is its breeding pair of trumpeter swans. Their call must be heard to be fully appreciated.

This is an easy walk through gentle terrain, with mud and water as its only challenges.

Route Description: Your hike begins in a large recreational area, among broad fields featuring a variety of services. A sign panel prominently displays a map and other information as soon as you begin, and you also immediately sight a bronze plaque commemorating the park's namesake, Joseph "Mac" Johnson. The crushed-stone path, the Wild-

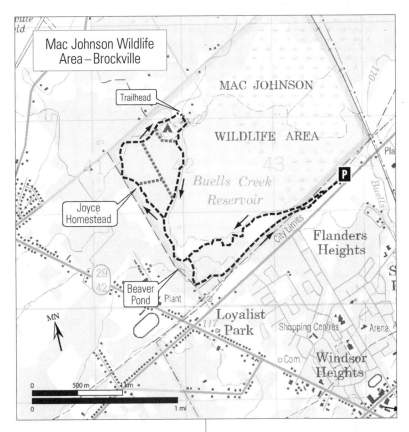

Mac Johnson Wildlife
Area–Brockville

Trailhead

MAC JOHNSON

WILDLIFE AREA

Buells Creek Reservoir

Joyce Homestead

Beaver Pond

Plant

Flanders Heights

Loyalist Park

Shopping Centres

Arena

Com

Windsor Heights

MN

0   500 m   1 km

0   1 mi

flower Loop, splits within 50 m/yd, marked by a numbered signpost. The activity centre and washrooms are right, should you wish to visit. For this hike, keep straight, heading toward the water.

On your left, you will probably hear, and might see, the trumpeter swans. You certainly have a great view of the reservoir and pass a number of tables and benches. This gentle path continues a further 300 m/yd before reaching the junction with Trail 2, the Railway Trail. Turn left, onto its more natural surface.

The Railway Trail is wide and flat, paralleling the water's edge with occasional benches for viewing waterfowl. Evidence of beaver activity is everywhere, including dozens of half-gnawed trees. You cross a small stream 500 m/yd along, and at 1.1 km (0.7 mi) arrive at the junction with Trail 3, the Old Woods Trail. Continue straight, through significantly wetter terrain with the reservoir and its cattails lapping right up to the treadway. Only 300 m/yd later, you reach the junction with trails 3 and 4; keep left on Trail 4, the Boardwalk Trail.

You return to drier ground, even onto some rock, sighting some magnificent old maples to your right. At 300 m/yd, there is an unmarked path branching right; keep left, because you soon reach the promised boardwalk, which crosses over the Beaver Pond. A delightful handmade, wood-burned signpost explains that this small body of water was created in 1916 as a private fishing hole by Albert Debruge. The boardwalk skirts the edge of the water along the original dam, with the wetland and reservoir to your left. About 200 m/yd later, you reach a signed junction, where you turn right, still on Trail 4, and head away from the water.

This next section passes through fairly dry terrain, mostly hardwoods, and encounters more informal junctions. You are approaching the perimeter of the conservation area, and visitors from nearby houses have created their own access. Keep left and you will emerge onto a grassy field only 100 m/yd from Centennial Road, the southern boundary. Your path now parallels a buried gas pipeline, continuing in the open to reach the junction with Trail 5, the Jack Pine Trail, about 3 km (1.9 mi) from the trailhead. Continue straight, still in the field, almost 1 km (0.6 mi), ignoring the many unofficial intersecting side trails. You draw closer to the reservoir, linking with the trail along the water's edge, at what can be a very wet area. Keep right, and in an additional 100 m/yd, you will reach the trail's end, the parking area on Centennial Road. There is a trailhead map, but there are no other facilities. If you continue along Centennial Road for a further 500 m/yd, you will reach the Broome-Runciman Dam, where there is a small picnic area.

It is time to return. Retrace the first 100 m/yd, keeping right at the first junction. You will reach an attractive area where the walking is dry, passing through a rocky area shaded by cedars growing right to the water's edge. There is even a tiny hill on this section, the first of the hike, about 1 km (0.6 mi) from the parking area, and I found this the prettiest woods of the walk. At the top, you reach the junction between trails 4 and 5.

An informal path heads right to

the water; keep straight as your route meanders through some younger cedars before returning to the edge of the reservoir. As wetlands replace open water, the cedars give way to hardwoods. Some 700 m/yd further, after about 6 km (3.75 mi) of walking, you reach the junction where you first turned away from the water toward Centennial Road. Keep straight/right, re-cross the Beaver Pond, and at the junction with Trail 3, turn left.

Trail 3 leads away from the water initially through a regenerating field, though white pine soon begin to take over, indicating higher, better drained soil. Although the path is generally drier, there are occasional places where the trail is almost like a drainage ditch or pond. At 500 m/yd, you reach another junction; keep straight on a lovely grassy path as you gently climb to the Joyce Homestead. Only fences and foundations remain, but an interpretive panel relates the site's history. For the next 800 m/yd, Trail 3 continues through the forest, until it meets Trail 2. Just before reaching that point, you should sight houses to your left. Keep straight, passing through the former campground, past rotting picnic tables and locked outhouses, on the former service road. After 400 m/yd, you reach the junction with Trail 1. Keep straight, ignoring many side routes, until the crushed-stone path comes up to the Activity Centre and back to the trailhead, a total distance of 8.5 km (5.3 mi).

Cautionary Notes: Often wet.

Cellphone Reception: Excellent.

Further Information: www.cataraqui region.on.ca/lands/macj.htm.

Marble Rock

Length: 11 km (7 mi) return
Hiking Time: 3-4 hrs
Type of Trail: natural surface
Uses: walking, snowshoeing
Facilities: none
Gov't Topo Map: 031C08
Rating (1-5): 4 [rugged terrain, steep climbs, navigation]
Trailhead GPS: N 44° 23' 38.5" W 76° 09' 10.0"

Access Information: From the Highway 416/417 split, follow Highway 416 for 75 km (46.75 mi) to Highway 401. Turn onto Highway 401 west and follow for 73 km (45.5 mi) to Exit 648. Turn right onto Highway 2, and 800 m/yd later, turn left onto Hiscocks Road/County Road 34. Follow CR34 for 4.5 km (2.8 mi), turning left onto Marble Rock Road. Follow for 1.7 km (1.1 mi); the trail begins in the open area on the right about 250 m/yd after crossing a river. Look for the trailhead sign and blue triangular markers.

Introduction: Although not terribly long, the Marble Rock Trail passes through difficult terrain, including rocky, sometimes steep slopes. Navigation is its principal challenge, however, as one extended stretch crosses a nearly treeless expanse of flat stone, where it is very easy to become disoriented. Coincidentally, cellphone reception in this area is very poor.

The Marble Rock Trail is organized into two loops. The South Loop, approximately 6 km (3.75 mi), is strenuous but should be comfortably within the capabilities of most fit hikers. The North Loop, an additional 4 or 5 km (2.5 or 3.1 mi), is more poorly signed and should be undertaken only by experienced navigators.

Route Description: Well marked by blue triangles, the path heads immediately into the forest, where a map of the route is affixed to a tree on the left less than 25 m/yd from the road. Although the trail begins as a wide track, within 300 m/yd it splits right onto a narrow, rocky, climbing footpath. Within 150 m/yd, you reach the Leaning Rock Lookout, a short but extremely challenging

scramble onto the top of a massive rock. This should serve as an indication of what will follow.

At 500 m/yd, you reach the junction for the South Loop, where there is another map; turn left, and follow the winding track as it twists through the rugged terrain, gradually descending. The trail reaches low ground, where there are no rocks but it is often wet, and you should be able to see open land to your left. You emerge from the vegetation at 1 km (0.6 mi), your route through flattened grass on a causeway, an expanding wetland on your right. Note the drowned pines, their dead needles rust brown.

The path has had to be rerouted around the rising waters, so it veers left before the end of the causeway, and passes through several hundred metres/yards of semi-open land before crossing a wood road and beginning to climb again. Rocks intrude into the path as you climb, and the grasses can be quite thick in the summer, almost hiding the path. You soon reach the top of the rocky ridge, Barn Hill, where the trail takes you to the crest of the slope and views of the field below and the surrounding ridges.

After only a few hundred metres/yards, the route descends through a narrow ravine and emerges from under the trees to link up with an ATV trail; it then turns left, but in less than 25 m/yd, it splits right and starts climbing again. The path, well marked by blue triangles, follows the ATV track for another 200 m/yd, then separates to the right, briefly paralleling, then crossing it.

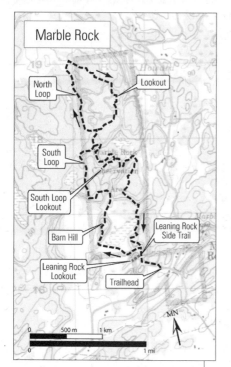

Marble Rock

North Loop

Lookout

South Loop

South Loop Lookout

Barn Hill

Leaning Rock Side Trail

Leaning Rock Lookout

Trailhead

MN

0   500 m   1 km

0   1 mi

leafy canopy, permitting cool breezes to pass through. This attractive section continues for more than 350 m/yd, until you cross a small brook feeding a small pond to your right. The trail turns sharply right and then follows the brook exiting the pond down to the junction with the North Loop, approximately 3 km (1.9 mi) from the start.

There is another map posted here as well as a directional sign. To hike the North Loop, turn left and climb the rough knolls for 300 m/yd to the next junction. Turn left again, and follow the poorly signed ATV track through the forest for the next 1 km (0.6 mi). You should see No Name Lake to your right, but just before reaching it, the footpath separates teasingly from the ATV track and proceeds left, away from the water, reconnecting with the ATV track about 150 m/yd later.

Turn left again; within 150 m/yd your route splits right, at first on an unused wood road, then 200 m/yd later diverging from it at a large flat rock, turning right onto an indistinct footpath. The next 800 m/yd are challenging, as the route passes over bare rock with few trees for route markers. Watch for blue paint on the rocks and occasional cairns.

When you finally return to the

Crossing a makeshift bridge over a tiny creek, the trail then gradually turns left, working its way around the base of a ridge for maybe 200 m/yd before turning sharply right and climbing steeply through a notch.

Now higher and drier, the footpath turns left again and continues to meander through the dense forest. It gradually climbs, making another sharp right turn, then another short steep climb. The woods change, with the understorey disappearing, replaced by lush grass beneath a forest, the path crosses a tiny brook and then reaches the shores of No Name Lake, a great location for lunch. The trail leaves the shoreline, climbing quickly to the North Loop Lookout, where there are views of Howard Lake, before returning briefly to the water's edge. A challenging 400 m/yd follows, as the path picks through rocky outcroppings, before it reaches an ATV trail. Continue straight, and at a junction 150 m/yd later, turn left onto the footpath, which leads you 300 m/yd back to the South Loop.

Turn left at this junction, descending alongside a tiny creek before crossing it to work around the base of a rocky ridge. Some 500 m/yd from the North Loop junction, you exit the forest next to a large wet area. The path now climbs the ridge, and in 50 m/yd reaches the junction with the South Loop Lookout side trail, a rugged 200 m/yd climb to your right. This provides excellent views of the surrounding terrain.

The main trail turns left at this junction, works around a hillside, then drops steeply to reach a former major beaver dam at 300 m/yd. From the dam, the path follows a former road gently uphill for 200 m/yd before your route splits right on a narrow footpath. You climb another 400 m/yd, the entire distance beneath a hardwood canopy, before

the trail begins to descend again. This next 300 m/yd is fairly steep, with a wicked cross-slope — very slippery when wet. Once at the bottom, you have 400 m/yd of very wet, flat, thickly vegetated ground to cross to the next ridge. On your right, an open wetland should be visible. Following this, about 150 m/yd of broken rock with treacherous footing must be traversed. Another 150 m/yd of wet ground follows before the trail begins to climb another, and final, ridge.

This next 400 m/yd includes some of the steepest, most difficult walking, as it winds its way over and down this rocky knoll. It even includes an open area, where the route is signed only by painted rocks. When you reach the junction at the end of the South Loop, turn left and retrace the remaining 600 m/yd to the trailhead.

Cautionary Notes: Animals, cliffs, rugged terrain, tricky navigation.

Cellphone Reception: Poor at the trailhead and low-lying areas; good on hilltops.

Further Information: None.

Murphys Point Provincial Park

Length: 7.5 km (4.7 mi) return

Hiking Time: 2 hrs

Type of Trail: compacted earth, natural surface

Uses: walking, snowshoeing, cross-country skiing

Facilities: benches, interpretive panels, outhouses, picnic tables

Gov't Topo Map: 031C16

Rating (1-5): 2

Trailhead GPS: N 44° 46' 03.6"
W 76° 15' 16.9"

Access Information: From the Highway 416/417 split, follow Highway 417 west for 14 km (8.75 mi) to Exit 145 with Highway 7. Turn onto Highway 7 and continue for 55 km (34 mi) to Perth, turning left onto Highway 43/Wilson Street West. Follow Highway 43 through Perth, continuing straight on County Road 1 when Highway 43 turns left at Craig Street, 2.9 km (1.8 mi) from Highway 7.

Follow CR1 for 5.8 km (3.6 mi) beyond Craig Street, turning right onto County Road 21/Elm Grove Road. Drive for 10.7 km (6.7 mi) to the main park entrance. Turn left and continue to the park's registration gatehouse and obtain day-use park permit. Return to Elm Grove Road; turn left. The pavement ends 200 m/yd later, and the road name changes to Lally Road. Continue for 2.4 km (1.5 mi). A designated parking area is on the left.

Introduction: Murphys Point Provincial Park is a compact, but diverse, natural preserve bordering the Rideau Waterway near the community of Perth. It boasts considerable attractive hardwood forest cover, camping, numerous short walking paths, canoe access, swimming, archaeological sites, former mines, and is bisected by the wandering Rideau Trail — all situated on the rolling, interesting topography of the Frontenac Arch.

This route is made up of two loops, each of which can be walked separately. One, 2.5 km (1.6 mi) in length, takes you to the site of the former Silver Queen Mine. The Silver Queen Mine Trail interpretive booklet, available at the park office, is a superb companion to this walk and will greatly add to the experience of this trail.

The other loop, 5 km (3 mi), heads to the McParlan Homestead, a former farm and an archaeological site. Both are suitable walks for families, although the later is more challenging, crossing rougher terrain. Neither features difficult climbing, although the descent to Hoggs Bay over Black Creek is steep in places.

Route Description: From the parking area, follow the orange triangles that mark the Rideau Trail down the small hill, past an old foundation, and across the grassy field toward the old farm buildings: the Lally Homestead. The grass-covered pathway passes left of the two standing buildings and briefly connects with Lally Road before veering right and into the forest.

As soon as you enter the woods, you encounter a junction with a cross-country ski trail, which happens to be signed by orange plastic squares. Keep right, following the triangles. Your path is delightfully uneven, an unimproved track climbing up and down the many little rocky ridges — mostly grass covered, but occasionally bare rock. As it mostly follows the top of the ridge, the trail is quite dry, the only exception being a 150 m/yd section where it drops low. Once out of this minor depression, the forest opens up into attractive hardwoods, providing wonderful views of the contoured ground around you.

After 900 m/yd, the trail reaches the Black Anse Point Road. A sign on the opposite side indicates that Murphys Point Campground is 1.8 km (1.1 mi) ahead and that the Rideau Trail is rerouted to the right, down the road, because of a washed-out bridge.

Follow the narrow road downhill, crossing Black Creek 100 m/yd later, and climbing on the far side. This is a pleasant walk, the road is tree lined, and there are no houses. About 300 m/yd beyond the creek, the Rideau Trail branches right. Ignore this, continuing to follow the road an additional 500 m/yd until you sight a prominent sign on the left. Turn onto the wood road, which passes a metal fence. After 200 m/yd, you reach the brook, where the path turns right and parallels it on a ridge above. After 300 m/yd, the trail makes a sharp turn to the left, and in 200 m/yd you emerge into the grassy grounds around the McParlan homestead.

The homestead, where the old house still stands, is an archaeological survey site, and also a protected place. It is also a great place for a picnic, as there are several picnic tables, a large grassy field,

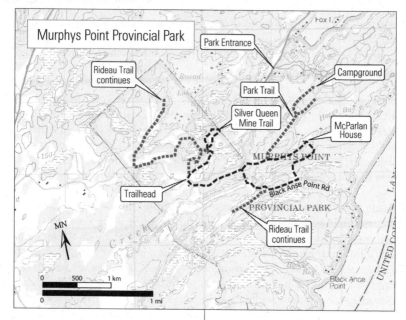

Murphys Point Provincial Park

Fox I.

Park Entrance

Rideau Trail continues

Campground

Park Trail

Silver Queen Mine Trail

McParlan House

MURPHYS POINT

Black Anse Point Rd

Trailhead

PROVINCIAL PARK

Rideau Trail continues

Black Anse Point

MN

0   500   1 km

0   1 mi

and easy access to Hoggs Bay and its good swimming.

The washed-out bridge over Black Creek, expected to be replaced in 2011, is less than 100 m/yd southeast of McParlan House. If in place, then you may cross it and follow the well-signed trail 900 m/yd back to the Black Anse Point Road. If there is no bridge, retrace your original route, about 1.6 km (1 mi), and from here the 900 m/yd back to the Lally Homestead.

Once back at the trailhead, cross the Lally Road and enter the Silver Queen Mine Trail. This 2.5 km (1.6 mi) loop — although one sign says 2 km (1.25 mi) — begins on an old road that borders an abandoned farm field. An interpretive panel at the trailhead provides good background. Immediately you have the option to divert onto the Beaver Pond Trail, but continue along the road; the two trails reconnect 900 m/yd later.

The next several hundred metres/yards are fascinating, as the trail works along the base of the hillside and visits the remains of a site where mica, feldspar, and apatite were mined. In this 700 m/yd loop, you will find numerous pits where the minerals were extracted — some open and fenced, some gated and shut — old equipment, and samples of the minerals.

In the middle of the loop sits a restored bunkhouse and in the field around it may be found several picnic tables, making it a pleasant location to sit and relax after your walk. There is also an outhouse nearby, just in case. From here, you follow the old mining road back about 1.2 km (0.75 mi) to the Lally Homestead and your car. Choosing to return along the Beaver Pond Trail adds about 200 m/yd and is slightly more challenging.

Cautionary Notes: Animals, road crossing, possible missing bridge.

Cellphone Reception: Excellent.

Further Information: www.ontario parks.com/ENGLISH/murp.html, www.friendsofmurphyspoint.ca, Silver Queen Mine booklet available at park for $1.

Hunting Season

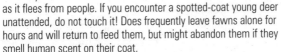

In the fall, hikers share the woods with hunters. If this worries you, limit your excursions to national parks, most provincial parks, and similarly restricted areas. Otherwise proudly wear your orange, stay on posted trails, and avoid dawn/dusk.

White-tailed Deer

Sighting one of these graceful, delicate-looking animals can be the highlight of anyone's hike, despite its being the most numerous of all large mammals. Reddish-brown on its back and sides during the summer, darker grey-brown in the winter, this deer is most recognized for the long, brilliantly white tail it raises in alarm as it flees from people. If you encounter a spotted-coat young deer unattended, do not touch it! Does frequently leave fawns alone for hours and will return to feed them, but might abandon them if they smell human scent on their coat.

The Greenbelt surrounding Ottawa is home to one of the densest populations of white-tailed deer in North America.

Rideau Trail – Tay Towpath

Length: 8 km (5 mi) return
Hiking Time: 2 hrs
Type of Trail: compacted earth,
    natural surface
Uses: walking, biking*, snow-
    shoeing, cross-country skiing
Facilities: benches, interpretive
    panels, picnic tables, washrooms
Gov't Topo Map: 031C16
Rating (1-5): 2
Trailhead GPS: N 44° 53' 58.3"
    W 76° 14' 53.6"

Access Information: From the Highway 416/417 split, follow Highway
417 west for 14 km (8.75 mi) to Exit
145 with Highway 7. Turn onto Highway 7, and continue for 55 km (34 mi)
to Perth, turning left onto Highway
43/Wilson Street (then Foster Street,
then Gore Street East). Follow Highway 43 for 1.7 km (1.1 mi), turning
left onto Colbourne Street. Park in
the lot 50 m/yd ahead and start the
walk at the northwest corner of Tay
Basin by the interpretive display.

Introduction: The community of
Perth was founded in 1816 as a military settlement, the first in Canada.

Initially its inhabitants were dis-
charged soldiers and its leaders
British half-pay officers. By 1822
the village was opened to general
settlement.

When work began on the Rideau
Canal in 1826, the residents of Perth
were concerned that it would not
connect to their community. They
decided to build their own canal,
and in 1834 the First Tay Canal
opened. This was extensively improved and upgraded between 1885
and 1891, and the route is currently
operated by Parks Canada as part of
their Rideau Canal operations.

The Rideau Trail, connecting
Ottawa and Kingston, follows the
Tay Towpath from its basin in downtown Perth to the Beveridge Locks
on the Rideau, making occasional
detours around private property.
This route is a pleasant walk suitable for almost every fitness level,
and it is very easy to follow.

Route Description: From the interpretive display, follow the boardwalk alongside Tay Basin toward
the bridge to the northeast, passing

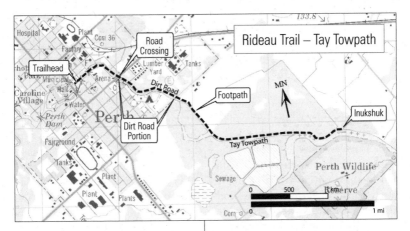

Rideau Trail – Tay Towpath

underneath it through a narrow tunnel. On the far side, you cross a grassy field, your route paralleling the river. To the left is the Armoury, where there is another historical plaque. After 250 m/yd, you cross Beckwith Street, and your route follows quiet Riverside Drive, where there is no sidewalk but little traffic, for the next 150 m/yd.

The road turns left 90°, but the path continues straight through a gap in a guardrail. With the exception of the occasional Rideau Trail orange triangle, there is no signage whatsoever. For the next 350 m/yd, Riverside Drive is closed to automobiles and is a pleasant walking route, following the Tay as it curves right in a sweeping turn. There are even some benches overlooking the water through here.

Rather abruptly you reach busy Highway 43, which you must cross, about 750 m/yd from your start. There is neither crosswalk nor signage, so be extremely cautious. On the far side, Riverside Drive returns to vehicle use but is now surfaced in dirt, which makes the following section quite dusty in the summer. Your route continues close against the Tay, sharing Riverside Drive for 900 m/yd until it turns away from the towpath. This is a more pleasant section than it may sound, as the opposite bank is the green space of Last Duel Park, and the narrow towpath is frequently busy with pleasure craft cruising past.

After 1.6 km (1 mi) of walking on the road, a prominent sign directs you into a field, which it cautions is private property, and onto the footpath that will be your route for the remainder of the walk. The sign also warns that the trail is closed during deer hunting season, which is usually late October to early November.

Once off the road, the trail changes considerably. It dwindles to a slender, unimproved track, suitable for hiking but occasionally wet and uneven. Following this route, however, is never an issue as it hugs the banks of the Tay for its entire length. For the next 600 m/yd, large fields stretch away to the left until the trail finally enters the forest through a gate in a split cedar-rail fence. If the gate is closed, there is a ladder provided to climb the fence; do not try to open the gate.

There follows a delightful woodland walk of 1.75 km (1.1 mi), with the trail paralleling the Tay Towpath. No houses or roads can be seen, except maybe when all the leaves are gone, and the marshy lands on the opposite bank are often busy with waterfowl. During the spring and summer, the thick young vegetation around you is full of activity with songbirds, such as the yellow and the chestnut-sided warblers. Your route is dry and usually level, although there is one section where the bank has eroded and the path is almost in the water.

The Rideau Trail Association maintains several rickety-looking but structurally safe bridges over a few drainage lanes in the towpath bank, and so you may amble unconcernedly until you reach the point where you should turn back, 4 km (2.5 mi) from the start in downtown Perth. Here the stream is unbridged, and a fence has been erected to block the opposite bank. A sign indicates that no trespassing is permitted.

The Rideau Trail turns left, heading away from the towpath. However, this is an excellent location to relax and have lunch. If you look to the left, you should find a picnic table hidden beneath a tree atop a rocky knoll. The towpath here is lovely, the water fine for swimming should you wish to do so. Hikers have erected a substantial inukshuk, apparently an irresistible attraction to photographers, and although you can see a farmhouse in the distance, this spot possesses a relaxing sense of remoteness.

When you are ready, return to Perth along the same route.

Cautionary Notes: Road crossings.

Cellphone Reception: Excellent.

Further Information: Rideau Trail Guidebook: Map 9.

Rideau Trail – Westport

Length: 9 km (5.6 mi) return

Hiking Time: 3-4 hrs

Type of Trail: board-walks, natural surface, roadside

Uses: walking, snowshoeing, cross-country skiing*

Facilities: barbecues, beaches, benches, camping, covered tables, garbage cans, interpretive panels, outhouses, payphone, picnic tables, playground

Gov't Topo Map: 031C09

Rating (1-5): 3

Trailhead GPS: N 44° 41' 07.3" W 76° 24' 36.1"

Access Information: From the Highway 416/417 split, follow Highway 417 west for 14 km (8.75 mi) to Exit 145 at Highway 7. Turn onto Highway 7 and continue for 55 km (34 mi) to Perth, turning left onto Highway 43/Wilson Street (then Foster Street, then Gore Street East/County Road 1). Continue through Perth for 3 km (1.9 mi) to Scotch Line Road/County Road 10. Turn right and follow for 29 km (18.1 mi) to Westport. Turn right onto Bedford Street/County Road 12 and follow for 900 m/yd. Turn right onto Mountain Road/County Road 36 and drive 700 m/yd, turning left at the Westport Lion's Club Beach, 63 Mountain Road, and park in their lot.

Introduction: Most of this route is found within the Foley Mountain Conservation Area, part of the Rideau Valley Conservation Authority. Although "mountain" might seem an ambitious name for a granite knob barely 80 m/yd high, the view from the Spy Rock observation platform is unquestionably panoramic. Foley Mountain sits on the edge of the Frontenac Arch, and the lush farmland spreading away to the south appears to be part of another world.

Foley Mountain played an important part in the history of the more than 300 km (188 mi) Rideau Trail connecting Kingston with Ottawa. It was here, on November 7, 1971, that the footpath was officially opened. One of the highlights of this walk is the bronze plaque, affixed to a massive boulder, commemorating that event. This is a challenging walk with considerable elevation change and occasionally rugged terrain but eminently worthwhile.

Route Description: You begin by walking uphill on Mountain Road for 250 m/yd. Watch for blue metal triangles on some telephone poles; these are Rideau Trail Association side-trail symbols. Just before the sign for Old Mountain Road, you should see, on the right, a wooden ladder bridging a fence, marked with the orange triangle of the main Rideau Trail. Cross this fence, and you will find a Rideau Trail informational sign, and a slender footpath that continues up the hillside. This is a delightful path, meandering fecklessly around rocks and trees, beneath a lush canopy of mostly hardwoods. It settles in to paralleling the ridge but below its crest. In spring and fall you should have views of Westport and the surrounding countryside. At 550 m/yd, the path descends briefly, passing an open rock face, and crosses a tiny, unbridged brook 25 m/yd later.

On the other side, the path climbs again, picking its way through rugged footing and over bare rock where the route has been worn into the moss. At 750 m/yd, the path levels somewhat and becomes more open, providing better views. White pine and jack pine predominate. You

descend into one shallower gully, crossing a larger brook on a modest bridge, before climbing back to the bare rock and continuing an additional 200 m/yd to reach Perth Road, 1.5 km (0.9 mi) from the trailhead.

You will sight the large entrance sign to the Foley Mountain Conservation Area on the opposite side, and about 25 m/yd uphill, you should notice the orange triangle marking your route. Once across the road, the trail, which is used for cross-country skiing in the winter, is broad and grassy. The path initially parallels the entrance road, coming close to the gate kiosk. It then returns to the ridge and slope. Within 250 m/yd, you pass a bench; look for the plaque that commemorates the official opening of the Rideau Trail.

The next 600 m/yd are among the most challenging of the hike, but your reward is an elaborate platform with benches, outhouses, picnic tables, and even a wheelchair ramp. This is Spy Rock, undoubtedly the highlight of the hike, towering 80 m/yd above the community of Westport. After enjoying the view, follow the ramp into the picnic area, then turn right to follow the orange arrows.

You soon come to a junction where there are blue markers; keep right and continue down onto the open rocky slopes as the trail meanders

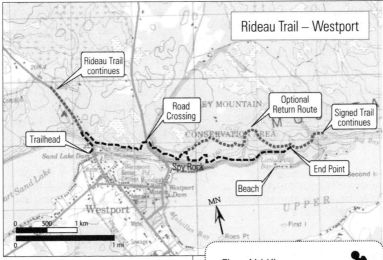

Rideau Trail – Westport

confusingly. It will be somewhat easier to follow once you reach what appears to be a former wood road. Keep right, keeping the lake to your right as much as possible. However, the Rideau Trail shares this trail with the conservation area's ski paths, which have their own symbols, and numerous side routes branch off. Once you reach a couple of benches, the Rideau Trail turns into the forest again

You should soon reach a signed junction with the choices for parking lots, one 500 m/yd away and the other 1 km (0.6 mi) distant. Keep right, as indicated by the orange triangle. You turn 90°, descending rapidly along an old wood road into a ravine.

First Aid Kit

When you are out in the woods, even little problems can suddenly become very important. A small first aid kit with bandages, gauze, tape, moleskin, etc., can permit you to deal with the blisters and bruises that might require attention.

After 200 m/yd, you reach a sign that reads "Rock Slide Lookout — Hikers Only." This is a narrow, twisty path, to the right, that contorts down the hillside until it ends almost at the water. This is not for casual walkers, and I do not recommend it.

The main Rideau Trail continues left, where it reaches another

Layering

Instead of having a separate outfit for each weather condition, put together a variety of clothes for different purposes: base (underwear), insulation, and outer shell. Mix and match according to conditions, adding, removing, or changing items as you warm up or cool down and if weather conditions change. Synthetic clothes for layering tend to be lighter, more durable, and provide greater flexibility.

junction 100 m/yd later, where you keep straight. It drops steeply now, downhill for 300 m/yd through an area of gorgeous hardwoods. Continue straight; you will cross a few little streams, another junction, and Mediation Point to your right. Ahead you can see a house, the field centre of the conservation area, and you have arrived at the large picnic area of Little Bay, where there are tables, outhouses, and barbecue pits. By now, you are slightly more than 3.5 km (2.2 mi) from your start.

The trail skirts the building and through the parking area onto a wide service road. After 300 m/yd, the road turns left and your route goes back into the forest, emerging onto the beach within 100 m/yd. The path crosses the sand, past some interpretive panels, and on the far side, leaves the lake to skirt a wetland at the mouth of the bay. It follows a wide track up a shallow ravine through a lovely forest. At 4.5 km (2.8 mi), you come to the junction with the blue side trail.

From here, there are three possibilities. First, you could continue on the main trail: this soon leaves the conservation area, and after a wooded walk of slightly more than 2 km (1.25 mi), it reaches the North Shore Road, where you must turn about to return to the trailhead. Second, you could follow the blue trail, the 2.5 km (1.6 mi) Foley Mountain Highland Loop: this turns inland for 2.5 km (1.6 mi), connecting back to the main trail near Spy Rock. Third, the option I recommend, you simply retrace your approach route: this route returns to the beach and revisits the best views on the escarpment.

Cautionary Notes: Animals, poison ivy, road crossings.

Cellphone Reception: Excellent.

Further Information: www.rvca.ca/careas/foley/index.html. The route is found on Map 6 in the Rideau Trail Guidebook.

Rock Dunder

Length: 6 km (3.75 mi) return

Hiking Time: 2 hrs

Type of Trail: compacted earth, natural surface

Uses: walking, snowshoeing

Facilities: cabins, firepits, outhouses, trailhead map

Gov't Topo Map: 031C09

Rating (1-5): 3

Trailhead GPS: N 44° 31' 55.3" W 76° 12' 10.8"

Access Information: From the Highway 416/417 split, follow Highway 417 west for 14 km (8.75 mi) to Exit 145 with Highway 7. Turn onto Highway 7 and drive for 21 km (13 mi) to Carleton Place. Turn left onto Highway 15 and continue for 76.5 km (47.5 mi), passing through Smiths Falls, to the village of Morton. Turn right onto gravelled Stanley Lash Lane, also marked by blue rectangular trail-marker triangles, then continue for 400 m/yd to the trailhead.

Introduction: Hikes with grand views are always popular, and Rock Dunder has been attracting hikers to its summit for more than 100 years. In 2006, the Rideau Waterway Land Trust purchased this property from Scouts Canada and invited the Rideau Trail Association to develop its path system. Their volunteers have done an excellent job and created a loop that provides views of wetlands, beaver ponds, a variety of woodlands, rocky ridges, and the Rideau waterway. Take time to read the bronze plaque mounted at the trailhead.

I recommend completing this hike as a figure eight, starting with the Morton Bay Loop. This saves the Rock Dunder Lookout and the section between Cabin 2 and Cabin 1, the most scenic portions of the hike, for the end.

Route Description: From the trailhead, follow the clearly marked wide, wood-chip-covered footpath. Note the route markers affixed to trees: blue metal triangles. Within 100 m/yd, you reach the first junction: a narrow footpath branching left. Continue straight, following the wide path over a bridge draining a

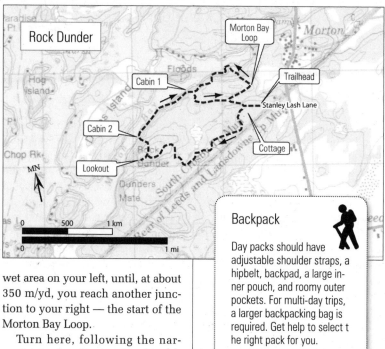

Rock Dunder

Morton Bay Loop

Cabin 1

Trailhead

Stanley Lash Lane

Cabin 2

Lookout

Cottage

MN

0   500   1 km

0   1 mi

Backpack

Day packs should have adjustable shoulder straps, a hipbelt, backpad, a large inner pouch, and roomy outer pockets. For multi-day trips, a larger backpacking bag is required. Get help to select the right pack for you.

wet area on your left, until, at about 350 m/yd, you reach another junction to your right — the start of the Morton Bay Loop.

Turn here, following the narrowing track as it meanders through very thick young vegetation for 250 m/yd before beginning to climb onto a pine-covered ridge. At 700 m/yd, the trail makes a sudden, sharp 90°+ turn onto a much narrower and less distinct path. It climbs briefly then quickly begins a steepening descent toward the bay, passing a great dead woodpecker-damaged tree and a magnificent huge maple within 150 m/yd. There are a few more descents and gentle climbs, and at 900 m/yd, you reach a small knoll overlooking the water of

Morton Bay and the cottage on the far bank. The trail turns left, following the shoreline, and soon reaches a grassy point of land at water level that is a great location for swimming. From here, the path skirts a tiny bay along an indistinct footpath, climbing as it negotiates past intruding rocks and a steepening slope.

Within the next 200 m/yd, nearly 40 m/yd of climbing is required before you approach the top of the ridge, moving away from the water.

A few more gentle dips and climbs are required in the next 300 m/yd, but it is fairly easy walking the rest of the way to Cabin 1.

The cabin is open to the public, providing shelter from bugs and weather. There is also a firepit and an outhouse on-site. From here, turn left and head back in the direction of the parking area. The broad path passes under pine between meadows on both sides, and within 400 m/yd, you reach the junction with the Morton Bay Loop on your left. Continue an additional 200 m/yd, then turn right onto the narrow, unsigned trail heading right. You have begun the Summit Loop.

This is a narrow footpath, with rocks and roots intruding. You im-

Garbage Bag

Always, always pack out your trash. And unless you want to make a mess of your pack, you will probably need a waterproof bag to do so. You might even pick up any other garbage you find along the trail, and make it a better experience for the next person.

mediately climb, and within 100 m/yd, you will sight the Cottage — a locked shelter for staff — on your left. The path continues past it, working around the rocky ridge line above the open meadow. For the next 100 m/yd, the path meanders through several open areas, climbing and descending constantly, negotiating rocks and trees and rarely following a straight route. It also gradually becomes more difficult. Watch for rocky cairns and painted rocks signing the path in the open areas.

Around 800 m/yd from the Cottage, as you are descending, you will notice a large pond on your right. The trail drops to pond level, working its way around the shore until heading up rocky walls, where you will gain an excellent view of the pond. You begin your final climb toward the lookout, not too steeply, as views open up to your left. When

you reach a large open area 300 m/yd later, continue straight an additional 100 m/yd, and you reach Rock Dunder, a steep cliff on exposed rock with superb views in almost every direction.

To return, retrace your route for about 100 m/yd, watching for the directional arrows. Turn left at the junction, and follow the path as it very steeply descends 70 m/yd over the next 400 m/yd to Cabin 2. The trail turns right, paralleling the river as it works along the slope facing the lake. At 200 m/yd, you pass a sheer rock face; in another 200 m/yd, there is a great lookout on the left. Never staying level for long, the slender path follows the contours of the slope, crosses a runoff, traces a rock wall, and emerges from the woods at Cabin 1. Retrace the 600 m/yd main trail to the parking area to finish.

Cautionary Notes: Animals, eastern rattlesnake, steep cliffs, ticks.

Cellphone Reception: Adequate on hilltops and slopes; some dead spots in low-lying areas.

Further Information: www.rideau trail.org/trailadj.htm.

Acknowledgements

There are so many people who provided me with information and feedback that it would be impossible to name them all without missing a good number. For example, representatives from each one of the provincial parks, municipal trails, and the National Capital Commission's Greenbelt, Capital Pathways, and Gatineau Park divisions reviewed my draft text for errors or omissions, as did volunteers from the Macnamara Nature Trail, Glengarry Trails, Rideau Trail, and several other groups. I do not even have a complete list of names of those who participated in this exercise, but through them, I received many constructive comments and excellent suggestions that improved this book. Thank you for helping me make *Hiking Trails of Ottawa, the National Capital Region, and Beyond* far better than I could on my own.

Some individuals, of course, require special mention. Ron Hunt, President of the Rideau Trails Association, hiked with me (never easy), discussed the text over numerous coffee meetings, and offered encouragement every step of the way. Gershon Rather, a trail coordinator for the Greenbelt, now retired, provided me with considerable information on lesser-known trails in the region. Heather Newson, who prepared all the maps for the routes on NCC properties, did so with an enthusiasm that reanimated my passion for this project. Rob Clipperton, long-time host on CBC Radio's *In Town and Out*, let me speak about the region's trails on his program for five years, until budget cuts ended my regular segments. Elina Farmanova-Haynes, a very special friend, refused to allow me to give up on the project, although several times I came close.

Finally, I would be unforgivably remiss if I did not acknowledge the debt I owe to the publisher, Goose Lane Editions. Susanne, Akou, and Julie have been tremendously supportive, flexible, and infinitely patient as I muddled my way toward completion. Their trust and encouragement deserves my unreserved thanks.

Web Pages

A. Outdoor Associations:

Alpine Club of Canada — Ottawa:
www.alpineclubottawa.ca
Canadian Volkssport Federation:
www.walks.ca
  Kingston — King's Town Trekkers
    Volkssport Club
  Ottawa — Nepean Nomads
    Walking Club
  Ottawa — Ottawa-Carleton
    Volkssport Association
  Ottawa — Ottawa Voyageurs d'
    Ottawa Walking Club
Ottawa Bicycle Club:
www.ottawabicycleclub.ca
Ottawa Field-Naturalists' Club:
www.ofnc.ca
Ottawa Hostel Outdoors Club:
ohoc.ncf.ca
Ottawa Orienteering Club:
ottawaoc.ca
Oxygène — Club de randonnée
de l'Outaouais:
www.cluboxygene.qc.ca
Rideau Trail Association:
www.rideautrail.org

B. Park/Trail Websites:

Capital Pathways:
www.canadascapital.gc.ca/
bins/ncc_web_content_page.
asp?cid=16297-16299-9970-
9971&lang=1
Cataraqui Trail: www.rideau-info.
com/cattrail
Centre de plein air du Lac-
Leamy: www.gatineau.ca/
page.asp?p=quoi_faire/
nature_plein_air/lac_leamy
Charleston Lake Provincial Park:
www.ontarioparks.com/English/
char.html
Cycloparc PPJ: cycloparcppj.org
Ferguson Forest Nursery: www.
seedlingnursery.com/trails.htm
Forêt-la-Blanche: www.lablanche.ca
Frontenac Provincial Park:
www.ontarioparks.com/English/
fron.html
Gatineau Park: www.canadas
capital.gc.ca/bins/ncc_web_
content_page.asp?cid=16297-
16299-10170&lang=1
Glengarry Trails:
www.glengarrytrails.com

L'Escapade: ville.rigaud.qc.ca/
modListText/content.do?oid=18
67377847&menuElementOid=1
242505339

Marlborough Forest: www.ottawa
forests.ca/Marlborough/index_e.
htm

Murphys Point Provincial Park:
www.ontarioparks.com/English/
murp.html

Ontario Trails Council: www.onta
riotrails.on.ca/trail-regions

Ottawa Greenbelt: www.canadas
capital.gc.ca/bins/ncc_web_
content_page.asp?cid=16297-
16299-9735&lang=1

Parc de la Plaisance: www.sepaq.
com/pq/pla/en

Parc du Lac-Beauchamp: www.
gatineau.ca/page.asp?p=quoi_
faire/nature_plein_air/
parc_lac_beauchamp

Prescott-Russell Recreational Trail:
www.prescott-russell.on.ca/
counties.jsp?section=recreatrail

Rideau Trail: www.rideautrail.org/
trailadj.htm

Rideau Valley Conservation
Authority: www.rvca.ca

South Nation Conservation:
www.nation.on.ca

C. Wildlife:

Bear Information, Ontario
Government: www.mnr.gov.
on.ca/en/Business/Bearwise/
index.html

Bear Brochure, Parks Canada: www.
pc.gc.ca/pn-np/inc/PM-MP/visit/
visit12a_e.pdf

Cougar Information: www.hww.ca/
hww2.asp?id=87

Coyote Information: www.hww.ca/
hww2.asp?id=88

Moose Information: www.hww.ca/
hww2.asp?id=93

Tick Information, Public Health
Agency of Canada: www.phac-
aspc.gc.ca/id-mi/tickinfo-eng.
php#es

Wolf Information: www.hww.ca/
hww2.asp?id=107

D. General Interest:

Cataraqui Region Conservation
Authority: www.cataraqui
region.on.ca

City of Ottawa – Dogs in Parks:
www.ottawa.ca/residents/
animal_care/cats_dogs/dogs/
parks/index_en.html

Friends of Charleston Lake: www.
friendsofcharlestonlake.ca

Friends of Frontenac Provincial
Park: www.frontenacpark.ca

Hike Ontario: www.hikeontario.
com

Hinterland Who's Who:
www.hww.ca

Mississippi River Conservation: www.mvc.on.ca

National Capital Commission Dog Regulations: www.responsible dogowners.ca/docs/NCC_lands.pdf

Ottawa Outdoors Magazine: www.ottawaoutdoors.ca

Raisin Region Conservation Authority: www.rrca.on.ca

Rideau Valley Conservation Authority: www.rvca.ca

The Big Wild: www.thebigwild.org

Trans Canada Trail: www.tctrail.ca

E. Weather

Weather Network: www.theweather network.com/weather/caon0512

F. Cellphone Coverage

Bell: www.bell.ca/support/PrsCSrv Wls_Cvg_Travel.page

Rogers: www.rogers.com/web/ content/wireless_network? setLanguage=en&cm_mmc= Redirects_Consumer_Wireless_ Eng_Nteowrk_0909_fastest

Telus: www.telusmobility.com/en/ ON/Coverageandtravelling/ canadavoicemaps.shtml

G. Transit

La Société de transport de l'Outaouais: www.sto.ca

OC Transpo: www.octranspo.com

Wild Turkey

A relatively new resident in eastern Ontario is the wild turkey. Nearly wiped out by the early 1900s, except for its domesticated cousin, recent conservation efforts have been wildly successful, and it has not only reclaimed most of its original range but moved into areas where it was not previously known, such as around Ottawa.

Turkeys congregate on the ground in flocks as large as 200, especially in the winter. In spring, males make their distinctive blue-faced, fan-tailed mating display. Bow hunting is permitted in season, from late April to early May.

Index

Please note: All **quick tips** are indicated with subject and page numbers in bold.
All *sidebar* subjects are indicated with page numbers in italics.

A

Adirondack Mountains 242
Alexandria ON 181, 184
Andrew Haydon Park 38
Arab Gorge 247-250
Arab Lake 252, 255
Arboretum Loop 47, 67
Arbraska aerial adventure camp 172
Arkon Lake 252
Arkon Lake Loop 252
Arnprior ON 197
Ascent Trail 202-203
Ashdad ON 193
Ault Island ON 224
Aventure douce, L' 174
Aviation Museum 33, 34, 36
Aviation Pathway 35
Aylmer QC 75, 115

B

Back Pond 256
backpack 276
Baie Dubé 161
Baie Noire Est 161
Baie Noire Ouest 160
bandana 144
Barn Hill 261
bear 14, 17, 86, **204**
  black 14
beaver 40, 64, 92, 116, *134*, 168, 174,
  182, 183, 195, 196, 197, 216, 242, 244,
  246, 248, 249, 253. 256, 262, 174
Beaver Pond 246, 258-259
Beaver Pond Trail 266-267
Beaver Trail 64

Bedford Township ON 241
Beryl Gaffney Park 236
Beveridge Locks 268
Bibliothèque Minérale, La 163
Big Salmon Lake 251, 254
blackbird, red-winged *212*
Black Creek 266
Black Sheep Inn 176
Blanchet Farm 119
blisters 58, **250**, 274
blue jeans 12, **161**
Blue Mountain 243
Boardwalk Trail 258
bobcat 14, 17
Bob's Cove campsite 246
Bonnie Glen 184
Boucle Est 143-144
Boucle Quest ski route 142
Bourget ON 218-220
Britannia Beach 38, 41
Britannia Park 37-40
Britannia Village ON 40
Brockville ON 256
Broome-Runciman Dam 258
Buck Lake 254
bullfrog 192

C

Calabogie ON 193-196
Calabogie Lake 203
Calabogie Peaks Resort 200
call of nature 203
Camp Fortune 113
Camp Gatineau 117
Canada's Capital Region 36

Canadian Central Railway 213
Canadian Forces Naval Reserve. *See* HMCS *Carleton*
Canadian National Railway 239
Canadian Pacific Railway 153, 193, 213
Canadian Parliament Buildings 34, 35, 40, 45, 53, 87, 138, 206
Capital Memorial Gardens 234
Capital Pathway 36
Capital Pathways pavilion 36
Captain's Gap Campsite 246
cardinal 111, *117*
cardinal flower 231
Carleton Place ON 140, 213, 217, 239, 275
Carleton University 52, 53, 56, 59
Cataraqui Region Conservation Authority 239
Cataraqui Trail 226, 239-242
Cataraqui Trail–Chaffeys Locks 26, 241
Cedar Grove Walking Trail 208-209
Cedar Lake Loop 253
Cedar Lake Trail Junction 255
cedar, eastern white *49*
cell phone 254
Central Experimental Farm 51-52
Centre de plein air du Lac Leamy 137, 140
Chaffeys Locks ON 226, 239-242
Champlain Lookout 123
Champlain Sea 85, 159, 181
Charleston Lake 242-243, 246
Charleston Lake Provincial Park 227, 243-246
chickadee 25, *27*, 40, 49
  black-capped 27
  boreal 27
Chipmunk Trail 64
Clé des bois, La 171, 173-174
compass 76
Connaught Rifle Range 73
Corridor Trail 251, 255
corydalis, golden 112
cougar 14, 17

County of Renfrew 193
Covey's Gap Campsite 246
coyote 17
Crosby ON 239
Cycloparc PPJ 128-131

D

Debruge, Albert 258
deer 205
  white-tailed *267*
Deschênes Rapids 41
Devils Gorge 254
Dewberry Trail 28
Dickson Mountain 200, 203-204
Doe Lake 229, 247-250, 252, 255
Doe Lake Loop 247
Doe Lake Trail 229, 247
Domain Chez Philias 219
Dominion Arboretum 51-52
Dow's Lake 51-52, 54
dragonfly, Fletcher's 25
Duck Islands 34, 45
Dunbar Bridge 59
Dutchman's breeches 111

E

E. *See* Boucle Est
Eardley Escarpment 84, *85*
Eardley QC 115
Earth Star Loop 209
Earth Star Shelter 209
Eastern Ontario Model Forest 46
Embrun ON 210, 212
Envolée du Castor Trail, L' 173

F

Farran Park campground 223
first aid kit 273
First Tay Canal 268
Flagpole Hill 255
Foley Mountain 232, 271
Foley Mountain Conservation Area 271-272
Foley Mountain Highland Loop 274

food 250
footwear 58
Forêt-la-Blanche 132-135, 145
Forêt-la-Blanche Ecological Reserve 132
Foulée du cerf, La 174
Friends of Glengarry Trails Association 181
Frontenac Arch 7, 9, 240, *242*, 264, 271
Frontenac Arch Biosphere Reserve 242
Frontenac Provincial Park 228-229, 242, 247-251, 253-255
Frontenac Provincial Park–Slide Lake Loop 252

G
GPS 76
garbage bag 277
Garry Fen Boardwalk 184
Garry Fen Trail 183
Garry River 181
Garter Lake 240, 242
Gatineau QC 45, 85, 104, 139, 141
Gatineau Hills 7, 42, 44, 75, 79
Gatineau Park 7, 9, 11, 14, 36, 71, 78, 80, 83, 85, 87, 95, 99, 103, 104, 115, 119, 123, 140, 149, 175, 178, 251
Gatineau River 7, 78, 137-138, 175-176
Gatineau River Pathway 138
Gatineau Valley 91
Geodetic Survey of Canada 86
Glengarry Snowmobile Club 182
Glengarry Trails 181-184, 279
Glengarry Trails–Alexandria 180
goose, Canada *158*, 159-160, 164
Green Creek 42-45
Green Road Trail 182-184
Greenbelt. *See* Ottawa Greenbelt
Greenbelt Pathway West 75, 76
Greenway Pathway West 73
groundhog *157*

H
HMCS *Carleton* 52
Hammond ON 218-220

Harrington Lake Estate 81
Hartwells Lock 52, 53
Haut-Lieu, Le 173
Herridge, Duncan 79
Herridge Shelter 79-81
Hidden Cove Campsite 246
hiking equipment 12, 14
Hoggs Bay 266
Hog's Back Falls 51, 53-54, 69
Hog's Back Lock Station 54
Hog's Back Park 58
Howard Lake 263
Hull QC 153, 175
hunting season 267
Hurdman Transit Station 59
Huron Trail 125
hypothermia 98

I
Indian Creek 219
Indian Pass 202, 204
Indian pipe 205
Island Park 181, 184

J
Jack Pine Trail 62-63
Jock River 233-234
Johnson, Joseph 256
Joyce Homestead 259

K
Kazabazua QC 156
Kemp Mine 248
Kettle Island 34
King Mountain 82-86, 110
King Mountain Trail 83-86, 110
Kingsmere QC 83, 86-87, 103
Kingsmere Lake 87
Kingston ON 53, 61-62, 206, 221, 242, 251, 268, 271
Kingston & Pembroke Railway 193
K&P Trail 193-196

L

La Pêche River 178
Lac Amik 134-135
Lac aux Hérons 134
Lac Beauchamp 144
Lac Black 83-84
Lac Brown 175-177
Lac Clair 116
Lac de la Vase 116
Lac en Ciel 134
Lac Howard 135
Lac Kidder 116
Lac la Blanche 133-134
Lac Leamy 136-140
Lac Lusk 93
Lac Meech 119, 121, 123, 125-126
Lac Mountains 85
Lac Mousseau Estate. See Harrington
  Lake Estate
Lac Mulvihill 90
Lac Philippe 79, 81, 91, 94
Lac Philippe campground 94
Lac Pink 99-101. See also Pink Lake
Lac Ramsay 115
Lac Richard 115, 117
Lac Robert 135
Lac Taylor 93, 116-117
lady's slipper 151
Lake Ontario 239
Lally Homestead 265-267
Lancaster ON 221
Lansdowne ON 243
Larose Forest 207, 219
Last Duel Park 269
Laurentian Highlands 78
Lauriault Lookout 88
Lauriault Trail 87-90
layering 274
Leamy Lake Pathway 140
Leaning Rock Lookout 260
Library of Parliament 140
Lièvre River 7
lily
  trout 185

water 149
Lime Kiln 61-62, 198
Lime Kiln Loop 60-64, 70
Little Bay 274
Little Renaud Lake 93
Long Sault Parkway 221
Long Way 201, 204
loosestrife, purple 215
Lost Valley Loop 203-204
Low QC 140, 153-157
Lusk Cabin 91, 93-94
Lusk Cave 72, 91-94
Luskville, QC 96
Luskville Falls 95-98, 105
lynx 14, 17

M

Mac Johnson Wildlife Area–Brockville
  256-259
Macdonald-Cartier Bridge 11, 79, 83,
  87, 91, 95, 99, 103, 115, 119, 123, 129,
  132, 137, 140, 141, 153, 159, 162, 167,
  175
Mackenzie King, William Lyon 87, 90
Mackenzie King Estate 90
MacLaren Cemetery 178
MacLaren House 178
Macnamara, Charles 197
Macnamara Nature Trail 187, 197, 199,
  279
Madawaska River 7, 193, 195
Mahingan Lookout 120
Maison Charron 140
Maison du vélo, La 139
Maison Galipeau 160
Manitou Lake 202-203
Manitou Mountain 188, 200-204
Manitou Mountain Lookout 202
Maniwaki QC 153, 157
map 86
maple, sugar 166
Marais Perras 160
Marble Rock 230, 260-263
Marble Rock Trail 260

Marlborough Forest 189, 206-209
McCloskey Farm 124
McKinstry Shelter 96, 121
McParlan Homestead 265-266
Mediation Point 274
Medicine Pine Pond 204
Mer Bleu 65
Mer Bleue 24, 25, 26, 28
Mer Bleue Bog 25
Métronome Organique, Le 163
Mink Lake Lookout 254
Mississippi River 7
moccasin flower 151,
Montagnes Blanches Ski de Fond 162
Montée Neuve 173
Montée-Neuve ATV Trail, La 172, 174
Mont Grand Pic 169
Mont Rigaud 171
Mont Tremblant 167
Montréal QC 34
Mooneys Bay 54
Mooneys Bay Park 54
moose 14, 205
Moreside Gardens 90
Morrisburg ON 221
Morton ON 275
Morton Bay 276
Morton Bay Loop 275-277
Mud Lake 40
Mud Lake Conservation Area 38, 40
Murphys Point Campground 265
Murphys Point Provincial Park 264-267
Museum of Civilization 136-140

N
Nakkertok Nordic Cross Country Ski
    Club 8
National Capital Commission 36, 206
National Capital Commission's Greenbelt
    Capital Pathways Division 279
    Gatineau Park Division 279
National Gallery of Canada 140
National Hiking Trail 80, 103
New York Central Fitness Trail 210-212

Nicolls Island ON 235
No Name Lake 262-263
Nopiming Game Preserve 197
North Glengarry ON 181
North Loop 260, 262
North Loop Junction 263
North Loop Lookout 263
North Slide Junction 254
Norway Lake 196
Nut Tree Trail 28
Nylene Canada Incorporated 197

O
O. See Boucle Quest ski route
O'Brien Beach 79, 80
Old Chelsea QC 83, 104, 113
Old Quarry Trail 29-32
Ontario Ministry of Natural Resources
    207
Opeongo Hills 7
orchid, wild 151
Orléans ON 42, 45
Ottawa-Carleton Trailway 29, 31-32,
    213-217
Ottawa New Edinburgh Club 35
Ottawa ON 7-9, 11, 14, 17, 23-76, 78, 85,
    104, 115, 134, 139-140, 153, 158, 162,
    166, 181, 204, 206, 207, 210, 218, 221,
    242, 251, 267, 268, 271
Ottawa River 7, 25, 33-35, 37, 39, 42-45,
    66, 73, 75, 78, 85, 116, 120, 134, 137-
    138, 159, 160, 161, 181, 193, 198, 199,
    214, 242
Ottawa River Pathway 34, 36, 38, 40, 45
Ottawa River Valley 84, 85, 121, 142,
    197
Ottawa's Greenbelt 23-76
Our Lady of Sorrows Church 156
Outlet ON 243

P
Papineau, Municipalité Régionale de
    Comté de 162
Papineauville QC 162

Parc Chartier de Lotbinière 171
Parc du Lac Beauchamp 141-144
Parc Écologique du Lac Leamy 138
Parc Jacques-Cartier 138
Parc linéaire de la Vallée-de-la-Gatineau
  153-157
Parc national de Plaisance 146-147,
  158-161
Parcours Louis-Joseph-Papineau 148,
  162-166
Parks Canada 53, 268
Parks of the St. Lawrence 221
Parliament. *See* Canadian Parliament
  Buildings
Parliament Hill 140
Pearson, Lester 175, 178
Pembroke ON 193
Perth ON 206, 264, 268, 270, 271
Petite Nation River 7
Petrie Island ON 42, 45
Pine Grove Forestry Trail 46-49, 67
pine, white *142*
Pink Lake 99-102, 106. *See* also Lac Pink
Plage Parent 91, 93-94
Plage Smith 94
poison ivy 15, 28, 35, 36, 41, 43, 45, 94,
  126, 157, 161, 174, 178, 184, 204, 212,
  217, 220, 224, 236, 242, 246, 274
Pontiac Lookout 96, 98
Pontiac Pacific Junction Railway 129
Pontiac Regional County Municipality
  QC 129
Porcupine Path Trail. *See* Beaver Pond
  Trail
Prescott-Russell Recreational Trail 190,
  218-220
Presqu'île QC 160-161
Promenade du Lac Leamy 138

Q
Quiddity Trail 244

R
railroads *214*

Railway Trail 257
rain gear 131
Red Arrow Rock Lookout 201
Red Trail 182
Renfrew ON 193
Renfrew County ON 193
Rideau Canal 50-54, *53*, 235, 239, 240,
  268
Rideau Canal Eastern Pathway 52-53
Rideau Canal Western Pathway 51
Rideau Canoe Club 54
Rideau Falls 138
Rideau River 7, 53, 55-59, 68-69, 138,
  233, 234, 268
Rideau River Park 59
Rideau River Pathway 58-59
Rideau Trail 29, 31-32, 40, 60-64, 70,
  206, 208, 209, 239-241, 252, 254, 264,
  265, 268-274, 279
Rideau Trail-Tay Towpath 269
Rideau Trail-Westport 232, 273
Rideau Trail Association 8, 209, 270,
  272, 275, 279
Rideau Valley Conservation Authority
  271
Rideau Waterway 264, 275
Rideau Waterway Land Trust 275
Rigaud QC 171, 218
Ripon QC 167
Riverglen Farm 76
Rivière Petite Blanche 160
Robinson Field 58
Rockcliffe Airport 34, 36
Rockcliffe Park 42
Rockcliffe Yacht Club 35
Rock Dunder 275-278
Rock Dunder Lookout 275
Rock Slide Lookout 273
Rogers Pond 208-209
Ron Kolbus Lakeside Centre 38
Round Lake 242
Russell ON 210-212

S

SAJO youth camp 164
Saguenay River 78
Saint-André-Avellin QC 162
St. John the Baptist Ukrainian Catholic National Shrine 53
St. Lawrence Heritage Corner 221
St. Lawrence Recreational Path 191, 221-224
St. Lawrence Recreational Trail 221
St. Lawrence River 181, 223
St. Theresa's School 211
Sandy Hill 56
scilla 228
Scouts Canada 275
Sector Philippe 116-117
Sentier de la Caverne 94
Sentier de l'Escapade 186
Sentier des Loups. *See* Trail 62
Sentier des Montagnes Noires 167, 169-170
Sentier des Outaouais 146-147, 158-161
Sentier la Baie Noire 160
Sentiers L'Escapade 171-174, 186
Sharbot Lake ON 228, 247, 251
Shawville QC 131
Shirley, Thomas 73
Shirleys Bay–Trail 10 73-76
shoelaces 143
Silver Queen Mine 264
Silver Queen Mine Trail 266
Skyline 102-104, 113
Skywalk Loop 202-203
Slide Lake 253-254
Slide Lake Loop 251-255
Slim Bay 246
Slim Bay Bridge 246
Small Lake Trudel 81
Smiths Falls ON 140, 239, 240, 275
socks 54
South Loop 260-261, 263
South Loop Lookout Side Trail 263
South Nation River 7
South Otter Lake 229, 248

South Slide Junction 254
Spy Rock 271-272, 274
squirrel
    black *113*
    eastern grey *113*
Stittsville ON 213, 216-217
Stonebridge Trail 233-236
Stony Swamp 29, 49, 63, 142
Strathcona ON 239
Strathcona Park 56
Sucrerie de la Montagne, La 171, 173
Summit Loop 277
sunscreen 249

T

Tallow Rock Bay 245
Tallow Rock Bay Loop 244
Tallow Rock Bay Trail 227, 243-246
Tawadina Lookout 119-121
Tay Basin 268-270
Tay Canal 53
Tay Towpath 268, 270
Thurso QC 159-161, 167
Thurso Park 160
tick 15, 224, *236*, 246, 278
Tincap ON 256
Totem Pole Pond 203-204
Trail 8 110
Trail 56 114-117
Trail 62 (Wolf Trail/Sentier des Loups) 108, 118-121
Trans Canada Trail 31, 40-41, 80-81, 103, 139, *140*, 154, 216, 239-240
Trans Canada Trail Pavilion 139
Transitway Bridge 58
Traverse de la Mine 143-144
trillium *80*
    purple 80
    white 80
turkey, wild *283*
turtle, spotted 25

U

United Nations' Ramsar Convention 25

Upper Canada Migratory Bird Sanctuary 221, 223-224
Upper Canada Village ON 221, 224

V

vaseline 135
Venosta QC 156
Via Rail station 58
Village Square Park 213, 216
Vincent Massey Park 56, 59
Virée gourmande, La 173-174
Voyageur Pathway 138

W

W.C. Levesque Fields 233
Wakefield QC 79, 81, 109, 140, 150, 152, 153, 175-178
Wakefield Mill 176, 178
Wakefield Trail Junction J 176
warbler, common yellow 65
water 44

water filtration 249
watershield 225
Wattford's Lookout 103-104, 113
Wendigo Way 204
Wendover ON 161
West Hunt Club 63
West Slide Junction 254
Westboro Beach 38, 41
Western Shelter 107, 123-126
Westminster Palace 87
Westport ON 271-272
Westport Lion's Club Beach 271
Westside Trails 243
whistle 155
Wild Bird Care Centre 64
Wildflower Loop 257
Wilson Ruins 111
Wolf Howl Pond 202-203
Wolf Trail. *See* Trail 62
wolves 14, 17, *205*
Wyman QC 131